T0374831

2006

Map showing Hundreds and Parishes

THE PUBLICATIONS OF THE BEDFORDSHIRE
HISTORICAL RECORD SOCIETY
VOLUME 85

HOW BEDFORDSHIRE VOTED, 1685–1735

THE EVIDENCE OF LOCAL POLL BOOKS

VOLUME I: 1685–1715

James Collett-White

THE BEDFORDSHIRE HISTORICAL RECORD SOCIETY

THE BOYDELL PRESS

First published 2006

A publication of
Bedfordshire Historical Record Society
published by The Boydell Press
an imprint of Boydell & Brewer Ltd
PO Box 9, Woodbridge, Suffolk IP12 3DF, UK
and of Boydell & Brewer Inc.
668 Mt Hope Avenue, Rochester, NY 14620, USA
website: www.boydellandbrewer.com

ISBN 0 85155 071 1

ISSN 0067–4826

The Society is most grateful for financial support from
the Simon Whitbread Trust and other donors who have
helped make the publication of this volume possible.

Details of previous volumes are available from
Boydell & Brewer Ltd

A CIP catalogue for this book is available
from the British Library

This publication is printed on acid-free paper

Printed in Great Britain by
Athenaeum Press Ltd., Gateshead, Tyne & Wear

Contents

Illustrations

Tables

This book is dedicated to my wife, Ann, and our children, Elizabeth, Francis and Richard, whose love, support and practical assistance have so much helped in its creation.

Acknowledgements

My interest in eighteenth-century politics was first kindled at University, studying with Dr Piers Mackesy. My interest in Bedfordshire political history was fostered by Michael Hurst with whom I studied the county's nineteenth-century politics in the 1970s. I am grateful for the way in which he showed me the importance of 'outsetters' in the Bedfordshire context. In my job as Search Room Archivist, I began to realise the potential of poll books for family historians. Such a project as publishing poll books for both Bedford Borough and Bedfordshire required a lot of help from a lot of people: from depositors allowing their documents to be published to checkers of my transcript and friends giving encouragement when the task seemed too great.

I gratefully acknowledge permission to publish items from their archives given by the Duke of Bedford and the Trustees of the Bedford Estate, Major Chester, and W.A. Wade Gery. I am also grateful for permission to use documents belonging to Bedfordshire and Luton Archive and Records Service, Bedford Borough Council, Bedford Library, Cecil Higgins Art Gallery and Museum and Lincolnshire Archives Service.

Colin Chapman's permission to use his invaluable County Codes has been much appreciated.

The photography work for the illustrations has been done by Dave Stubbs to his own high standards.

For help with producing the book, my heartfelt thanks go to my family, Patricia Bell, Mark Humphreys, Penny Stanbridge, Gordon Vowles and Peter Wood, without whose skill and enthusiasm this book would never have been completed. Above all this book is a tribute to the professionalism, care for detail and unfailing support of the Society's general editor, Barbara Tearle. The value of a book of this kind depends largely on the indexing of names. Her experience of indexing and her particular interest in family history made her the ideal person to undertake that task – not thankless because I shall not be the only person to be grateful! Many thanks, too, to my colleagues at BLARS, whose dedication, camaraderie and support have made it such a pleasant task working with them.

My appreciation goes to the staff of Boydell & Brewer for their skill and professionalism in producing another meticulous volume.

I am most grateful to Michael Orlebar and Sam Whitbread, who have given me the chance to work in Hinwick House and Southill Park, in the houses, if not the rooms, where the political arguments were conducted and the alliances forged that underlay the elections discussed here.

James Collett-White
May 2006

Abbreviations

BHRS	Bedfordshire Historical Record Society
BKM	Buckinghamshire
BLARS	Bedfordshire and Luton Archive and Records Service
CAM	Cambridgeshire
DNB	*Dictionary of National Biography*
ESS	Essex
GEC	*The Complete Peerage of England*
HRT	Hertfordshire
HUN	Huntingdonshire
LEI	Leicestershire
LIN	Lincolnshire
LND	London
MDX	Middlesex
NTH	Northamptonshire
NTT	Nottinghamshire
ODNB	*Oxford Dictionary of National Biography*
SRY	Surrey
VCH Bedford	*The Victoria History of the County of Bedford*
WAR	Warwickshire

For abbreviations to BLARS and Lincolnshire Archives, see the Bibliography at the end of the volume.

General Summary of Election Results

Bedford Borough Election Results 1685–1715

1685	Sir Anthony Chester Thomas Christie		
1688–1689	Thomas Hillersden Thomas Christie Sir William Franklyn	(failed petition)	
1695	Thomas Hillersden William Farrer		
1697	William Spencer in place of Thomas Hillersden deceased		
1698	Sir Thomas Alston William Spencer		
1701	William Farrer William Spencer		
1702	Henry Edward Carteret William Spencer		
1705 (11 May)	William Farrer Sir Philip Monoux Samuel Rolt William Spencer	385 340 225 151	elected elected
1708	William Farrer William Hillersden		
1710	William Farrer John Cater		
1710	William Farrer re-elected on obtaining office		
1713	Samuel Rolt John Cater William Farrer		
1715	William Farrer John Thurloe Brace		
1715	William Farrer re-elected on obtaining office		

Bedfordshire County Election Results 1685–1715

1685 (9 and 10 March)	Sir Villiers Chernocke	841	elected
	William Boteler	904	elected
	Edward Russell	744	
	Sir Humphrey Monoux	634	
1688 (abortive election)	Edward Russell		
	William Duncombe		
1689 (January)	Edward Russell		
	Thomas Browne		
1695 (31 October)	Lord Edward Russell		elected unopposed
	William Duncombe	1108	elected
	Thomas Browne	906	
1698 (20 July)	Lord Edward Russell		elected
	Sir William Gostwick		elected
	William Duncombe		
	Thomas Bromsall		
	(unsuccessful petition of 12 December)		
1700	Lord Edward Russell		
	Sir William Gostwick		
1701	Lord Edward Russell		
	Sir William Gostwick		
1702 (July)	Lord Edward Russell		
	Sir William Gostwick		
1705 (11 May)	Sir Pynsent Chernocke	1408	elected
	Sir William Gostwick	1276	elected
	Lord Edward Russell	1239	
	John Harvey	764	
1708 (5 May)	Lord Edward Russell		
	Sir William Gostwick		
1710 (October)	Lord Edward Russell		
	Sir William Gostwick		
1713 (2 September)	Sir Pynsent Chernocke	1261	elected
	John Harvey	1264	elected
	John Cater	1254	
	William Hillersden	1241	
1714 [i.e. 1715](16 February)	Sir Pynsent Chernocke	1241	
	John Harvey	1264	elected but unseated
	John Cater	1254	elected
	William Hillersden	1261	elected
	John Cater in place of John Harvey unseated on petition		

Introduction

The purpose of publishing this book is twofold: firstly, to provide data useful for family historians and, secondly, to use this data to explore why people voted in the way they did. The poll books give an important insight into the structure of land-owning in Bedfordshire and the patterns of local allegiance and loyalty. Both county and parish historians should find the book useful. The data will also provide material that will assist social, economic and political historians with interests beyond Bedfordshire.

Sources for Family History 1671–1841

For family historians the period 1671–1841 is so often the bottomless pit, where they can lose their ancestors for ever. For 1671 there is the hearth tax,[1] which covers the names of heads of most of the households in the county. The 1841 census lists all the people living in a household. Between them there is no comprehensive list. Having exhausted parish registers and wills, family historians can be at a loss what to do next.

For the poorer people the records, generated by parish poor relief, such as removal orders, settlement examinations, bastardy bonds and the like, can give important clues, especially now that the Bedfordshire Family History Society has published an excellent index.[2] Unfortunately, the records do not cover every parish. A manuscript index in the Search Room of the Bedfordshire and Luton Archives and Records Service (BLARS) of such records held in Quarter Sessions supplements this. This second source covers the whole county.

Poll Books

For those in the middle ranks of society, neither very rich nor very poor, research is much more difficult. Poll books[3] provide some answers, as they are a record of how people voted in parliamentary elections. Up to 1734 these occurred reasonably frequently, both for the Borough of Bedford and the Bedfordshire County seat. There is then a gap until 1774. There was at least one contested election in the

---

[1]   Lydia M. Marshall, *The Bedfordshire Hearth Tax Return for 1671*, BHRS, vol. 16 (Bedford, repr. 1990).
[2]   *Bedfordshire Parish Poor Law Papers 1622–1834: an index*, Bedfordshire Family History Society, Occasional Paper No. 2 (Bedford, 1991).
[3]   For a general introduction to Poll Books, see John Cannon, 'Poll Books', in K.M. Thompson, ed., *Short Guides to Records: first series – guides 1–24*, repr. edn by the Historical Association (London, 1994), No. 2.

Guild Hall with John Bunyan preaching, c. 1659. The view looks down towards the old bridge, with the Swan on the left of the picture. The spire is St Paul's. This shows the area where the elections took place.

period in the Borough (1768), but no poll book has survived. Poll books record the parish where the voter held property that entitled him to vote and, if resident elsewhere, the place of that residence. Many voters appear, for example, from Huntingdonshire, London and Middlesex. On one of the poll books for the 1727 election John Orlebar recorded whether a voter had died or sold his property between 1727 and 1734. The records are not always accurate and are based on what someone heard at the husting. Distortion from lack of local knowledge and the broadness of the accent happened frequently. The numerous differences between the two surviving poll books of the 1727 County election show this. The totals of voters are similarly suspect, but nonetheless give a good idea of how a parish or hundred voted.

If a voter is no longer recorded in a subsequent election, it may be a sign that he has died, and burial registers may confirm this, or it may be that the voter has moved away from the county. The deeds of the parish at BLARS, often in the archive of a family that subsequently became great landowners, such as the Dukes of Bedford or the Whitbreads, may reveal that he sold up. Voters having property in two counties may well have had their will proved at the Prerogative Court of Canterbury, thus giving another area to search. For the Borough seat there were normally around 400 voters and for the County over 2000. Some of the names will be duplicated as a considerable number of voters were entitled to vote for both seats.

The Franchise: by what right did a man claim a vote?

Unlike today, the right of voting was not universal and differed from place to place. Voters had to be male and over 21. English and Welsh peers, minors, lunatics and women were disenfranchised. Bedfordshire returned four members of Parliament, two for the County of Bedford and two for the Borough of Bedford. There were no rotten boroughs with tiny electorates beholden to one landlord. Voters in towns, such as Luton, Leighton Buzzard and Dunstable, could vote for the County seat.

The County covered all present-day Bedfordshire, with some exceptions. The boundaries were those prior to the late nineteenth-century changes and those of the local government review of the 1960s, changes in which the county lost the urban part of Eaton Socon and gained Linslade. Holwell was part of the county. Swineshead, however, was part of Huntingdonshire. The freeholders of the town of Bedford had the right to vote in County elections and a number voted in both Borough and County elections.

Voters for the County had to be '40 shilling freeholders'. Under an Act of 1429, electors of members of parliament had to possess land to the value of 40 shillings a year.[4] Note that there was no provision for tenants to have the vote. The £50 copyholder and long leaseholder were only enfranchised in 1832. The 1774 election for Bedfordshire[5] shows that some tenants had the vote, but only as a result of owning small pieces of freehold. Before 1832, the greater landowner could not dominate elections purely by the size of his rent roll. The steward's correspondence of the Bedford estate from the 1740s shows that more subtlety was required.[6]

The franchise for Bedford was completely different. By an order the House of Commons of 12 April 1690, the right to elect two MPs for the Borough of Bedford was vested in the burgesses, freemen and householders not receiving alms.[7] Robert H. O'Byrne, in his *Representative History of Great Britain and Ireland* (1848)[8] explains that 'the office of burgess is both hereditary and elective; every son of a burgess born after his father's admission, is entitled to be admitted a freeman, and by such admission becomes a burgess. Honorary burgesses are created by the common council without any restriction either as to number or qualification.' They had to be sworn before the aldermen, 'denying for ever the usurped power and unlawful jurisdiction of the Bishop of Rome, here most justly abolished'. They were also expected to help with the apprehension and attachment of traitors. From this group alone could be elected the higher officers of the Council.

Freemen were appointed by birth, apprenticeship and gift: 'the son first born after his father's admission is entitled to becoming a freeman at 21, apprenticeship for seven years and faithful service for another seven years also entitled a man to become a freeman'. Purchase of the right to be a freeman was at a rate decided by the Borough; the highest before 1832 was £20. Honorary freemen could be appointed at the will of the Council without any restriction of place of residence, ownership of property etc. From the ranks of freemen could be appointed the lesser officials. Crucially, freemen could vote in Parliamentary and municipal elections.

---

4   Electors of Knights of the Shire Act 1429, 8 Hen. 6 c. 7.
5   BLARS, RV 13.
6   H. Wellenreuther, 'Activities of an Estate Agent in Mid-Eighteenth Century England: Robert Butcher and the Town of Bedford', in *Bedfordshire Historical Miscellany: Essays in Honour of Patricia Bell*, BHRS, vol. 72 (Bedford, 1993), pp. 156–76. Transcripts at BLARS of letters relating to Bedfordshire (shelf mark 160).
7   *Journals of the House of Commons*, vol. 10, p. 376.
8   R.H. O'Byrne, *The Representative History of Great Britain and Ireland*, p. 7.

Householders who claimed a vote were not allowed to have received poor relief. Receiving alms from the Harpur Trust was a grey area, which provided for plenty of dispute. Politicians sought to overturn the 1690 decision when it suited them.

This was the framework of Bedford's electoral system until the Great Reform Bill of 1832.[9] The power to create freemen was capable of huge abuse but probably was reasonably controlled at least until the late 1730s. The practical effects of all these regulations of the borough franchise are shown in the poll book for the 1727 election: '116 burgesses voted; 275 freemen; 124 householders paying scot and lot; 132 not paying scot and lot, 37 certificate men, 19 no voters on any pretence'.[10]

'Scot and lot' was used as a general description for parish payments such as rates. 'Certificate men' were people who had obtained a certificate from their parish of settlement, indemnifying the parish where they were working, in the event of their being chargeable to the poor rate. The complexity of the system meant that people voted, who were not entitled to, and there were disputes over results, causing petitions to the House of Commons. Yet, despite everything, nationally, Bedford was in the second tranche of borough electorates with over 700 voters, of whom the majority during this period were local.

Who were the Voters?

The County electorate was led by local landowners with estates covering more than one parish and the beneficed clergy. These were followed by a whole host of smaller men, independent farmers and some practitioners of local trades. In the towns, shopkeepers, stonemasons and innkeepers might all have the vote, as long as they owned land to the value of 40 shillings. Entitlement to vote can increasingly be gauged by the land tax returns, and it is no accident that the first full land tax of the County in 1784 coincided with the closest election battle for the County seat.

The number of voters in a parish varied greatly. Clapham, even then quite a populous parish (in 1801 it had 157 inhabitants), was owned by an absentee landlord, Lord Ashburnham. At most elections only one or two people voted, with a high point of six in 1715. Bromham, an estate village, had four voters in 1685, one in 1705 but by 1727 it had stabilised at six voters, with nine in 1734. Biggleswade in 1722 (1801 population: 1794) had just seven votes cast, and it was only in 1734 that votes reached fifty-one. The low figure is explained by much of the centre of the town being copyhold rather than freehold. Expansion of the town onto freehold land meant the creation of new voters.

If we compare Clapham and Biggleswade with Eaton Socon and Dunstable, the population of the latter in 1801 was 1625 and 1296 respectively. Eaton Socon was physically a large parish in multiple ownerships. In 1722, 150 votes were cast and in 1734, 112. Figures for Dunstable for the same elections were 53 and 78 respectively. Cardington, an open village in the ownership of a number of people, had 39 voters

---

9   Representation of the People Act 1832, 2 & 3 Will. 4, c. 45.
10 BLARS, OR 1784.

in 1722. By 1826 this number had reduced to 22, owing to the purchases of the Whitbreads and their cousin John Howard.

Bedford had a considerable role in deciding County elections, having 137 voters in 1705. Not all householders could vote in the County election as they did not have a 40 shilling freehold in the town. In 1705, 21 voted for the County but not the Borough, and 469 for the Borough seat but not the County.

One of the peculiarities of the electoral system was that people could vote even if they did not live in the constituency. For the County in 1727, for example, there were 428 'outsetter' voters out of 2382. For the Borough election of that date, the house-holders and others were outnumbered by the burgesses and freemen. However, the majority of this last group were from Bedford. Some of those burgesses were resident in the county, with only one from Hertfordshire. The 275 freemen included 19 from elsewhere in Bedfordshire and 29 from out of the county.

Although the occupations of voters is given all too infrequently, these can be gauged from parish registers, which often recorded such information from the 1690s to the 1720s, and from wills. Taking Bedford as an example, using the baptism registers of St Paul's, the 1730 poll book for the Borough and wills proved in the Archdeaconry of Bedford, some tentative conclusions can be drawn. Of 247 voters whose occupation can be ascertained, 75 were of the landowning class (baronets, esquires and gentry), to whom may be added the 15 clergy voters. Of the remainder, 43 were involved in some way in the food and drink trade (brewing, malting, innholders, bakers, butchers etc.), 19 worked in the clothing industry (tailors, shoemakers and a small cloth-making industry), 17 were involved in either farming or market gardening, 16 in a whole miscellany of local trades and 13 in the building industry (carpenters, joiners, bricklayers and masons). A small group of voters worked in a service industry ranging from coal merchant to barber. There was even a hair seller. Many of these men would have worked as one-man or family enterprises. There is also a group of 31 labourers, a number of whom left wills, so they would have had possessions of their own and be above the poverty line. It may well be that some of them were small cultivators of land on the outskirts of what was quite a small town geographically. The 'scot and lot' franchise indeed produced a broad-based electorate in which all ranks of society within the town were repre-sented, apart from the very poor.

How did they Vote for the Candidates?

After the election had been called, negotiations were started between leading gentry to select the candidates. This could be followed by a public meeting to endorse the candidacy. A general meeting of the freeholders was called. The candidates were nominated by well-known local supporters. If there were more than two candidates, there was a show of hands. The two most successful were then elected. The losers, often, would thereupon demand a poll.

The sheriff conducted the poll for the County. After the 1685 election the polls tended to be held at Bedford in the St Paul's Square area. The result would have been declared from the Guildhall (opposite where Wilkinson's is now). What it must have looked like is captured in an engraving of 1659 showing Bunyan preaching in front of the Guildhall with St Paul's spire, the old Swan and the old bridge as back-cloth.[11] There was no Shire Hall until 1750.

Each voter had to vote publicly on a platform known as a husting. Each voter had two votes. If he decided to use just one vote, this was allowed. It was called 'plump-ing'. This gave the candidate 'plumped for' an added advantage, as the other candi-dates were deprived of a vote. This tactic was particularly used when a party, such as the Tories, fielded one candidate against the opponents' two. Alternatively, if it was feared that neither candidate from one party might win, voters could 'plump' for one of the candidates. Particularly strong support for a candidate in one region of the county could also lead to 'plumping', often recorded in the headings on poll books as 'single votes'.

In the Borough the election would have been the responsibility of the mayor, but he had to send in a writ of return, which the sheriff passed on to the Clerk of the Crown. The process of selection must have been similar but would have included negotiations between the leading figures on the Borough Council and the recorder, who was of a leading local family and whose responsibility was to ensure the smooth running of the Borough courts and to represent the town's interests at royal court.

Voters came considerable distances to the polls, both from outlying parts of the county and from London. A Winchester man voted in the Borough election of 1727. Considerable 'treating', that is, giving drink and food, took place at the candidates' favoured inn, such as the Russell supporters at the Swan in Bedford and the Tories at the Bell opposite, both conveniently close to the hustings. Further treating took place when a candidate canvassed before the election. After the election giving beer and bread to the 'rabble' was expected of the successful candidate. The considerable expenses involved to candidates are indicated in Russell's expense accounts for the 1688 and 1695 elections and Chernocke and Harvey's expenses for 1715 (see Chap-ters 2 and 4).

Politics and Society in Bedfordshire 1680–1735

In determining which candidates were chosen and why they were supported by voters, the power structure of the county was critical. As the qualification for voting for the county seat was based on land, it was inevitable that the most important players were landowners. So, was there one great landowner and a lot of lesser ones cowed into submission to him?

Linda Colley states in her *In Defiance of Oligarchy*:[12] 'Even the great Duke of Bedford owned only a tenth of Bedfordshire, which was one reason why the Tories were able to maintain a presence in the county.' The conclusions Colley drew were correct, but in this period, the Dukes of Bedford did not own a tenth of the county, even if they did so in 1873. The big expansion of the estate started with the rebuilding of Woburn in the 1740s and continued unabated until the acquisition of

---

11 Taken from J. Brown, *John Bunyan (1622–1688) . . . His Life, Times and Work*, Tercentenary edn, rev. F.M. Harrison (London, 1928). Photograph copy at BLARS, Z50/143/40.
12 L. Colley, *In Defiance of Oligarchy: the Tory Party 1714–60* (Cambridge, 1982), passim.

the Ossory/Holland estate in 1842. The purchase of outlying estates at Oakley, Cople and Willington and huge additions both before and as a result of enclosure from 1760 onwards, as well as systematic buying-up of smaller landowners, led to the creation of the great estate that only existed in embryo in 1700.[13]

In the 1680s the Russells were important, more because of the martyrdom of Lord William than because of their Bedfordshire estate, which at that time was concentrated on Woburn and its immediate neighbourhood.

There were three other resident peers in Bedfordshire. Most important in 1685 was Robert Bruce, Earl of Ailesbury, Lord Lieutenant, Recorder of Bedford and holder of the Honour of Ampthill, with a considerable power-base in the parishes round Ampthill. Anthony Grey, Earl of Kent, was based at Wrest Park and had estates near there, as well as at Blunham and Harrold. The third, Oliver St John, Earl of Bolingbroke, owned an estate at Melchbourne and Bletsoe. Others were added during the period 1685 to 1734, such as George Byng, who bought Southill in 1693 and became 1st Lord Torrington in 1721.

Peers could exercise considerable influence on who was elected. Their sons could be elected MP, such as George Byng's son, Pattee, who was MP for Bedfordshire from 1727 to 1733, or Edward Russell, second son of the future 1st Duke of Bedford.

Below the peers in influence were the baronets. Although having a title, they could vote and, more importantly, be elected as members of Parliament. They dominated local society, both socially and economically.

For the County seat in the period 1685 to 1734, of nineteen candidates, three came from peers' families, nine from baronets' families and seven from gentry families. For the Borough, there were none from peers' families, three from baronets' families and fifteen from gentry and others, who included two lawyers and a merchant.

The baronets tended to be the natural leaders of the local parties, such as Chester and Chernocke for the Tories and Alston for the Whigs. Together with the esquires and gentry, they numbered 112 in the 1685 election.

The narrow basis for selection of candidates is reflected by the fact that, as two men stood at various times for both seats and two from a family were candidates, the MPs were selected from only 28 families. A number of these families were connected by marriage. Helen, second daughter of William Boteler MP (1634–1703), married Sir Pynsent Chernocke, Bt of Hulcote, MP for the County whose father (Sir Villiers Chernocke) and son (Boteler Chernocke) were at different times also local MPs.[14] William Boteler's third daughter, Mary, married William Farrer (1653–1737), MP for Bedford at various times between 1701 and 1722. However, the family relationship between the politicians did not always decide their politics. Samuel Rolt seems to have been a Tory while his son-in-law John Orlebar was a Whig.

The Farrers' third daughter, Elizabeth, married William Hillersden of Elstow, MP for Bedford, and candidate for the County in 1715. Boteler was also related to John Orlebar, MP for Bedford, through his father-in-law. The Duke of Kent was related

13 BLARS, Russell Estate documents and catalogues, ref. R, RH and RO.
14 BLARS: see Introduction to the TW Catalogue.

through the Crewe family of Steyne, Northamptonshire to the Alstons, MPs from Odell Castle, even if he disliked Sir Rowland.

Family and personal ties of friendship and sense of loyalty created little 'interests'. The chief players in the political manoeuvring knew they could rely on the support of their own 'interest'. The key was to add other 'interests' to form a strong candidacy.

The vast majority of the 112 landowners were squires with estates in individual parishes of considerable sway in their own area and allied to others of importance on the County political scene. The parishes in which their estates lay would be likely to look up to them and follow their lead.

The Clergy

In 1685 the clergy, mainly incumbents of the various parishes, overwhelmingly backed the Tories because they saw them as the protector of their privileged status vis-à-vis the nonconformists.

As time went by clergy became more flexible in their voting patterns as the Church seemed less in danger. John Bolton, vicar firstly of Felmersham and then of Harrold and Sharnbrook, voted in Borough elections: in 1721 for Farrer and J.T. Brace, and in 1730 for Thomas Browne, all Whigs. For the County in 1705 he voted for Gostwick and Russell, then in 1715 for Cater and Hillersden, and in 1730 for Thomas Browne. His Whiggism was helped perhaps by his friendship with the Braces, going over to Astwood to help supervise Mr Brace's brewing.[15]

Reverend Alexander Leith, vicar of St Paul's Bedford and a key figure in the town, voted in County elections for Duncombe in 1695 and 1705; in 1715, he voted for Chernocke and Harvey, the Tories. However in the Borough elections he backed J.T. Brace in 1722 and George Huxley in 1725, both Whigs. In 1730 Leith walked through the town with the Tory gentlemen when Sambrooke was named their candidate and promised them his interest. Overall at this election, four clergy voted for Sambrooke and two for Browne.

The Pattern of Politics in Bedfordshire

While in 1685 the leading landowning families almost unanimously followed the lead of the Bruces and voted for two Tories to give James II the benefit of their doubts as to his intentions, by 1705 they were supporting the two parties almost equally. The even balance of Bedfordshire politics is shown by the fact that there were nine contested elections for the County between 1685 and 1734, producing six Tories and eight Whigs as members of Parliament. However, the Tory County of 1685 was considered by 1734 to be a Whig one. The Tories managed to top the polls in 1685, 1705, 1713, 1715 and 1722. Thereafter the Whigs won comfortably.

One factor in this instability was the changed role of the Lord Lieutenant. The

---

[15] BLARS, ABCP 110.

Bruces had used this position to ensure MPs favourable to the King. His replacement, the 1st Duke of Bedford, was too old to fulfil that type of role. Wriothesley 2nd Duke became Lord Lieutenant in 1701, aged 21, and held the post until his death from smallpox on 26 May 1711.

The office of Recorder of Bedford, which was in a way the patron of the Borough, was held by Paulet St John, 3rd Earl of Bolingbroke from 1689 to 1711. He was replaced by Charles, Lord Bruce, showing Bedford's longing for the old days of Charles's exiled brother, Thomas, the Earl of Ailesbury. Bruce could be expected to support the Tories but hardly be at the forefront of politics in Bedford, as he had been MP for Great Bedwyn in Wiltshire since 1705. His lack of concern for the Borough led to a sustained, yet unsuccessful, attempt to remove him in 1728–29.

The uncontested elections for the County from 1734 to 1774 followed national trends. In Bedfordshire they were greatly influenced by the fact that a number of leading landowning families were running out of money and could no longer afford to fight an election. Long-term Whig MP Sir William Gostwick ruined his Willington estate so that it had to be sold in 1774 to Sarah, Duchess of Marlborough for £50,000, all of which had to be paid to creditors. The Chernockes, Rolts and Duncombes all sold land, and the Chesters of Chicheley sold Lidlington. John Orlebar escaped enforced sale by being appointed a Commissioner of Excise in 1738, a government post that he held until his death in 1765.

The actual election costs were augmented by the need to give widespread hospitality and keep up a London house, at least during the season. The Orlebars leased a house in Piercy Street.

Why did Voters support the Candidates?

Influence of party

What was it that bound the voters to support candidates in sufficient strength for there to be so many elections during the period 1685 to 1734? If 'party' was an important determinant in people's voting, there needs to be evidence of consistent support for candidates from the same political alliance, especially in both County and Borough, a vaguely common ideology and support for MPs who vote consistently on party lines in the House of Commons.

Beginning with 1685, there was a heightened spirit of conflict in which ideological splits can be detected. Chernocke, Boteler and their leading supporters signed the *Loyal Address to James II*. They supported the Bruces, the House of Stuart and the Church of England. They were prepared to give the King the benefit of the doubt. Their role as the Church of England party was underlined by the overwhelming support of the clergy. These were the Tories. The degree to which they regarded the Russell family with suspicion is an interesting one. As people at least influenced by the doctrine of the divine right of kings and 'passive obedience', Lord William Russell's involvement in the Rye House plot coloured their attitude to his brother, Edward.

Their opponents, the Whigs, saw Lord William as a martyr. They were opposed to James II as they feared he would be an arbitrary and despotic ruler, leading

England to Roman Catholicism and subservience to the hated French. They were opposed to the exclusivist position of the Church of England and its oppression of nonconformity.

In 1695, Edward Russell did not have to contend with opposition from the King and Lord Lieutenant, as he had to in 1685. Consequently he was elected by acclamation. The contest for the second seat was between a court politician, who commanded support from both parties, and a Whig, who was comprehensively defeated.

From 1698 to 1705, Russell and Sir William Gostwick were elected as Whigs for the County. Only in 1705 did the Tories feel strong enough to make a determined challenge by fielding two candidates, Sir Pynsent Chernocke and John Harvey, for the County. The result was a curious one with Chernocke top and Harvey bottom of the poll. Gostwick was the preferred Whig candidate, with Russell just losing his seat. Clearly the parties were now evenly balanced in the County.

Despite the Tory revival nationally, 1708 and 1710 saw the two Whigs, Russell and Gostwick, as the County's MPs. Yet in 1713 the two Tory candidates of 1705 were triumphant over two new Whigs, Cater and Hillersden. After a petition to the House of Commons against irregularities in the 1715 election, the tables were reversed.

In 1722 a strong Tory, Charles Leigh, stood on his own and was top of the poll. The other MP elected was Sir Rowland Alston, a Whig. In 1727 the seesaw swung again, with Pattee Byng and Alston, both Whigs, winning the two seats. In 1734 Leigh stood again but was comprehensively defeated by two Whigs.

Parties were not homogeneous. The accession of George I split the Tories between Jacobites and Hanoverian Tories. The jostling for power among the Whigs led to disunity and feuds. Lord Carteret of Hawnes Park, who had been Whig Secretary of State for the Southern Department 1721–24 and Lord Lieutenant of Ireland 1724–30, refused any further office under Walpole. In 1732 his daughter married John Spencer, grandson of Sarah Duchess of Marlborough, a formidable opponent of Walpole. Two other granddaughters had married Wriothesley, the 3rd Duke of Bedford, and John, the 4th Duke. From 1726 to his death in 1732, Wriothesley favoured Tory candidates. John was an opposition Whig, who joined with Carteret in opposition to Walpole. The great local political interest of the Russells, that was so much a feature of the late eighteenth and early nineteenth century, was only in its infancy. In 1735, despite the Duke having nominated Orlebar as the Whig candidate for the County, Sir Roger Burgoyne was chosen instead.

Regionalism within Bedfordshire

Within the overall election, there were marked differences in performance from one area to another. The first section of tables at the back of this book shows how the candidates fared in the different hundreds. (See the frontispiece for a map of the hundreds and p. 232 for a simplified version.)

The northern hundreds of Willey and Stodden remained Whig throughout the period 1685 to 1734. The large number voting in favour of Alston, when he stood, shows that he had a considerable following in this area. In neighbouring Barford hundred, the two Tories and the Whig, Lord Edward Russell, were almost equal in the number of votes they gained in 1685. The hundred supported the Whigs for the rest of the period.

There was near equality in Bedford in 1685 but thereafter the Whigs were always in front, if by a small margin. Sir William Gostwick won spectacularly for them in 1705.

The three eastern hundreds were more profitable for the Tories, who were always in the lead in Biggleswade, apart from 1734 when it went Whig. In Clifton, the Tories won from 1685 to 1715 and the Whigs from 1722 to 1727. Wixamtree hundred was Tory in 1685 and Whig in 1705, with local Whig, Sir William Gostwick, in the lead. In 1715 it went Tory, thanks to local man, John Harvey; his not standing in 1722 led to it going Whig.

Redbornestoke, given the residual influence of the Bruces, was Tory at all the elections apart from 1715. Flitt was Tory between 1685 and 1715 but went Whig in 1727. The large Manshead hundred was Whig in 1685, thanks probably to Lord Edward Russell. From 1705 to 1722 the Tories predominated but in 1727 the Whigs achieved parity.

In the County elections two Tories won in 1685; between 1705 and 1722 there was one Tory and one Whig, and in 1727 and 1734 two Whigs. In 1685 the Tories won despite doing badly in Manshead. They overwhelmed their opponents in Biggleswade, Clifton and Wixamtree. For one Tory MP to be elected, they had to get a substantial majority of votes in Manshead. From 1705 to 1722 they took Manshead, and in consequence one of their candidates was elected. Then parity and later lagging behind in Manshead led them to lose the election.

These widespread divisions and contrasts can be found at parish level, shown in the tables at the back of this volume. Despite the almost universal support for the Alstons and the Whigs in the north part of the county, there were odd pockets of support for the Tories. Sharnbrook, Felmersham and Pavenham were Whig throughout. Nearby Riseley was Tory throughout. Milton Ernest, home of Samuel Rolt, was Tory to 1715, thereafter Whig. In this hundred any parish, such as Bletsoe or Melchbourne, on the St John estate tended to be Tory.

Barford hundred contained Eaton Socon with its large electorate. Having a Tory majority in 1685, thereafter it was a key element in the Whigs' success. Next-door Roxton was Whig until 1715. In 1722 the influence of James Metcalfe was felt and the parish went Tory. Sir William Beecher's parish of Renhold was Whig throughout.

The eastern hundreds of Biggleswade, Wixamtree and Clifton were among the most Tory areas in the County, but this pattern altered when the Byngs of Southill and their relations the Osborns became involved in local politics. Southill, Campton and Shefford were all Tory till 1722 but with the candidacy of the local man, Pattee Byng, went Whig. Northill, home of John Harvey MP, remained Tory throughout. Dunton showed a more volatile voting pattern. In 1685 the Whigs predominated, from 1705 to 1722 the Tories, and then, in 1727, back to the Whigs. The Spencers owned the manor of Millo in the parish and may well have had an effect on how the vote went. Everton was Tory from 1685 to 1722 but in 1727 the two parties were equal. Langford remained Whig throughout. The small towns of Sandy and Potton were Tory till the latter went Whig in 1734. Willington and Blunham were Whig, including the major estates of Sir William Gostwick and the Duke of Kent, both Whigs.

Flitt hundred contained another strong Tory area, centred on the Napiers of Luton Hoo. The important market town of Luton always had a Tory majority, as did nearby Caddington and Streatley. Barton was Tory to 1722. That year, and in 1727, the Tories were in the lead. Pulloxhill was, in contrast, Whig, perhaps influenced by its proximity to Wrest Park and the Whig Duke of Kent.

Manshead hundred had the largest number of electors and included the two important towns of Dunstable and Leighton Buzzard, both strongly Tory. Yet next to Dunstable was the equally strongly Whig Houghton Regis led by the Brandreths of Houghton Hall and Houghton Manor House. Within the hundred were some more varied voting patterns such as at Eaton Bray where in 1685 the Whigs predominated. In 1705 the poll was headed by a Tory and in 1715 by a Whig and a Tory. Thereafter it was Whig. Toddington had a slightly different pattern, being Tory from 1715 to 1727. It went Whig in 1734. Woburn was always Whig, apart from 1727, when the 3rd Duke of Bedford supported Tory candidates. Woburn's near-neighbour Eversholt remained Whig throughout, turning a deaf ear to the Duke of Bedford in 1727.

At the heart of Redbornestoke hundred was the Ailesbury fiefdom of Ampthill, Maulden and Milbrook. They all remained Tory until 1734 when the parties were equal. Houghton Conquest, however, went over to the Whigs in 1715 and did not return to the Tories. At the other end of the hundred was the strong Whig area of Kempston, home of John Cater MP.

Bedford Borough

As the Borough poll books are not arranged by parishes, it is not possible to analyse them in the same way as for the parishes in the County election. However, parish registers for the five ancient parishes and the Minute Book of Bunyan Meeting[16] will give clues as to the relative strengths of Anglicanism and nonconformity within the Borough. The Minute Books of the Borough Council[17] and Borough Quarter Sessions reveal how the rivalries and divisions panned out in detail. The Apprenticeship register gives details of those who would ultimately seek to be freemen, because of their apprenticeships.[18] This document offers useful information on the trading base of the town's prosperity.

Bribery and corrupt practices

Loyalty to a local landowner, loyalty to party and self-interest are motivations for people deciding on how to vote. The extensive treating that took place during the canvas and around the time of the election itself has already been highlighted. But what about direct bribery? There were five petitions to the House of Commons in the forty years from 1690 to 1730 about Borough elections.[19] Those of 1705, 1727 and 1730 alleged direct bribery. In 1690 there was corruption alleged in that the wrong writ was returned to the Clerk of the Crown by the under-sheriff. In 1713

---

[16] H.G. Tibbutt, ed., *The Minutes of the First Independent Church (now Bunyan Meeting) 1656–1766*, BHRS, vol. 55 (Bedford, 1976).
[17] BLARS, BOR. BB2/3 Minutes 1688–1718.
[18] BLARS, BOR. BC1/2 Inrollments of indentures for apprentices 1663–1713.
[19] O'Byrne, *The Representative History of Great Britain and Ireland*, pp. 6–12. *Journals of the House of Commons*, vol. 10, pp. 360, 375–7, 380; vol. 15, p. 12; vol. 17, p. 487; vol. 21, pp. 34, 50, 138–9, 635, 666.

Rolt, although elected, was not qualified to stand as he had not taken the requisite oaths. The petitioners accused the under-sheriff and mayor of malpractice over sending in the election return.

There were two petitions over malpractice in elections for the County seat.[20] In 1698 complaints were made against votes being procured by entertainments and voters prevented from voting. In 1715 John Harvey was unseated for using illegal practices, specifically using unqualified voters to support him.

Bribery was likely to be more effective in the Borough, because of its smaller electorate, at least some of whom lived in a compact area, close to public houses and the hustings. The Tories quite clearly intended to buy the Borough in 1727 and 1730. The Whigs also did their treating but claimed that they never actually bribed. Full-scale bribery was probably endemic in boroughs throughout the country, adding to the great cost of elections especially under the Triennial Act, where new Parliaments had to be elected every three years. After 1715, septennial Parliaments were the rule.[21]

Conclusion

It is hoped that this introduction and the texts in this volume and its successor will clarify the role of individual people and parishes in Bedfordshire politics from the 1680s to the 1730s. The story of the somewhat frenzied politics of Bedford Borough and County will be continued to 1734 in a subsequent volume. There were a number of elections in the years 1716 to 1734 and therefore plenty of chances of finding out where people were. Some useful correspondence towards the end of the period gives a clear insight into the manoeuvrings of the principal players.

---

[20] *Journals of the House of Commons*, vol. 12, p. 352; vol. 13, pp. 2, 90–1.
[21] Septennial Act 1714, 1 Geo. 1, sess. 2, c. 38.

Chapter One

1685 Election

Prelude

The first poll book transcribed here dates from 1685. To understand it properly, the deep political divisions that surfaced in the last years of Charles II's reign must be looked at. Underlying these were the, as yet, unhealed wounds of the trauma of the Civil War and the Commonwealth. For one side the bogey of a monarch acting without Parliament could be paraded to stiffen the resolve of the faithful. For the other side the judicial murder of Charles I, the destruction of the Anglican Church and the rule of nonconformists had a similar effect. On both sides was a deep hatred of Roman Catholicism. Louis XIV, the autocratic and expansionist King of France, crystallised Bedfordshire people's fears. This underlying anti-Roman Catholicism was to surface in the Gordon riots in London a century later but was always in the background.

The later years of Charles II intensified these tensions, as it became clear that his heir was going to be his brother, James Duke of York, a convert to Roman Catholicism in the late 1660s. This was made public by his resigning his post as Lord High Admiral, because he was unwilling to take communion in the Church of England as was required by the Test Act of 1673[1] of all office-holders. In the same year he married Mary of Modena, an Italian Roman Catholic.

The actual size of Roman Catholic support in Britain was tiny, estimated by W.A. Speck at 2 percent of the population.[2] In Bedfordshire,[3] the proportion was probably even less, with the only prominent family being the Conquests of Houghton Conquest, some of whom were Roman Catholics and some Anglican. There were a few Roman Catholics at Turvey on the Mordaunt estates and others at Shefford.

The Stuarts' main support came from the remnants of the Cavaliers and others who wanted the dynasty to be the main bulwark of the Church of England. They were nicknamed 'Tories'. They favoured the legitimate succession of James, as long as he protected the Church of England's privileges as the established Church and the exclusion from national and local power of all those who did not conform to it, namely, nonconformists. The Cavaliers/Tories had used their power after the restoration of 1660 to pass legislation severely restricting people, like John Bunyan, Independent Minister of Bedford, who was imprisoned for his beliefs from 1660 to

---

[1] Test Act 1673, 25 Car. II, c. 2.
[2] W.A. Speck, *Reluctant Revolutionaries: Englishmen and the Revolution of 1688* (Oxford, 1988), p. 170.
[3] BLARS, Introduction to RO Catalogue.

William Lord Russell (1639–83). The Whig leader was executed for his part in the Rye House Plot. Engraving by Thomas Cook. (BLARS, Casebourne Archive)

1672 and again in 1675 or 1676.[4] Their local leaders were the Bruce family, Robert, 1st Earl of Ailesbury (d. 1685) and his son, Thomas, 2nd Earl (1656–1741).

Those who still felt sympathy with the ideas of greater religious and political freedom of the 1640s and 1650s were nicknamed 'Whigs'. They tended to resent the predominance of the Church of England and favoured relaxing the Tories' legislation against nonconformists. They saw a Protestant King as essential. Some in their desperation supported the Duke of Monmouth, Charles II's illegitimate son. Their local leaders were the Russells of Woburn Abbey and were supported by most of Bedfordshire's substantial number of Independents, Baptists and Congregationalists.

In 1678 there was a vicious anti-Roman Catholic outburst fuelled by Titus Oates, who unveiled what he saw as a popish plot. Charles II dissolved Parliament to save his minister, Danby, who was found to have secretly communicated with France. The ensuing election of 1679 was a triumph for the Whigs. This success was repeated in two further general elections: later in 1679 and in 1681. The two members of Parliament for the County seat for Bedfordshire were Lord William Russell, heir to Woburn Abbey, and Sir Humphrey Monoux of Wootton, a newcomer to the county. Both were staunch Whigs. About the earlier election Edmund Verney wrote on 24 February 1678/9: 'I hear the Bedfordshire election cost £6,000. They were three days a polling. But Lord Bruce and his party lost by 500 votes, whereat the Earl of Ailesbury, his father, was extremely angry.'[5] Bruce's fellow candidate had been Sir John Napier of Luton Hoo. The Whig Sir William Franklyn of Mavourn, Bolnhurst, replaced Sir William Beecher of Howbury, Renhold. William Paulet St John was re-elected. They won again later in the year and in 1681, contributing towards a Whig domination of the House of Commons.

The Whig leader, the 1st Lord Shaftesbury, tried to introduce two bills for James's Exclusion, one of which was presented by Lord William Russell, member for Bedfordshire. Both failed.

On 25 March 1681 Charles II dissolved Parliament and did not summon another. His Declaration blamed this on Parliament, which he accused of obstructing attempts to carry out the laws against nonconformists. It was ordered to be read in all churches and chapels. In June, Lord Ailesbury, as Lord Lieutenant, arranged a *Loyal Address from the Lieutenant, Deputy Lieutenants, Justices of the Peace, Military Officers, Clergy, Gentlemen, and Freeholders of the County of Bedfordshire.*[6] Referring to the 'benign influence' of the King's 'most equal and prudent government', they were grateful for the 'Royal Assurance you are pleased to give us therein to remove all the reasonable fears and causeless jealousies which some ill men (whose attempts we abhor and detest) have endeavoured to insinuate into the people, thus weakening your Majestie's prerogative (which by law we are bound to support) and defaming the true sons of the Church of England, which as now Established, is the best, if not the only, bulwark against Popery.' The address was signed by some 200 people, showing the strength of the Bruces in mobilising opinion.

---

4   J. Brown, *John Bunyan*.
5   Ibid., p. 295.
6   Ibid., p. 315, where the full text is transcribed.

The Effigies of the Earle of Ailesbury, and of Ampthill, Baron Skelton, and Kinlos, County of Bedford; of ÿ Honour of Ampthill his Ma:ties most Hon:rbl

P. Lelÿ Pinxit.

IVIMUS

Right Hon:rbl Robert Elgin, Viscount Bruce Bruce, of Wharlton, L:d Leiutenant of the Hereditary high Steward And one of the Lords of Privy Councell.

R. White Sculpsit.

Robert Lord Ailesbury (d. 1685). Lord Lieutenant of Bedfordshire 1660–85. Engraving by Robert White of a portrait by P. Lely. (BLARS, Casebourne Archive)

Although determined to govern as much as possible without Parliament, Charles II prudently prepared for the inevitable day when he would have to summon one by ensuring that any new House of Commons was as subservient to the crown as possible. He turned his attention to boroughs, which elected members of Parliament. By using the device of granting new charters, Charles granted a new power to enable his Council to remove any official or member of the Borough Council that it wished. This would ensure a permanent majority in favour of royal policy.

The Rye House Plot and the death of Lord William Russell

The Whigs could see that the consequence of Charles II's policy would be their permanent exclusion from power. It is not surprising that direct action began to be talked about. A plot was mooted of kidnapping Charles II and James, as they travelled back from Newmarket on 22 March 1683, and forcing them to recognise Monmouth as the heir to the throne. The so-called Rye House Plot was a non-event. Indeed, it has been suggested that it was no more than talk. It was not even discovered until the following June. However, Lord William Russell was convicted by Monmouth turning King's evidence. As a proposer of the 1680 Exclusion Bill, Russell could not expect royal mercy. The King and his brother saw they had a golden chance to eliminate a major enemy. William was therefore executed on 21 July 1683. Unwittingly, a Whig martyr had been created.[7]

Reaction in Bedfordshire

Surprisingly, the reaction in Bedfordshire at Russell's execution was mixed. The Whigs, and especially the Russell family itself, were appalled at what they saw as judicial murder. The Tories, however, applauded. Lord Ailesbury, as the Lord Lieutenant of Bedfordshire, organised the following Loyal Address, significantly from Ampthill, close to his house, Houghton House:

The London Gazette[8]
From Monday November 5 to Thursday November 8 1683
Whitehall, November 7
The following Address was presented to His Majesty by the Right Honourable the Earl of Ailesbury, Lord Lieutenant of the County of Bedford, accompanied with my Lord Bruce, and the High Sheriff of the County, which His Majesty received very Graciously,
We the Grand Jury Sworn to enquire for the Body of this County of Bedford, at the General Quarter Sessions held for the said County at Ampthill, this Third day of October, One thousand Six hundred Eighty and Three, Having heard His Majesties Declaration read on the day by him appointed for a Thanksgiving for His and his Royal Brother's, and the Nations deliverance

---

[7]   Speck, *Reluctant Revolutionaries*, p. 39; Georgiana Blakiston, *Woburn and the Russells* (London, 1980), pp. 71–2.
[8]   Copy in Bedford Borough Archives, BLARS, BOR B. A3/6.

from the late Damnable and Fanatical Plot; And having amongst other things contained in it, seriously considered what his Majesty hath been pleased to express, particularly relating to the dangerous Consequences and Results which have and might arise from Conventicling and Caballing Meetings. We think ourselves bound in Duty, to the Care we ought to have of his Majesties Safety and the security of the Government as now by law established in Church and State, to present all Conventicles, and pretended Religious-Meetings, and all Clubs and Cabals of such whose Religion or Loyalty is much and justly to be doubted; And also all such who can be proved to have lessened either the certain Truth or Fatal Consequences of this last Plot, or have spoken anything contradictory to what His Majesty hath been pleased to publish in the aforementioned Declaration, which we conceive so high a Reflection on his Majesty and His Government, that we presume them not only unfit to bear any office in this Government, but likewise deserve to be bound to their Good Behaviour.

We the Custos Rotulorum, and the rest of His Majesties Justices of the Peace for the said County, do heartily concur in Opinion with the Gentlemen of the Grand-Jury, in this their seasonable Presentment. And do declare our Resolutions upon all Occasions, to put the laws in execution against all such dangerous Persons as are therein mentioned.

The Tories were using the plot to try to enforce legislation against Protestant nonconformists, who were in no way implicated in the plot and could not protest at this unjust slur.

The new Charter for the Borough of Bedford 1684

From 1681, Ailesbury had gradually been preparing the ground for persuading Bedford to accept one of Charles II's new-style charters. Soon after Parliament had been dissolved, enquiry was made at Bedford and it was found that two Chamberlains, Miles Wale and Andrew Freebody, had not taken the sacrament at church in the twelve months before and were therefore not qualified to act until they did so. In December the Privy Council accused Robert Audley, Deputy Recorder, of being 'an enemy to the Government and the Church of England, and a great countenancer of conventicles and phanaticks in the town of Bedford. And yet he was the great head and pillar of the disaffected party.'[9] Lord Ailesbury, the town's recorder, moved that Audley and other aldermen should be removed. Audley, as someone who had fought for Charles I and in consequence had had his estates sequestrated, was understandably aggrieved. He claimed that he had never been to a conventicle but might be forced to because of the superior preaching there! Although the complaint was dropped at the Privy Council, Audley's enemies on the Borough deprived him of a vote at their meetings. Paul Cobb, the mayor and hand in glove with Lord Ailesbury, managed to get Audley replaced. In October 1683, 53 new burgesses were appointed, all supporters of the Bruces, including two of Ailesbury's younger sons, Sir Francis Wingate and the Fosters. The latter two families had been involved in the

9   J. Brown, *John Bunyan*, pp. 317–18.

Num'b. 1875

The London Gazette.

Published by Authority.

From **Monday** November 5. to **Thursday** November 8. 1683.

Whitehall, November 7.

THe following Address was presented to His Majesty by the Right Honourable the Earl of *Ailesbury*, Lord-Lieutenant of the County of *Bedford*, accompanied with my Lord *Bruce*, and the High Sheriff of the County, which His Majesty received very Graciously,

WE the Grand-Jury Sworn to enquire for the Body of this County of Bedford, at the General Quarter Sessions held for the said County at Ampthill, this Third day of October, One thousand Six hundred Eighty and Three, Having heard His Majesties Declaration read on the day by Him appointed for a Thanksgiving for His and his Royal Brother's, and the Nations deliverance from the late Damnable and Fanatical Plot; And having amongst other things contained in it, seriously considered what His Majesty hath been pleased to express, particularly relating to the dangerous Consequences and Results which have and might arise from Conventicling and Caballing Meetings. We think our selves bound in Duty, to the Care we ought to have of His Majesties Safety, and the security of the Government, as now by Law established in Church and State, to Present all Conventicles, and pretended Religious-Meetings, and all Clubs and Cabals of such whose Religion or Loyalty is much and justly to be doubted; And also all such who can be proved to have lessened either the certain Truth or fatal Consequences of this last Plot, or have spoken any thing contradictory to what His Majesty hath been pleased to publish in the aforementioned Declaration, which we conceive so high a Reflection on His Majesty and His Government, that we presume them not only unfit to bear any Office in this Government, but likewise deserve to be bound to their Good-Behaviour.
We the Custos Rotulorum, and the rest of His Majesties Justices of the Peace for the said County, do heartily Concur in Opinion with the Gentlemen of the Grand-Jury in this their reasonable Presentment. And do declare our Resolutions upon all Occasions, to put the Laws in execution against all such dangerous Persons as are therein mentioned.

Venice, October 16. We have an account from *Bossina* and *Albania*, that they had there the news of the defeat of the Turkish Army before *Vienna*, and that it put the Turks in those Countries into a great consternation. And from several Parts of *Turkey*, we are told, that they have received orders from the Grand Signior, to send what Troops and Provisions they possibly can to *Hungary*. The Marquis *de la Torre*, Ambassador Extraordinary from the Emperor, parted from hence the last

Emperor on his behalf, but that the King had let him know, that he could not expect to make his Peace, unless he immediately lay down his Arms, or else employ them against the Turks. We are told that the King of *Poland* will have his winter quarters at *Presbourg*, and that the Queen is on her journey to meet his Majesty there.
Lintz, October 16. The Emperor has received Letters from the Duke of *Lorrain*, giving his Imperial Majesty an account, that having repaired *Barkan*, and put a good Garison in it, he had passed the *Danube* with the Imperial Army on the 10th Instant, and Besieged *Gran*; That at the same time the King of *Poland*, being reinforced with the Troops of *Lithuania*, was marched towards *Agria*, to possess himself of that and some other places in the *Upper Hungary*, for the security of their winter quarters. That they had advice that the Grand Visier had been forced to quit his Camp near *Stoel-Weissenburg*, for that his Troops refused to remain any longer in the Field and disbanded, and that he was retiring towards *Belgrade*, having first put what men he could into *Buda*, under the command of two Bassa's, whom he had charged to be answerable for the place, and had promised them in case they were attacked, a powerful assistance in the Spring. The Elector of *Bavaria*, who was forced to leave the Army after the Battle of *Vienna*, by reason of his illness, rejoyned it the 19th Instant near *Barkan*, with 7000 Foot; His Horse, as likewise the Cavalry of *Franconia*, are it's said, coming back to winter in the Empire, there being a great scarcity of Forage in *Hungary*.
Lintz, October 30. This day arrived here the Count *d'Averspeg* from the Imperial Army in *Hungary*, being sent by the Duke of *Lorrain*, to give the Emperor an account of the happy success of his Arms against *Gran*. On the 20th Instant the Duke of *Lorrain* understanding by some Prisoners that were taken, that the Turks who were posted in the Fort upon *Thomas Hill*, had orders so it on as they perceived the Christians approach to attack them, to retire into the Cittadel; His Highness resolved to intercept them, and commanded the Count *de Scherffenberg*, being supported by two Regiments of Horse, to invest the Hill, and to take the said Fort, which was accordingly done, and of 380 Ja-

arrest of Bunyan in 1672 and were strongly opposed to nonconformists. In November, another 23 new burgesses were added, including the Dives of Bromham and Chesters of Lidlington.

The purpose of all this was revealed on 8 January 1684, when the Borough Council decided to surrender the town charter to the King in exchange for another one. The new charter was brought to Bedford by the Earl of Ailesbury with a large retinue of local gentry. They met a deputation from the town between Wilstead and Elstow. The procession numbered around 500 people on horse. The charter was handed over in front of the Guildhall in Bedford with much rejoicing, after which there was a feast. The Borough now had the right to have two new fairs a year but the King had the right by an Order in Council to remove any or all of the members or officials of the Borough Corporation.[10] Had the town lost its birthright for a mess of pottage?

In the last months of Charles II's life, Ailesbury made another determined effort to enforce the law on attendance at Church of England churches. Quarter Sessions was held on 14 January 1684/5 and resolved: 'That all such Laws as had been provided for the reducing all Dissenters to a thorow Conformity shall be put into a speedy and vigorous execution.' All clergy had to report on non-attenders, people who did not kneel at prayers or sat during the gloria, creed and hymns.[11] This resolution was supported by the diocesan bishop, Thomas Barlow of Lincoln. Such a policy would have been deeply unpopular among Bedfordshire's nonconformists, with John Bunyan at their head.

Death of Charles II and Accession of James II

On 6 February 1685, Charles II died and his brother ascended the throne, surprisingly peacefully. He immediately made a statement in the Privy Council: 'I shall make it my endeavour to preserve the government both in church and state, as is by law established.' He added, somewhat ironically in the light of his later actions, that 'as I shall never depart from the just rights and prerogative of the Crown, so I shall never invade any man's property'.

Henry Mordaunt, 2nd Earl of Peterborough, who owned an estate at Turvey, commented: 'Every thing is very happy here. Never king was proclaimed with more applause than he that raignes under the name of James the Second. He is courted by all men, and all orders pay him Duty and Obedience . . . I doubt not to see a happy reign.'[12] Peterborough was a Privy Councillor and two years later became a Roman Catholic.

It was politic as well as customary to send a petition to congratulate the new King. The Earl of Ailesbury organised this petition of congratulation, which was expected to be signed by people of both political persuasions. Ailesbury characteristically put his own twist to it by specifically welcoming James's declaration that he would preserve the Government according to the established laws both in Church

10   Ibid., pp. 319–21; VCH *Bedford*, vol. II, p. 58.
11   J. Brown, *John Bunyan*, p. 323.
12   Speck, *Reluctant Revolutionaries*, pp. 42–3.

and State, that is, continue the oppression of nonconformists of all religious hues. Secondly, Ailesbury included the pledge that at the next election the MPs for Bedfordshire would be 'agreeable to your Majestie' and support the declaration. Ailesbury's intention was that they should be Tories. The party nature of the document is shown by the fact that at least 41 out of the 86 signatories voted for the Tory candidates at the subsequent election. It was a difficult document for Whigs to subscribe to and the Earl of Bedford's name, being added in another hand, perhaps implies that he signed it late.

Petition of Congratulation from the County of Bedfordshire[13]
To the King's most Excellent Majesty
We your Maj[es]ties Loyall Subjects the Lords, Gentlemen and Freeholders of the County of Bedford. As we heartily condole the Death of his late Majesty of Blessed Memory, your deer Brother, So wee most chearfully Congratulate Your Majestie's happy access to the Crowne And do begg Your Majestie's Acceptance of Our most humble thanks for your gracious Declaracon wherein your Majesty is pleased to assure your Subjects that you will preserve the Government, according to the established Laws, both in Church and State, which as it hath confirmed those who always believed your Majestie would do what you now declare; so wee hope it will give such satisfaction to others who formerly made doubt there of that they will endeavour for the next Parliament to choose such Representatives for this County as shall be agreeable to your Majestie and promote the end of the said Declaration And according to both our Duty and Interest Wee shall pray for your Majestie's long and prosperous Reigne over us.
[underlined names were added later]

[Earl of] Kent
[Earl of] Ailesbury
[Lord]Bruce
[Earl of] Bedford

Edward Russel	Jo. Ventris jnr	A. Chester	Cooper Orlebar
John Osborn	George Walker	Humphrey Monoux	Henry Bassett
Creswell Levins	Jo. Marshe	Villiers Chernocke	Jo. Pemberton
St John Moor	Daniel Marshe	G. Blundell	Jo. Goodwine
John Duncomb			
Jo. Francklin	Samuel Bedford	Francis Wingate	Jo. Davyes
Clement Armiger	Thomas Cheyne	W. Bicher	Robert Montague
James Astrey	Jo. Marsh jnr	William Boteler	Oliver St John
John Osborn	S. Hanwell	E. Browne	Thomas Sickling
Francis Dive	Thomas Upwood	T. Hillersden	Matthew Denis
William Geary	Thomas Brace	Benjamin Conquest	George Orlebar
John Ventris	Ralph Baldwyn	Richard Orlabear	Anthony Chester jun
Charles Gery	Thomas Christie	Thomas Taylor	Thomas Snagge
George Edwards	William Berkley	W. Dyer	George Snagge
William Foster	John Cockayne	St John Thomson	Ralph Sadlier
Lewis Monoux	Nicholas Luke	Ditto jnr	William Stone
William Farrer	Jo. Willsheiere	William Livesay jnr	Edward Hall

13 BLARS, CH 921.

Edmund Gardner	John Smith	George Hide
Simon Urlin	George Mourdaunt	G[a]i[us] Squires
Charles Dimocke	William Symcotts	Thomas Browmsell
C. Dymocke jnr	William Daniel	Ralph Broomsell
Richard Helder	Nicholas Granger	James Edwards
Humphrey Taylor	Mountague Pickering	William Boteler
Francis Brace	Richard Orlebar	James Boteler
Paul Cobb	Georg Cob	Richard Stone

Bedford Borough Election 1685

Early in March, the Borough of Bedford elected its two MPs, Sir Anthony Chester of Chicheley and Lidlington and Thomas Christie, a prominent local man. Both were Tories. Christie was a staunch Anglican, worshipping at St Paul's, Bedford. He was interested in helping the poor, and the almshouses that bear his name are the successors of those he endowed in 1682.

It is not known if Chester and Christie were opposed by other candidates. There was an influential nonconformist presence in the town centred on John Bunyan and his followers. Dr Browne saw the tribulations in Mansoul in Bunyan's *Holy War* of 1682 as a commentary on the evil times Bedford was enduring. In 1683 there had been a prosecution at the assizes of someone for speaking slanderously of James, then Duke of York. Added to which, the new charter would have made it difficult to elect an opposition candidate.

The 1685 County Election

Using this unexpected goodwill, James II called a Parliament as soon as he could to obtain generous grants to help pay for the costs of government. He came to the throne on 6 February, and by 9 March votes were being cast in the general election in Bedfordshire. The two County seats were contested by four candidates. The two Tories, backed by the Bruces, were William Boteler of Biddenham and Sir Villiers Chernocke of Hulcote. The Whig candidates were Edward Russell of Woburn and Sir Humphrey Monoux of Wootton. Boteler was the grandson of the Cromwellian MP of the same name and, unusually, had joined the party of the Cavaliers. Chernocke was a relative of the Duke of Buckingham, Charles I's favourite. His father, Sir John, had been granted their baronetcy in 1661. Villiers had succeeded in 1680. Boteler, with estates in Harrold and Biddenham, was likely to have support in the Ouse Valley, including Bedford. Chernocke was best known in the south and west of the county. Both formed part of a tight net of independent country gentry, owning their estates but lacking London links. In 1691 Villiers's son was to marry Boteler's daughter, and another daughter married William Farrer, an MP for Bedford at the start of the eighteenth century.

The Honourable Edward Russell was the younger brother of Lord William, the martyr. He had been forced to take a leading role with his brother's widow in running the family estate, as his father was old and his nephew was a minor. He took up his brother's mantle and stood for an uncompromising Whiggism, bitterly opposed to James II. The father of his fellow candidate Sir Humphrey Monoux had received a baronetcy in 1660. He had been elected in 1679 with Lord William and was the sitting member. His estates were based in Wootton and Sandy.

The election was held just after the assizes.[14] Many of the leading gentry formed part of the calendar of the county or names of ministers preserved in the assize records. On this list were the chief ministers of state, including the Archbishop of Canterbury and Judge Jeffreys, whose Bloody Assize in the West Country later in the year was to make him famous. To these were added the leading gentry, as justices of the peace, the mayor of Bedford and bailiffs for the several towns and hundreds. Out of this group was selected the grand jury, who decided what cases should be tried by the petty jury. The justices of the peace were selected by the Earl of Ailesbury as lord lieutenant. At the assize he needed some form of minimal military force to ensure order. Ailesbury was trying to ensure a maximum turn out of his own supporters with the added bonus of being able to have a useful meeting to decide electoral tactics.

The assizes were held on 4 March and polling took place five days later. In between there was a general meeting of the County voters, probably held at Bedford. The Whig candidates were elected on a show of hands but the Tories demanded a poll.[15] The polling towns were Ampthill and Biggleswade. Ampthill was close to the Earl of Ailesbury's seat at Houghton House. Biggleswade was near estates of leading Tory supporters such as Sir John Cotton of Stratton, the Bromsalls of Moggerhanger and Northill and John Harvey of Ickwell. Significantly, Bedford was not to be used for polling, despite being the county town.

The poll book[16] for the election comes from the Chester family archives. Sir Anthony Chester of Chicheley, Buckinghamshire, was Tory MP for Bedford from 1685 to 1688. He was also the High Sheriff for Bedfordshire and therefore responsible for the running of the County election. The result was a triumph for the Tories. Indeed, the King, looking at the results of the general election as a whole, saw there were only forty MPs whom he would not have chosen himself. The Bedfordshire results were: Boteler 901, Chernocke 841 (elected), and Russell 744 and Monoux 634 (not elected), making a total of 3120 votes. However, the names in the poll book and their votes only add up to 2833.

Thus 287 votes are not recorded. Was there another polling town, whose return has been lost? Looking at where the voters came from this is unlikely, as there are a number of voters recorded from possible alternative polling towns, such as Bedford, Luton or Leighton Buzzard. As these unrecorded votes seem to support the candidates roughly equally, it is unlikely that the winning party added votes corruptly. The most likely explanation is that they were outsetters, voters with qualifications to vote in Bedfordshire but living outside the county, often in London.

In his *Diary* for 10 May 1685, John Evelyn recorded: 'elections were thought to be very indirectly carried on in most places, and persons chosen who had no interest in the Country and places for which they served. God grant a better issue of it than

14 BLARS, Introduction to HSA.
15 J. Brown, *John Bunyan*, p. 334.
16 BLARS, CH 922.

some expect!'[17] The MPs elected for Bedfordshire were, as we have seen, all well known in the county.

Was the Tory triumph purely because of undue pressure from Lord Ailesbury? Analysis of the poll book shows far from uniform voting patterns. Bedford, for example, was about level, with a difference of eleven votes covering all four candidates. Other tight results were at Dunstable, Leighton and Turvey.

Boteler and Chernocke had substantial leads in Ampthill, Barton, Biggleswade, Bromham, Campton, Clophill, Cranfield, Eaton Socon, Flitwick, Lidlington, Luton, Maulden, Milbrook, Potton, Riseley, Sandy, Shillington, Southill, Sundon, Tilsworth, Tingrith, Whipsnade, Willington and Wrestlingworth.

On the other side, Cardington, Colmworth, Elstow, Felmersham, Flitton, Harrold, Houghton Regis, Husborne Crawley, Kempston, Marston Moretaine, Ravensden, Renhold, Toddington, Wilden, Wilstead, Woburn and Wootton all polled strongly for Russell and Monoux.

Normally voters voted for either one party or the other. Hockliffe broke the trend by giving most of its votes to Boteler and Russell.

This complex picture of neighbouring parishes voting for opposite sides suggests different reasons for the result. The territorial influence of Lord Ailesbury was important in his immediate area. Ampthill and the five parishes bordering on it all voted for Boteler and Chernocke. Yet parishes a bit further away such as Marston Moretaine voted the other way.

The main strength of the Tories was the support of the esquires and gentry: 112 voted for both Chernocke and Boteler, with some others voting for just one of them. Contrast this with the 12 who voted for Russell. None voted for Monoux. The 112 were dominant in their own parishes and were often related to one another. Sir Anthony Chester, with the help of Thomas Jones, gentleman, delivered the vote for them at Lidlington. He had large estates there. Some of the voters may have been tenants but they would have had to own land to the value of 40 shillings in the county to be able to vote. Later elections show that such a practice was widespread. Northill had a strong group of Tory gentry supporters, including Humphrey Fishe of Ickwell, the High Sheriff, who had the key job of administering the election. The result was 18 for the Tories, 2 for the Whigs. Regional influence of a local landowner could help the Whigs too, such as at Wootton, where Sir Humphrey Monoux lived. He won all but one vote from the parish.

The influence of the local landed gentleman was not always decisive, as at Elstow, where Thomas Hillersden voted for his relation Boteler and gave his second vote to Russell. The rest of the parish's voters all supported Monoux as well as Russell. Similarly at Cardington, William Whitbread voted for Boteler and Russell, while the rest of the Cardington voters supported Russell and Monoux.

The Boteler and Chernocke partnership was seen as a strong support for the Church of England: 42 clergy voted for them and none for the Russells. Macaulay writes with a little exaggeration, perhaps, that: 'The people were warned from a thousand pulpits not to vote for any Whig candidate, as they should answer it to Him

---

17 E.S. De Beer, ed., *The Diary of John Evelyn* (London, 1955), pp. 807–8.

who had ordained the powers that he, and who had pronounced rebellion a sin no less deadly than witchcraft.'[18]

The nonconformists would have been expected to vote for Russell and Monoux and against the clergy. Leading members of Bunyan's Meeting in Bedford[19] voted for them, such as Richard Eston and Thomas Woodward, as well as other Woodwards, who were probably his relations. However, John Eston plumped, giving the only vote he cast for William Boteler of Biddenham, whom he would have known and no doubt respected. William Wheeler of Cranfield, probably either a Quaker or a Baptist, as people with that name were prominent in both sects, voted for Boteler and Chernocke. Here again, living close to Chernocke, he was voting for someone he knew.

Voters tended to support either one pair of candidates or the other. If a candidate came from the voter's area, he might only support his local one. Some, mainly from the north of the county, voted for Boteler but not for Chernocke, and in the south the reverse happened.

As many as a hundred voters voted for Russell and did not give their second vote to Monoux. These came from all over the county and included a substantial number from Bedford itself within a few miles of Monoux's house. This suggests either that Monoux was seriously unpopular or that the Whigs, realising that they would be lucky to get one MP elected, backed Russell as more likely to have wider support.

Poll books show how individuals and families voted. This can be unexpectedly revealing. Christopher and Robert Foote of Great Barford both voted for the Whigs. Thomas Ward voted for the Tories, Edmund voted for Boteler alone and William for the Whigs. They are quite clearly voting as a family, trying to avoid annoying either of the parties or the local gentry. This pattern of voting is repeated countless times in the ensuing elections. Leading figures, such as William Whitbread, may well have wanted a balanced representation in Parliament for Bedfordshire, so that no one felt excluded and affairs would not be run in a partisan way. Some hope in 1685!

The actual campaigning in Bedfordshire was extraordinarily bitter. The Tories paraded with decapitated heads of cocks on the ends of their sticks, thus showing their hatred of the beheaded Lord William Russell and his brother Edward.[20] The importance of the gentry vote was well understood by the future Earl of Ailesbury. He wrote in his *Memoirs*: 'the gentry were generally for us: a great mark of the eyes of the nation being well opened, and so it appeared by the choice throughout the kingdom'.[21]

---

[18] T.B. Macaulay, *History of England from the Accession of James I* (London, 1854), vol. 1, p. 475.

[19] H.G. Tibbutt, ed., *The Minutes of the First Independent Church (now Bunyan Meeting) at Bedford 1656–1766*, BHRS, vol. 55 (1976), p. 13.

[20] Speck, *Reluctant Revolutionaries*, p. 46.

[21] Ibid., p. 46.

Poll for the County of Bedfordshire 1684 [i.e. 1685]

Source: manuscript, BLARS, CH 922. Voters are listed according to the candidate for whom they voted.

Poll Book of election on 9 and 10 March 1684 [1685]

Votes for Sir Villiers Chernock   841   Mr Boteler   901

Memorandum of all who voted twice: Monoux 18(857) and Boleler 14 (915)
Ampthill and Biggleswade 9 and 10 March 1685

The name of such Freeholders as poled for Sir Villiers Chernock Baronet and William Boteler Esq.

Aldridge, John of Ampthill, gentleman
Arnold, Thomas, jun of Ampthill, gentlemen
Abbis, Thomas of Gravenhurst, Clerk
Atkinson, Alexander of Potton
Atkinson, Richard of Potton
Atkinson, Henry of Sandy
Atkins, John of Sandy
Ashton, Thomas of Shitlington
Ansell, Francis of Shitlington
Aston, George of Shitlington
Apethorpe, Stephen of Barford
Amps, Edward of Maulden
Astry, William of Maulden
Astry, Ralph of Maulden
Astry, Henry of Maulden
Alborne, John of Southill
Augur, William of Litlington
Addams, Richard of Litlington
Amps, George of Sundon
Ashbolt, John of Willington
Avery, John of Totternhoe
Abbott, William of Bedford
Atkins, Richard of Eaton Bray
Atwood, Thomas of Eaton Socon
Atwell, William of Cople
Abbys, Thomas of Eyworth
Austen, Nicholas of Beeston
Atterton, Ralph of Dunstable
Albright, Thomas of Luton
Andrews, Richard of Luton
Ashwell, John of Leighton

Blundall, Sir George, Knight
Bedford, Samuell, of Henlow, Esq.
Bromsall, Thomas of Biggleswade, Esq.

Bromsall, Ralph of Mogerhanger, Esq.
Bromsall, Thomas of the same, gentleman
Barnardiston, George of Northill, [Esq. deleted] gentleman
Bassett, Henry of Eaton [Socon del], gentleman
Biddell, William of Willshamstedd, gentleman
Brace, Francis of Bedford, gentleman
Brace, Thomas of Shefford, gentleman
Bromsall, John of Blunham, gentleman
Butler, James of Harrold, gentleman
Barkerfeild, Thomas of Leighton
Broxton, William of Leighton
Bromsall, John of Sutton
Barnett, John of Roxton
Barlow, William of Chalgrave, Clerk
Bromsall, William of Sandy
Britten, Barron of Sandy
Bolton, John of Felmersham, Clerk
Bland, Robert of Cockayne Hattley
Bromsall, Thomas of Sandy
Bristow, Timothy of Wrestlingworth
Beaumont, William of Biggleswade
Burr, William of Shitlington
Barber, John of Southill
Barrett, Stephen of Cranfeild
Barber, William of Broome
Bourne, Edward of Bedford, Clerk
Browne, Henry of Risely
Beckett, Francis of Bedford, gentleman
Bayly, John of Luton
Bayes, Willson of Biggleswade
Boddington, William of Turvey
Bigg, Thomas of Barton

Beane, Thomas of Stopsley
Boston, Thomas of Wilden
Durkhead, Joseph of Barford, Clerk
Bedford, Pemberton of Henlow, Clerk
Bishop, Francis of Girford
Burrows, Thomas of Cranfeild
Bonner, William of Bedford
Blew, John of Wrestlingworth
Barber, William of Shefford
Burr, John of Harlington Grange
Boston, Richard of Eaton Socon
Barber, William of Farndish, Clerk
Brace, William of Millbrooke
Bowstredd, Joseph of Shefford
Bredsall, John of Bedford
Beale, Samuel of Houghton
Browne, Thomas of Maulden
Betts, John junior of Maulden
Betts, William of Maulden
Betts, John senior of Maulden
Baker, Thomas of Maulden
Baker, Andrew of Maulden
Benfeild, John of Risely, Clerk
Buckingham, John of Chalgrave
Bayes, John of Stagsden
Brand, Thomas of Turvey
Birden, William of Clophill
Brichmore, Richard of Whipsnade
Brichmore, William of Whipsnade
Boteler, John of Litlington
Browne, Edward of Litlington
Birt, John of Litlington
Bird, George of Houghton Conquest
Battison, Thomas of Bedford
Beale, John of Tuddington
Bundy, James of Bedford
Buckingham, Gabriell of Tillworth
Britten, John of Gravenhurst
Bland, William of Dunstable Houghton
Booth, Edward of Flitwick
Buckmaster, Edward of Eaton Bray
Buckmaster, Joseph of Millbrooke
Barnewell, William of Ampthill
Berry, John of Henlow
Berry, Thomas of Henlow
Berry, George of Henlow
Brace, Thomas of Millbrooke
Bonner, Thomas of Litlington
Barron, Thomas of Shitlington
Blowes, James of Wrestlingworth
Blith, Robert of Sandy

Bushby, William of Litlington
Bushby, Matthew of Litlington
Bedcott, John of Litlington
Browne, Evans of Eaton Socon
Browne, James of Eaton Socon
Boote, John of Eaton Socon
Baxter, William of Eaton Socon
Bisshop, John of Girford
Brittain, Thomas of Girford
Beckett, Thomas of Yevelden, Clerk
Bayes, Thomas of Tempsford
Blow, James of Wrestlingworth
Bouldstredd, William of Cardington
Brinkly, Thomas of Sandy
Burry, Thomas of Henlow
Boulton, John of Felmersham, Clerk
Burrow, John of Shitlington
Bedford, William of Ampthill

Chester, Sir Anthony of Litlington,
    Barronett
Cotton, Sir John of Stratton, Barronett
Chester, Anthony of Litlington, Esq.
Christy, Thomas of Bedford, Esq.
Cockayne, John of Cockayne Hatley, Esq.
Cockayne, John of Astwick, gentleman
Conquest, Benjamin of Haynes, Esq.
Cary, Walter of Everton, Esq.
Cheyne, Thomas of Sundon, Esq
Cheyne, Thomas of Luton, gentleman
Child, Henry of Roxton, gentleman
Crawly, John of Bedford, gentleman
Crow, William of Stoughton
Crane, William, Dr in Physick
Carr, Anthony of Leighton
Cooke, William of Leighton
Child, Thomas of Roxton
Child, Henry of Roxton
Chicheley, Richard of Bedford
Carrington, John of Broome
Clerke, John of Whipsnade, Clerk
Cumberland, William of Clifton
Cole, John of Northill
Carter, Thomas of Northill
Clarke, Robert of Northill
Calamy, James of the same, Clerk
Constable, Stephen of Shitlington
Cheyne, Thomas of Wootton, Clerk
Cleyton, Nathaniell of Risely
Cranfeild, Isaack of Luton
Chapman, Thomas of Luton

Corley, John of Risely
Chatterton, Joseph of Carleton, Clerk
Croote, Nicholas of Biggleswade
Chapman, John of Dunstable
Clerke, Henry of Sandy
Chapman, William of Luton
Cranfeild, William of Luton
Cautherell, John of Luton
Clerke, Richard of Southill
Coleman, Henry of Shitlington
Cawcock, George of Everton
Crouch, Robert of Cranfeild
Crawly, William of Southill
Clapham, John of Sandy
Carter, Edward of Wrestlingworth
Curfy, William of Litlington
Cranfeild, William of Shefford
Carter, John of Clophill
Cooke, Thomas of Sundon
Cooke, Francis of Sundon
Child, Francis of Maulden
Crouch, Thomas of Crawly [all deleted]
Carter, John of Ampthill, Clerk
Cooke, William of Tillsworth
Clerke, Thomas of Bedford
Cranidge, Robert of Houghton Conquest,
   Clerk
Curtis, John of Flittwick
Clerke, Thomas of Litlington
Cole, William of Litlington
Chapman, Josias of Litlington
Coleman, Thomas of Shitlington
Chapman, John of Potton
Cooke, Nearge of Potton
Corsby, William of Wrestlingworth
Child, Ralph of Malden
Crowe, Richard of Eaton Socon
Coote, William of Eaton Socon
Cotton, William of Eaton Socon
Chissell, Paul of Eyworth, Clerk
Child, John of Roxton
Chalkly, John of Luton
Cooper, Benjamin of Henlow
Carr, William of Houghton, Clerk
Cocker, John of Cople
Carter, Thomas of Beeston
Cole, Michaell of Clophill
Crawly, Robert, Doctor in Phisick of
   Dunstable
Cooper, Thomas of Thurleigh
Cotton, William of Eaton Socon [all deleted]

Conquest, Thimbleby of Houghton
   [Conquest]

Daniell, William of Newberry, Esq.
Dives, Francis of Bromeham, Esq.
Davies, John of Goldington, Esq.
Dodsworth, Francis of Ridgement, Esq.
Dockyra, Thomas of [blank], Esq.
Dillingham, John of Deane, gentleman
Dimock, Charles, senior of Cranfeild,
   gentleman
Dimock Charles, junior of Cranfeild,
   gentleman
Deane, John of Leighton
Deane, Henry of Leighton
Dix, Isaac of Cranfeild
Deere, John of Bedford
Day, Francis of Sandy
Dilly, Edward of Southill
Dilly, Thomas of Southill
Dennys, George of Everton
Day, Thomas of Luton
Davison, Robert of Tempsford
Dawborne, John of Litlington
Dawborne, Thomas of Litlington
Darling, John of Thurleigh
Deere, Solomon of Wrestlingworth
Dennys, John of Wrestlingworth
Denton, Nicholas of Houghton Conquest,
   gentleman
Davy, Thomas of Flittwick
Darling, Giles of Potton
Deere, John of Statfold
Day, William of Willshamstedd
Deere, William of Southill

Edwards, Richard of Arlesey, Esq.
Edwards, Jasper of Little Barford, Esq.
Everard, John of Beeston, gentleman
Etheridge, William of Eaton Bray, Clerk
Ellingham, Nathaniell of Stanbridge
Eling, John of Leighton [Luton deleted]
Ellis, Thomas of Sandy [Cardington
   deleted]
Earle, William of Thurleigh
Elmer, Thomas of Shitlington
Elmer, William of Shitlington
Ewsden, John of Shitlington, Clerk
Ewer, Edward of Luton
Emmerton, Richard of Stepingley
Eames, John of Kempston

Ekins, Henry of Wrestlingworth
Edwards, Thomas of Wrestlingworth
Edwards, Thomas of Clophill
Edwards, Peter of Cranfeild
Emmerton, William of Stepingley
Everard, William of Sandy

Fish, Humfry of Northill, Esq., High Sheriff
Foster, William, Doctor of Laws and
    Chancellor of Lincolne
Foster, William, junior of Bedford, Esq.
Faldo, William, senior of Bedford, gentleman
Faldo, William, junior of Bedford, gentleman
Francis, Jonathan of Biggleswade, gentleman
Fuller, John of Eaton Socon, Clerk [all
    deleted]
Frank, Richard of Eaton Socon
Frank, William of Eaton Socon
Faulkenham, William of Eaton Socon
Field, William of Cranfeild
Franklyn, Henry of Bromeham
Field, Thomas of Barford
Field, Phillip of Barton
Freeman, William of Sandy
Freeman, John of Pavenham
Frank, Thomas of Cranfeild, Clerk
Fage, Thomas of Southill
Fish, William of Southill
Fisher, John of Luton
Fossy, Daniell of Dunstable
Freeman, William of Statfold
Fenn, Samuel of Clophill
Fann, William of Hawnes
Field, Thomas of Maulden
Fensham, Richard of Maulden
Fowler, William of Luton
Fisher, William of Millbrooke
Field, Nicholas of Shefford
Fowks, Henry of Ampthill, gentleman
Farnell, Richard of Ampthill
Fowks, Richard of Ampthill
Finch, John of Houghton Conquest
Follett, John of Holcott
Field, Joseph of Cranfeild
Field, Thomas of Cranfeild
Fell, Thomas of Harlington
Field, Robert of Litlington
Finch, Henry of Potton
Freeman, John of Statfold
Fountaine, Robert of Hattley
Frank, John of Wyboston

Gostwick, Sir William of Willington,
    Barronett
Gostwick, Charles of the same, Esq.
Gostwick, William of Cople, Esq.
Grainger, Nicholas of Shitlington, Esq.
Grainger, Lancelott of the same
Gery, William of Clapham, Esq.
Goddard, Vincent, of Carleton, gentleman
Gates, William of Bolnhurst, Clerk
Gregory, James of Leighton
Gayton, John of Leighton
Groome, John of Dunstable
Gell, William of Risely
Goodwinn, John of Eaton Socon
Groome, Thomas of Dunstable
Gale, Robert of Oakely
Goldsmyth, Abraham of Barton
Gramant, William of Cranfeild
Goodship, John of Campton
Gibson, Thomas of Sandy
Gillam, William of Luton
Gasely, S[amue]ll of Cardington
Gaines, Edward of Mepersall
Goldsmyth, Peter of Shitlington
Graunt, James of Dunstable
George, William of Luton
Gibson, Edward of Hawnes, Clerk
Garrett, Thomas of Flitwick
Gilbert, Thomas of Bromeham
Good, James, senior of Bedford
Grey, Jeremy of Ampthill
Gregory, Thomas of Sundon
Greene, Robert of Sandy
Greene, Thomas of Houghton
Goodwinn, Robert of Litlington
Grundon, Simon of Oakely
George, John of Eaton
Goods, William, junior of Bedford
Gale, Simon of Oakely, Clerk
Goldsmyth, Daniell of Campton, Clerk
Gardner, John of Kempston
Griggs, William of Neither Standon
Grummant, Thomas of Cranfeild
Glinister, William of Standon
Gowler, John of Eaton Socon

Harvey, John of Ickwell, Esq.
Hanscombe, William of Shitlington, Esq.
Hide, George of Mepsall, Esq.
Halfehead, Edmund of Potton, gentleman
Halfehead, Thomas of the same

Hale, Olliver of Pulloxhill, gentleman
Hewett, Thomas of Millbrooke, gentleman
Halfepenny, Thomas of Faldo, gentleman
Hollowley, Christopher of Clifton, gentleman
Hanwell, Shem of Bedford, gentleman
Hooker, Jonathan of Sandy, Clerk
Houghton, Adam of Sundon, Clerk
Humfrys, Arthur of Barton, Clerk
Hawkins, Robert of Goldington, Clerk
Harding, Thomas of Marston
Hollingworth, John of Leighton
Honour, Henry, senior of Stanbridge
Honour, Henry, junior of Stanbridge
Hunt, Henry of Westoning, [Wrestlingworth deleted] Clerk
Hanscombe, John of Stretly
Holloway, S[amue]ll of Cople
Hill, Samuell of Broome
Honour, Richard of Luton
Haws, John of Bedford, gentleman
Harding, Thomas of Bedford
Hull, William of Barton
Hopkins, William of Barton
Higham, Richard of Luton
Harvey, Thomas of Cople
Harlow, Richard of Luton
Harris, Henry of Luton
Harper, Olliver of Everton
Heynes, Henry of Bidenham
Heyward, William of Bedford
Hanly, Robert of Wrestlingworth
Hill, Thomas of Luton
Hartwell, Joshua of Cranfeild
Hill, John of Maulden
Hales, Thomas of the same
Hancock, John of Bedford
Heyns, Lewis of Bromeham
Hummerstone, Thomas of Houghton
Howe, Thomas of Clophill
Hickman, Henry of Litlington [all deleted]
Hubbins, Benjamin of Marston
Hill, John, senior of Maulden
Harrowden, John of Clifton
Harrowden, Thomas of Clifton
Hills, Ralph of Ampthill [all deleted]
Harvey, Thomas of Ampthill
Hoggis, John of Henlow
Hill, Edward of Barton
Harper, William of Potton
Hawkins, Thomas of Potton
Hanscombe, Jeremy of Mepsall

Hickman, Thomas of Litlington
Hains, Thomas of Eaton Socon
Harris, George of Eaton Socon
Hall, John of Biggleswade
Holt, Baron of Sundon
Hey, William of Bedford
Hickman, William of Litlington
Halfehead, John of Southill
Hodden, John of Southill
Hurst, John of Southill
Haxby, Thomas of Potton, Clerk

James, Richard of Luton, gentleman
Jones, Thomas of Litlington, gentleman
Ironmonger, William of Harlington, gentleman
Jeffs, John of Leighton
Jenkins, Thomas of Billington
Inskipp, Thomas of Southill
Jones, William of Willington
Joy, Robert of Cople
Jackson, John of Luton
Jennings, John of Everton
Jennings, Robert of Everton
Jones, Robert of Stepingley
Jakins, Steevens of Eaton Socon

Kentish, William of Luton
Keyne, John of Luton
Knight, Daniel of Luton
Keofford, Richard of Roxton
Keppis, William of Roxton
Knight, Thomas of Harrold
King, Andrew of Sundon
King, John of Sundon
Knott, George of Eaton Socon
Killeson, Thomas of Sandy
Keyny, Ambrose of Ampthill
Knott, Robert of Goldington
King, Richard of Wrestlingworth
Kilby, Ralph of Ampthill

Lee, Charles of Leighton, Esq.
Luke, Nicholas of Cople, Esq.
Lawe, John of Ridgement, Esq.
Lee, Richard of Potton, gentleman
Leach, Theophilus of Deane, gentleman
Lawson, George of Wilshamsted, gentleman
Lithgold, Charles of Warden, Clerk
Love, John of [blank], Clerk

Lord, John of Dunstable, Clerk
Littlejohn of Holcott, Clerk
Lovell, William of Salford, Clerk
Leach, Samuell of Over Standon, Clerk
Litchfeild, Thomas of Risely
Lacy, Matthew of Shitlington
Leighton, John of Biggleswade
Lermouth, David of Potton
Legg, William of Flitwick
Lawford, John of Sandy
Lawford, Thomas of Sandy
Lucke, William of Sandy
Lebatt, Richard of Cranfeild
Lyce, Abraham of Luton
Lepar, Robert of Luton
Lame, Thomas of Bedford
Luke, Thomas of Everton
Lawrence, Richard of Standon
Lilly, Richard of Standon
Lake, John of Wrestlingworth
Lane, Edward of Sundon
Linford, Thomas of Bedford
Linford, Thomas of Clophill
Linford, John of Maulden
Limby, Paul of Ampthill
Luffe, Samuell of Eaton Socon
Leighton, William of Harlington
Lawrence, James of Mepsall
Lawman, Thomas of Maulden
Leighton, William of Ampthill
Lowe, Robert of Litlington
Lindsey, Thomas of Eaton Socon
Lewton, Thomas of Southill
Lawrence, William of Mogerhanger
Linford, William of Clophill

Mordaunt, George of Northill, Esq.
Mordaunt, John of the same, gentleman
Marsh, John, senior of Leighton, gentleman
Marsh, John, junior of Leighton, gentleman
Marsh, John, Doctor in Phisick
Marsh, Daniell of Dunstable, gentleman
Manly, William of Bedford, gentleman
Milward, Charles of Feilding, [Clerk deleted]
    gentleman
Merriden, Robert of Potton, gentleman
Merriden, Richard of Little Barford, Clerk
Merriden, William of Little Barford, Clerk
Miles, Thomas of Biggleswade, Clerk
Mole, William of Risely
Metcalfe, William of Dunstable

Moore, Sir St John, Knight
Mitchborne, John of Sandy
Mann, Robert of Dunstable
Moles, William of Marquet Streete
Moreton, Jeremy of Marquet Streete
Morgan, Richard of Potton
Merrywether, Francis of Everton
Meager, Edward of Shitlington
Martin, Thomas of Risely
Mash, George of Tempsford
Merrill, William of Gravenhurst
Moles, Henry of Sundon
Money, Thomas, junior of Kempston
Marriott, Samuell of Kempston
Milward, Henry of Litlington
Manfeild, William of Shefford
Merrill, John of Northill
Moore, John of Northill
Middleton, John of Northill
Miller, Thomas of Northill
Marshall, Samuell of Barton
Miles, William of Stanford
Miller, John of Potton
Meares, Thomas of Eaton Socon
Medbury, Thomas of Eaton Socon
Moaks, John of Eaton Socon
Mitchborne, Edward of Sandy
Mayduell, Thomas of Mogerhanger

Nodes, George of Southill, gentleman
Nasbitt, Alexander of Tingrith, Clerk
Newold, George of Sutton
Negus, Philipp of Barford
Nottingham, James of Kempston
Newman, William of Ridgement
Newman, Thomas of Eaton Socon
Noddings, George of Eyworth

Osborne, John, Esq.
Orlebear, Richard of Harrold, Esq.
Osborne, John of Wilshamstedd, gentleman
Oakely, John of Bedford
Olliver, Francis of the same
Odell, John of Salford
Ony, William of Luton

Palmer, William of Hill, Esq.
Pickering, Mountague, Esq.
Plott, John of Moggerhanger, gentleman
Pomfrett, John of Dunstable, gentleman

Peirson, Nathaniell of Eaton Socon, gentleman
Peddar, Joshua of Marston, gentleman
Price, William of Millbrooke, gentleman
Pulford, John of Leighton, Clerk
Price, John of Statfold, Clerk
Painter, Thomas of Houghton, Clerk
Pomfrett, Thomas of Maulden, Clerk
Procter, Thomas of Leighton
Procter, John of Leighton
Pratt, Thomas of Totternhoe
Peddar, William of Cardington
Pedly, John of Potton
Parker, Thomas of Wrestlingworth
Palmer, Tobias of Sandy
Parratt, Thomas of Cardington
Piggott, Thomas of Tingrith
Peirson, Thomas of Northill
Peake, John of Stagsden
Piggott, Thomas of Risely
Peacock, William of Risely
Peddar, Thomas of Stretly
Palmer, John of Sandy
Piggott, Thomas of Stopsly
Piggott, John of Stopsley
Palmer, Thomas of Cople
Perchmore, Richard of Luton
Phillips, William of Salford
Poole, Olliver of Kempston
Purton, John of Kempston
Peirson, John of Kempston
Peirce, Robert of Houghton Conquest
Pratt, James of Clifton
Partridge, Richard of Tilsworth
Pilkington, John of Clifton
Pawlin, John of Bedford
Phillips, John of Bedford
Phillips, William of Bedford
Page, Samuell of [blank]
Perry, Christopher of Hockliffe
Powell, William of Flitwick
Pennyfather, Joseph of 'Milcocke'
Piggott, William of Tingrith
Parrott, Richard of Potton
Phipp, Nicholas of Potton
Phipp, Nicholas, junior of Potton
Phillips, Richard of Eaton Socon
Palmer, John of Eaton Socon
Potton, Simon of Mogerhanger
Parrin, Thomas of Mogerhanger
Prior, Matthew of Statfold

Peck, John of Tempsford
Page, Thomas of Houghton
Parratt, Thomas of Risely
Peirce, Jeremy of Houghton Conquest
Peddar, Robert of Tilsworth

Rhodes, Samuell of Flitwick, Esq.
Rudd, William of Biggleswade, gentleman
Reynolds, Anthony of the same, gentleman
Reynolds, Francis of Carleton, gentleman
Rands, Olliver of Fensham, Clerk
Rands, Richard of Turvey, Clerk
Rixe, John of Bedford, Clerk
Radnell, Thomas of Eaton Socon
Richardson, John of Sandy
Richardson, Richard of Sandy
Rumbold, John of Shefford
Ryley, Edward of Dunstable
Rolph, William of Luton
Read, Nicholas of Maulden
Risely, John of Houghton
Reynolds, James of Sandy
Rose, Edward of Northill
Reeve, George of Tuddington
Rogers, Benjamin of Bedford
Reynolds, John of Bedford
Riddy, Robert of Milton Ernys
Rogers, Thomas of Southill
Rolfe, Samuell of Shefford
Roe, Richard of Sundon
Robinson, John of Sundon
Robinson, Robert of Langford
Read, Richard of Clophill
Roe, William of Sundon
Read, Nicholas of Millbrooke
Read, Robert of Millbrooke
Rayment, Andrew of Potton
Rossell, John of Wrestlingworth
Robinson, Robert of Eaton Socon
Rawson, Nicholas of Eaton Socon
Rawly, Thomas of Sandy
Rosin, John of Wrestlingworth
Robinson, William of Ridgement
Rawly, John of Sandy

Symcotts, William of Clifton, Esq.
Stone, Richard of Ridgement, Esq.
Squier, Gaius of Eaton Socon, Esq.
Skevington, John of Turvey, gentleman
Smith, Hugh of Sharpenhoe, gentleman

Shelden, Nathaniell of Southill, [gentleman deleted]
Shelden, Michaell of the same, Clerk
Stone, William of Aspley, gentleman
Sam, Richard of Salford, Clerk
Snagg, George of Marston, Clerk
Straight, Nathaniell of Leighton
Smith, Luke of the same
Smith, John of Eaton Socon
Samuell, Christopher of Leighton
Smith, Robert of Potton
Spring, Edward of Sandy
Samers, William of Sandy
Swetman, Richard of Sandy
Spring, William of Sandy
Spring, Edward of Sandy
Saffold, Simon of Eaton Socon
Smith, John, junior of Eaton Socon
Stanbridge, Marke of Eaton Socon
Stanbridge, John of Eaton Socon
Swaine, James of Eaton Socon
Stocker, Richard of Eaton Socon
Shepheardson, Thomas of Eaton Socon
Swift, John of Eaton Socon
Smith, David of Eaton Socon
Sam, John of Henlow
Sam, William of Henlow
Seaman, George of Cranfeild
Shreeve, William of Totternhoe
Stanbridge, Thomas of Dunstable
Stone, John of Luton
Swaine, Edward of Luton
Surry, Thomas of Luton
Smart, Simon of Rysely
Sam, Edward of Shitlington
Smith, John of Luton
Sims, John of Bedford
Skelton, Humfry of Bedford
Sexton, Thomas of Tempsford
Spring, Solomon of Malden
Smith, John of Cople
Spencer, James of Oakely
Steevens, William of Shefford
Sole, George of Flitwick
Stanbridge, Thomas of Litlington
Smith, Thomas of Bedford
Smith, Richard of Bedford
Saunders, Richard of Ampthill
Sole, George of Mepsall
Sellers, John of Flitwick
Shirrhogg, John of Flitwick

Smith, Francis of Potton
Stapler, William of Girford
Smith, William of Girford
Stacy, Henry of Girford
Simon, Lewis of Wrestlingworth
Sault, Robert of Wrestlingworth
Squier, Butler of Wrestlingworth
Sibtharpe, Thomas of Northill
Sockling, Francis of Stamford
Skilleter, Thomas of Sandy
Sutton, Edward of Sutton
Stanton, William of Beeston
Smith, Robert of Southill
Singlehurst, Abraham of Warden
Stratton, William of Clophill
Sellers, John of Silso

Thompson, St John junior, Esq.
Tayler, Humfry of Evershall, gentleman
Toller, Thomas of Cranfeild
Taylor, John of Cranfeild
Townsend, Joseph of Leighton
Thorne, Richard of Potton
Townsend, Henry of Sandy
Tilcock, William of Sandy
Thompson, John of Luton
Titford, Richard of Willington
Tompion, William of Northill
Tompson, Nicholas of Risely
Thomas, Isaack of Tempsford
Thomas, Isaack of Turvey
Tompson, Roger of Wrestlingworth
Taylor, Richard of Eaton
Tompkins, Matthew of Maulden
Tillingsly, John of Stagsden
Tayer, John of Goldington
Tompion, James of Northill
Terle, Thomas of Stanbridge
Thirley, John of Houghton Conquest [all deleted]
Turner, John of Litlington
Tompkin, John of Pulloxhill
Thompson, Edward of Potton
Taylor, Richard of Eaton Socon
Taylor, Thomas of Eaton Socon
Topham, James of Eaton Socon
Titford, Isaack of Willington
Thomas, Humfry of Blunham
Thurgood, Henry of Sandy
Tucker, John of Eaton Socon, Clerk

Ventris, John of Campton, Esq.
Ventris, John of the same, gentleman

Urlin, Simon of Ampthill, gentleman
Vaux, John of Whipsnade, gentleman
Vaux, John of Cranfeild, gentleman
Valentine, Thomas of Eggington
Valentine, Thomas of Leighton
Vaux, Michaell of Westoning
Usher, John of Wrestlingworth
Usher, Anthony of Wrestlingworth

Wingate, Sir Francis, Knight
Walker, George of Ampthill, Esq.
Wright, Gawen of Biggleswade, gentleman
Walker, Calebb of Ampthill, gentleman
Winton, Francis of Leighton, Esq.
Wiffen, John of Bedford
Warner, John of Dunstable
Walker, Edward of Beeston
Walker, Henry of Beeston
Walker, William of Beeston
West, John of Sundon
Woodward, William of Wrestlingworth
Wheeler, John of Cranfeild
Woodward, Michaell of Cranfeild
Whitly, William of Cardington
Woodham, Twiford of Risely
Woodward, Edward of Risely
White, Robert of Risely
Whitlock, John of Dunstable
Woodward, Thomas of Barton
Willows, Thomas of Shefford
Wye, John of Barford
Watford, Richard of Wilden
Ward, Thomas of Potton
Ward, Thomas of Barford
Wye, Thomas of Barford
Wagstaffe, Richard, senior of Wilden
Wells, Thomas of Luton
Wheeler, Edward of Sundon

Worland, Joseph of Eaton Socon
Wyan, Thomas of Eaton Socon
Wright, Robert of Eaton Socon
Wright, George of Eaton Socon
Wright, John of Eaton Socon
Wiles, Thomas of Eaton Socon
Woodward, Henry of Biddenham
Wells, Henry of Tempsford
Wells, Robert of Tempsford
Whitworth, John of Tempsford
Willsheir, Samuell of Luton
Wenwright, John of Tuddington
Webb, William of Houghton
Wallis, William of Litlington
Wardall, John of Maulden
Wester, John of Sundon
Wells, Jeremiah of Luton
Williams, Thomas of Oakely
Willymott, Thomas of Houghton Conquest
Webb, John of Leighton [all deleted]
Webb, Henry of Ampthill
White, John of Tilsworth
Walters, Richard of Maulden
Whitbread, John of Shitlington
Wood, Simon of Eaton Bray
Webb, George of Ampthill
Wallis, Henry of Potton
Whittingham, George of Statfold
Willymott, John of Barford
Wigmore, John of Girford
Wray, John of Sandy
Wilsheir, John of Harrold
Wells, Benjamin of Bedford, Clerk
Wye, Thomas of Eaton Socon
Whitridge, Robert of Maulden
Woodward, William of Wrestlingworth

Yarway, James of Kempston, gentleman
Young, William of Leighton
Yardly, James of Stanford

Votes for William Boteler, Esq. (without Sir Villiers Chernock)

Arnold, Thomas of Ampthill, Esq
Arnold, Thomas of the same, gentleman
Appleston, John of Harrold, Clerk

Briggs, George of Dunstable
Burr, John of Stanbridge

Blott, William of Harrold
Brisco, Thomas of Keysho, Clerk
Bell, Edward of Over Deane
Bell, Richard of Bedford
Bread, Bernard of Westoning
Burr, William of Westoning

Bell, Lewis of Ampthill
Beckett, William of Bedford
Banforth, Paul of Bedford
Bitheray, Thomas of Pertenhall
Bradly, William of Wilden
Bridgeman, William of Luton

Courtier, Marmaduke of Bedford
Cheyne, William of Hockliffe
Clarke, Anthony of Harrold
Carter, Matthew of Turvey
Cheyne, Wythers of Hockliffe
Crawly, Abraham of Luton
Cox, Samuell of Luton
Chalkely, John of Luton

Duncombe, William of Battlesden Esq.
Darling, John of Chellington
Dillingham, George of Pertenhall
Doggett, William of Hockliffe
Dennis, Thomas of Gravenhurst
Davy, John of Luton
Disney, Thomas of Arlsey

Eston, John of Bedford, gentleman

Faldo, John of Bedford, gentleman
Fosson, John of Dunstable
Fisher, William of Hockliffe
Farey, William of Barford

Gilpin, Richard of Hockliffe
Groome, John of Dunstable

Hammond, Richard of Bedford
Hubbins, Thomas of Kempston
Hildersdon, Thomas of Elstow, Esq.

Jennings, William of Maulden

Keeble, Thomas of Hockliffe

Larkin, John of Cardington
Lawrence, John of Harlington

Mountague, Robert of Sharnebrooke, Esq.

Maxey, John of Bletsoe
Maxfeild, John of Bletsoe
Meager, William of Clifton
Masham, William of Felmersham
Mole, John of Risely
Money, Thomas, sen. of Kempston

Newman, Simon of Ampthill

Parker, Richard of Thurleigh
Peddar, Richard of Harrold
Potts, Thomas of Tuddington
Poulton, John of Hockliffe
Peirce, Thomas of Great Barford
Peppar, William of Westoning
Peppiatt, John of Pulloxhill

Reddall, Ambrose of Bedford, gentleman
Ruffe, Francis of Kempston
Richards, Thomas of Keyshoe
Russell, John of Oakely
Rolfe, Edward of Shitlington

Scroggs, Richard of Tuddington

Toller, Robert of Pavenham
Toll, John of Chellington
Thorowgood, Henry of Girford
Thomas, Robert of Bedford
Thurgood, Henry of Sandy

Willsheire, John of Wilden, gentleman
Whitbread, William of Cardington
Woodward, William of Bedford
Woodward, Henry of Biddenham
Watford, Henry of Thurleigh
Wootton, Robert of Barford
Wallis, Robert of Potton
Winch, Thomas of Clifton
Wrentham, John of Pulloxhill
Wagstaffe, Richard of Sexton [sic]
Wylds, Richard of Bedford
Whitly, John of Luton
Ward, Edmund of Barford
Wells, John of Leighton

Votes for Sir Villiers Chernock, Barronett (without Mr Boteler)

Burr, Edward of Westoning
Dr Bringlehurst

Crouch, Thomas of Crawly
Cooke, Francis, sen. of Milton Bryant
Cooke, Francis, jun. of Milton Bryant
Cooke, Robert of Milton Bryant
Crawly, Thomas of Milton Bryant
Cooke, Robert of Herne
Crouch, Robert of Cranfeild
Cooke, William of Ridgement
Crawly, John of Asply Guise

Follett, Thomas of Holcott

Gale, Edward of Wooburne
Goodman, James of Litlington

Hall, Edward of Aspley, Clerk

Jones, Robert of Litlington

Lamb, Robert of [blank], Clerk
Lacy, John sen. of Milton Bryant

Manning, John of Litlington, gentleman

Parratt, Henry of Tilsworth

Sadler, Ralph of Aspley, gentleman
Sickling, Thomas of Maulden, gentleman
Stert, Thomas of Willington, Clerk

Turner, Francis of Wooburne
Turner, Michaell of Flitwick

Votes for Mr Russell 744; Sir Humfry Monax 634

Memorandum in all with those that poled twice over for Mr Russell (3) 747

Ampthill and Biggleswade Russell and Monax
The Names of such Freeholders as poled for the Honourable Edward Russell, Esq. and Sir Humfry Monax, Barronett

Aunger, Joseph of Colmworth
Abbys, Thomas of Hawnes
Alsop, Lewis of Risely
Ashwell, Thomas of Eaton Bray
Ashwell, John of Eaton Bray
Austen, Thomas of Aspley
Ayres, John of Northill
Alcock, Nathaniell of Keyshoe
Allen, William, jun. of Kempston
Aslendine, John of Marston
Alcock, William of Leighton
Allen, Thomas of Willshamstedd
Ashton, Thomas of Turvey
Albone, Thomas of Statfold
Anico alias Lewis, John of Elstow
Atkins, Simon of Marston
Ambridge, James of Aspley
Asby, Andrew of Wootton
Allen, Thomas of Wootton
Alden, John of Heath and Reach

Astwood, Luke of Potton
Addington, Silvester of Eaton Socon
Ashwell, James of Eaton Bray
Adkins, Thomas of Husband Crawly

Bawdry, William of Eaton Bray
Barker, Joseph of Kempston
Baldry, John of Houghton R[egis]
Banes, Matthew of Elstow
Bundy, Robert of Pertenhall
Betly, Richard of Stanbridge
Bisshop, Edward of Pulloxhill
Baker, William of Wyboston
Boulton, Thomas of Kempston
Buckingham, Henry of Houghton
Ballard, Samuell of Cardington
Battison, Thomas of Elstow
Boston, Thomas of Colmworth
Bayley, Francis of Leighton
Bardwell, John of Bedford

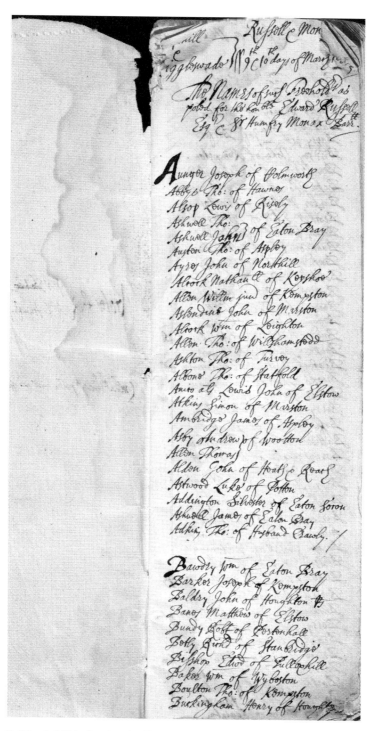

Poll book 1684, showing the first page of the list of Whig voters.
(BLARS, Chester Archive)

Bayly, William of Bedford
Birdsey, John of Kempston
Beech, William of Willshamstedd
Baker, Thomas of Cranfeild
Barker, Matthew of Wootton
Beckett, Edward of Aspley Guise
Barnes, William of Stanbridge
Bunnyon, William of Milton Bryant
Berridge, Edward of Bedford, jun.
Baldock, Thomas of Arelsey
Bowskill, Thomas of Bedford
Beaumont, Thomas of Flitton
Beaumont, Henry of the same
Bundy, Nathaniell of Wilshamstedd
Bunker, Thomas of Chalgrave
Badcock, Heritage of Cardington, Clerk
Brooks, Thomas of Felmersham
Brewer, William of Harrold
Berry, John of Felmersham
Boffe, Daniel of Dunton
Battison, John of Felmersham
Barnes, Richard of Marquet Streete
Bonner, John of Litlington
Bigg, Abraham of Litlington
Bayly, John of Stepingly
Burrow, William of Flitwick
Billingham, William of Bedford
Barton, George of Westoning
Bletsoe, Joseph of Ravensden
Buckingham, Thomas of Houghton R[egis]
Burges, Peter of Pulloxhill
Buckingham, John of Tuddington
Berry, John of Husband Crawly
Bray, Robert of Willstedd
Brace, Arnold of Little Stoughton
Barringer, Thomas of Carleton
Boston, Thomas of Wyboston
Bosworth, Thomas of Marston
Birdsey, William of Egginton
Bletsoe, John of Harrold
Baldock, George of Statfold
Ball, John of Chalgrave
Ball, James of Turvey
Birdsey, Thomas of Ridgement
Britwell, John of Evershall
Burrows, Thomas of Shitlington
Barber, William of Dunton
Berridge, Edward of Bedford
Barr, Richard of Mogerhanger
Barr, John of Mogerhanger
Button, Richard of Eyworth

Bushby, Thomas of Millbrooke
Berry, Richard of Husband Crawly
Berry, Robert of Felmersham
Barringer, Joseph of Steventon
Barker, John of Kempston
Botsford, Edmund of Milton Bryant
Barker, James of Kempstone

Cumberland, John of Oakely
Cooper, Robert of Stanbridge
Clarke, John of Biggleswade
Cooke, John of Bedford
Campion, Thomas of Risely
Cleyton, Thomas of Bedford
Cooper, Edward of Stanbridge
Crawly, Lawrence of Aspley
Coles, Henry of Keyshoe
Coles, William of Husband Crawley
Chambers, Michaell of Bedford
Chapman, Robert of Dunstable Houghton
Crow, Henry of Reynold
Carter, John of Keyshoe
Cooper, George of Cardington
Church, John of Bolnhurst
Conquest, John of Wilden
Cocks, John of Steventon
Cock, Thomas of Dunton
Cooper, Edward of Wilshamstedd
Carter, Thomas of Stanbridge
Chandler, Robert of Clifton
Chapman, William of Dunstable
Chester, William of Dunstable
Crow, Thomas of Stoughton
Chalton, Uriah of Shefford
Child, John of Cardington Cotton End
Curtis, Thomas of Chalgrave
Castleton, John of Felmersham
Cartright, John of Litlington
Child, John of Roxton
Crouch, John of Litlington
Crawly, William of Houghton R[egis]
Connisby, Robert of Wilden
Cumberland, Lawrence of Odell
Cranfeild, John of Cardington
Clarke, Richard of Keysho
Cole, William of Keysho
Cooke, Thomas of Ridgement
Cooper, John of Statfold
Cooke, Edmund of Eaton Bray
Cooke, Nicholas of Kempston
Cole, William of Dunstable Houghton

Cooke, Francis sen. of Milton Bryant
Cooper, Thomas of Silsoe
Cutbert, William of Wooburne
Crosly, William of Langford
Crouch, Edward of Statfold
Clare, Francis of Shefford
Cock, Thomas of Dunton
Climpson, Henry of Evershall
Cock, John of Dunton
Crocker, Joseph of Shefford
Chandler, John of Bedford
Carter, Robert of Bedford
Crawly, Thomas of Wooburne

Dye, Abraham of Dunstable Houghton
Day, Henry of Keysho
Doggett, Ralph of Leighton
Deane, Matthew of Leighton
Day, William of Deane
Doceter, Robert of Eaton
Dine, William of Dunstable
Deare, Matthew of Alcy
Day, John of Shitlington
Dorrington, John of Elstow
Dunckly, Richard of Harrold
Davy, John of Charlton
Davy, Thomas of Charlton [deleted]
Dickins, Richard of Kempston
Denbigh, Edwinn of Ridgement
Dearmer, William of Tuddington
Dix, Richard of Ampthill
Darling, George of Bedford
Davies, John of Evershall
Day, Stephen of Keysho
Davy, John of Husborne Crawly
Dearmer, Henry of Wilshamstedd
Davies, John of Luton
Dutton, Thomas of Langford
Davy, John of Houghton
Deacon, William of Evershall
Davy, Thomas of Felmersham

Edge, John of Leighton
Everett, Richard of Eaton Bray
Eston, Richard of Bedford
Edmunds, John of Tuddington
Emery, Francis of Eaton Socon
Edmunds, Silvester of Eaton Socon
Eastwell, Edward of Bolnhurst
Eastwell, Robert of Wilden
Elmer, John of Odell

Estwick, Stephen of the same
Essex, Matthew of Felmersham
Eldershaw, James of Wooburne
Emmerton, Richard of Husband Crawly
Emmery, Edward of Wyboston
Emery, John of Wyboston
Eastwell, Libias of Wilden
Endersby, Robert of Langford
Elson, John of Bedford

Favell, George of Renhold
Fox, Robert of Over Deane
Fenn, Robert of Bedford
Fisher, Leonard of Colmworth
Fortune, William of Colmworth
Franklyn, Robert of Bedford
Furr, William of Harlington Wood End
Fenner, William of Leighton
Folbigg, John of Keyshoe
Fossy, Edward of Tuddington
Fulby, John of Stoughton
Feery, Samuell of Deane
Flint, Richard of Bedford
Farr, Ralph of Aspley
Foster, Thomas of Leighton
Farey, Olliver of Harrold
Farey, John of the same
Franklyn, Nicholas of the same
Fowks, Hugh of Elstow
Fitzhugh, John of Wilden
Foote, Robert of Barford
Franklyn, Thomas of Litlington
Foote, Christopher of Great Barford
Franklyn, Thomas of Litlington [deleted]
Fowler, Thomas of Shitlington
Flint, John of Shitlington
Fowks, John of Wootton
Farr, John of Blunham
Found, George of Blunham
Fox, Thomas of Dunstable Houghton
Freeman, Michaell of Statfold
Franklyn, James of Evershall
Fosty, John of Houghton R[egis]
Favell, George of Wilshamstedd
Farr, Roger of Marston
Farrer alias Cooper, John of Kempston
Fowks, Richard of Wootton
Franklyn, Thomas of Marston
Fox, George of Elstow
Fuller, Robert of Evershall
Feery, Peter of Edworth

Gate, John of Dunstable
Grey, Samuel [James deleted] of Evershall
Groome, John of Dunstable Houghton
Gosby, Richard of Houghton R[egis]
Gresham, William of Husband Crawly
Greene, John of Renhold
Gardner, Thomas of Luton
Gurney, Thomas of Tuddington
Gregory, James of Evershall Church End
Grey, Robert of Eaton Socon
Garrett, John [Thomas deleted] of Dunton
Goldsmith, William of Tuddington
Gurry, Samuell of Bolnhurst
Gale, John of Bedford
Gregory, William of Evershall
Gregory, John of Evershall
Gregory, George of Evershall
Gibbs, Edward of Evershall
Goldsmith, Henry, sen. of Evershall
Goldsmith, Henry, jun. of Evershall
Gregory, James of Evershall
Gregory, Joseph of Leighton
Glover, Thomas of Ravensden
Greene, Henry of Ridgement
Groome, Benjamin of Chalgrave
Gill, John of Great Barford
Greene, Edmund of Husband Crawly
Griffin, William of Husband Crawly
Greene, George of Elstow
Greene, Thomas of Silsoe
Gifford, Robert of Roxton
Gamble, Thomas of Pulloxhill
Goldsmyth, Thomas of Charlton
Gwynn, Thomas of Silsoe
Giddings, Thomas of the same
Gregory, William of Marston
Gosley, Lawrence of Wooburne
Grant, Nathaniell of Goldington
Greene, Robert of Langford
Gregory, John of Thurleigh
Gregory, William of Thurleigh

Hitchcock, John of Elstow
Hows, Timothy of Houghton R[egis]
Harborough, John of Milton Bryant
Holliman, Stephen of Cople
Hammond, Richard of Bedford [deleted]
Hall, William of Keysho
Hebbs, John of Hockley
Hewitt, John of Eaton Bray
Higgs, John of Bedford

Hawkins, John, jun. of Houghton R[egis]
Hildersdon, John of Leighton
Honour, Thomas of Goldington
Hubbins, Thomas of Kempston [deleted]
Hawkins, Thomas of Houghton R[egis]
Hawkins, Edward of Houghton R[egis]
Haynes, Edward of Houghton R[egis]
Hall, Thomas of Keysho
Hall, Richard of Keysho
Helder, Richard of Little Stoughton
Hills, William of Keysho
Haynes, Edward of Bolnhurst
Hewett, John of Eaton Socon
Hawkins, Jeptha of Limby [Limbury]
Higgs, Edward of Milton Bryant
Hebbs, Henry of Dunstable R[egis]
Hinton, Henry of Arlesey
Holms, William of Kempston
Hawkins, Robert of Houghton R[egis]
Hartwell, John of Harrold
Harriott, Richard of Harrold
Hewlatt, Thomas of Harrold
Harrison, John of Charlton
Huckle, George of Cardington
Hanwell, Edward of Litlington
Harris, Robert of Wooburne
Hawks, Paul of Carleton
Hedding, Joseph of Wilshamstedd
Harris, William of Milton
Hewitt, John of Eaton Socon
Hill, Robert of Langford
Holdstock, Robert of Elstow
Hanscombe, William of Ravensden
Hollingworth, Matthew of Ridgement
Hawthorne, Thomas of Evershall
Herring, Thomas of Potton
Hopkins, Nicholas of Tuddington
Harrowdine, John of Shefford
Haddock, Walter of Tempsford
Hunt, John of Statfold

Jarvis, Stephen of Kempston
Impy, John of Milton Bryant
Impy, Godfry of Battlesden
Ind, Thomas of Colmworth
Jorden, John of Keysho
Ireland, Thomas of Wooburne
Jones, William of Kempston
Ironmonger, William of Eaton Bray
Jenkins, Thomas of Billington

Ibbott, John of Pertenhall
Jorden, Thomas of Harrold
Iselopp, John of Harrold
Impy, Richard of Marston
Impy, John of Houghton R[egis]
Jarvis, Richard of Roxton

Knott, Thomas of Tillbrooke
Knight, George of Totternhoe
King, Steph[e]n of Goldington
King, Thomas of Wilden
Kent, Thomas of Ridgement
King, William of Wilden
Knight, William of Carleton
Keeling, John of Dunton
King, Thomas of Colmworth
Kendall, Thomas of Wilshamstedd
King, William of Colmworth

Lamb, William of Bedford
Ligo, William of Leighton
Leach, Richard of Leighton
Love, Thomas of Risely
Lamant, John of Wilshamstedd
Lockwood, William of Bedford
Lane, Robert of Westoning
Lovell, John of Roxton
Love, Richard of Harrold
Lindopp, Henry of Wilden
Livett, William of Great Barford
Lucy, John of Milton Bryant
Leach, Thomas of Felmersham
Long, John of Houghton R[egis]
London, Edward of Hockley
Lucy, William of Milton Bryant
Lawrence, William of Langford
Lambert, Andrew of Evershall
Lawrence, John of Luton
Leach, Thomas, jun. of Felmersham

Munns, James of Bedford
Mea, James of Keysho
Martiall, Thomas of Odell
Martiall, John of Carleton
Martin, Thomas of Totternhoe
Mouse, Michaell of Totternhoe
Mouse, John of Totternhoe
Mayes, Thomas of Keysho
Munns, Joseph of Studham
Mann, Richard of Clipson
Maxey, Thomas of Knotting

Morris, Thomas of Pavenham
Maxey, John of Bletsoe
Mayes, Thomas of Tillbrooke
Marriott, James of Kempston
Moaks, William of Eaton Socon
Musgrave, Robert of Bletsoe
Miles, Richard of Aspley Guise
Munns, Benjamin of Studham
Morrison, Robert of Ridgement
Mason, John of Harrold
Milward, William of Malden
Males, William of Charlton
Moreton, John of Dunton
Mayes, John of Milton Bryant
Mawdlin, William of Willshamstedd
Messyter, Michaell of Dunstable R[egis]
Marlyn, Joseph of Bedford
Mea, Thomas of Wootton
Matthews, Robert of Shefford

Noell, Praise of Wootton
Nicholls, William of Bedford
Nottingham, John of Kempston
Newman, William, jun. of Houghton R[egis]
Negus, Thomas of Renhold
Negus, John of Oakely
Nicholls, Daniell of Potton
Norman, Lewis of Bedford
Newold, John of Elstow
Norris, Henry of Houghton
Norman, William of Harrold
Nottingham, William of Kempston
Negus, John of Langford
Negus, John of Clapham
Norman, Joseph of Carleton
Newman, William, jun. of Houghton R[egis]

Odell, John of Chalgrave
Olney, Thomas of Chalgrave
Osborne, John of Chalgrave
Odell, Stephen of Goldington
Osborne, Henry of Chalgrave
Olney, Thomas of Tebworth
Odell, John of Wootton
Ouen, John of Malden
Odell, Benjamin of Steventon
Osborne, John of Hawnes

Purney, John of Deane
Perrott, Robert of Leighton
Paine, John of Oakely

Peck, Thomas of Cardington, gentleman
Peck, Olliver of Cardington
Palladay, Edward of Wilden
Peirce, Thomas of Statfold
Pilkin, John of Kempston
Peares, Henry of Evershall
Peares, Thomas of Bedford
Peirson, William of Leighton
Palmer, John of Wilshamstedd
Perry, Gideon of Harrold
Piggott, John of Flitton
Parkins, William of Tempsford
Perrott, John of Chalgrave
Pymer, Henry of Cardington
Pennyfather, Edward of Flitton
Peacock, John of Keyshoe
Pestell, Walker of Colmworth
Potts, Theodore of Tuddington
Poynton, Samuell of Shefford
Pollard, Edward of Houghton R[egis]
Pearne, Joseph of Tuddington
Pilkington, Edward of Bedford
Phillipps, William of Dunton
Peirson, John of Hockly

Quincy, Thomas of Harrold
Quick, Edwinn of Bedford
Quarrell, William of Roxton

Rushead, Josias of Bedford
Reevs, Richard of Leighton
Rudd, Thomas of Bedford
Rolt, John of Bletsoe
Reynolds, William of Bedford
Robins, John of Totternhoe
Russell, Thomas of Husband Crawly
Russell, William of Ravensden
Reddall, Ambrose of Ridgement
Risely, John of Knotting
Richardson, George of Ridgement
Ridge, William of Odell
Russell, William of Aspley
Rushead, Thomas of Wilshamstedd
Richardson, Thomas of Roxton
Ravensden, Robert of Clophill
Robinson, Thomas of Bedford
Rudd, Gideon of Carleton
Risely, William of Harrold
Rush, Hugh of Wilden
Reeve, George of Tuddington
Reynolds, John of Kempston

Robinson, Thomas of Wilshamstedd
Richard, Henry of Keysho
Robinson, John of Luton
Rose, Robert of Elstow
Rudd, Edward of Milhoe
Rawlins, William of Shefford

Snoxall, John of Stanbridge
Smith, Olliver of Risely
Stopley, Richard of Keyshoe
Smith, Robert of Wooburne
Sheppard, John of Tillbrooke
Swayne, Thomas of Houghton R[egis]
Sutton, John [Thomas deleted] of Sandy
Swinsco, Edward of Thornecoate
Skevington, William of Turvey
Sheppard, William of Tillbrooke, Clerk
Stretch, Robert of Dunstable
Streete, John of Cardington
Swaine, Thomas of Lygrave
Sadler, Thomas of Husband Crawly
Sheppard, Clement of Luton
Smith, Thomas of Oakely
Spencer, John of Pavenham
Strange, John of Tuddington
Stanton, John of Bolnhurst
Sansome, Thomas of Cotton end
Savadge, Henry of Bletsoe
Stanbridge, William of Milho
Sheriffe, Spencer of Odell
Smart, William of Pulloxhill
Smith, William of the same
Smith, Stephen of the same
Smith, William of Felmersham
Steevens, Richard of Shefford
Swift, Thomas of Roxton
Smith, Richard of Wilden
Smart, Francis of Flitton
Smith, Henry of Charlton
Slingsby, Edmund of Husband Crawly
Stokes, Thomas of Kempston
Skevington, Jonathan of Turvey
Smith, Abraham of Wilden
Stratton, William of Wootton
Smith, George of Husband Crawly
Sibly, Thomas of Wyboston
Stanbridge, Humfry of Wootton
Sinfeild, Henry of Husband Crawly
Salisbury, William of Husband Crawly
Sinfeild, Robert of Wooburne
Searle, William of Dunton

Sears, Robert of Dunton
Samms, Michaell of Clifton [Clophill deleted]
Skevington, Thomas of Turvey

Taylor, John of Bedford
Taylor, Randall of Bedford
Tall, Gilbert of Bedford
Thompson, John of Bedford
Tyler, Henry of Dunstable R[egis]
Tombs, John of Luton
Threddar, Thomas of Flitwick
Taylor, Olliver of Leighton
Taylor, Giles of Cardington
Truelove, John of Leighton
Timberly, Bartholomew of Houghton R[egis]
Turkington, John of Sharnbrooke
Turney, Thomas of Wooburne
Tearne, John of Stanbridge
Teach, Henry of Cardington
Taylor, George of Great Barford
Thickpenny, Thomas of Blunham
Tapp, Robert of Felmersham
Thorowgood, Richard of Roxton
Tillcock, William of Aspley Guise
Timberlake, Thomas of Houghton R[egis]
Tannyford, Thomas of Wooburne
Taylor, Robert of Mogerhanger
Thomas, William of the same
Tomalin, John of Ampthill
Taylor, Stephen of Marston
Tompkins, Henry of Dunstable Houghton
Tompkins, John of Houghton R[egis]
Thomas, Robert of Mogerhanger
Turney, Thomas of Husborne Crawly
Taylor, William of Husborne Crawly
Tidd, John of Clophill
Toller, Joseph of Odell

Veale, James of Bedford
Veale, Edward of Bedford
Urland, Joseph of Evershall

Ward, William of Great Barford
Watts, John of Kempston
West, John of Wooburne
Whish, Thomas (John deleted) of Charlton
Watford, Richard of Goldington
Watmough, Thomas of the same
Whitbread, Stephen of Cardington

Worrall, Robert of Little Stoughton
Wooster, Thomas of Aspley Guise
Walker, Thomas of Leighton
Wildman, John of Wooburne
Wilson, James of Warden
Wagstaffe, Edmund of Colmworth
Whitly, John of Dunstable
Woodward, Thomas of Bedford
Whitbread, John of Elstow
Walker, Henry of Pertenhall
Wagstaffe, William of Wilden
Which, William [John deleted] of Stanbridge
Woodward, John of Kempston
Wakefeild, John of Cardington
Warner, Edward of Wilshamstedd
Wildman, Edward of Roxton
Whitbread, Ambrose of Evershall
Walls, Matthew of Sundon
Whiston, Henry of Tempsford [Kempston deleted]
Warner, Robert of Felmersham
Wheeler, William of Bedford
Watford, Thomas of Knotting
Willson, John of Cardington
Wagstaffe, Richard of Wilden
Whiston, Abraham of Tempsford
Wheeler, John of Flitton
Wheeler, Richard of Marston
Warner, William of Wilshamstedd
Watts, Thomas of Wilshamstedd
Woodfeild, George of Stondon
White, Thomas of Kempston
Wright, John of Wilden
Wright, John of Wyboston
Woodward, Matthew of Westoning
Wallis, William of Houghton R[egis]
Wootton, Richard of Carleton
Woodcraft, John of Wilshamstedd
Wilcocks, Anthony of Marston
Watts, William of Colmworth
Wooster, William of Husband Crawly
Walker, Thomas of Ravensden
Willows, Robert of Mepsall
Wootton, Thomas of Colmworth
Ward, George of Aspley
Ward, Thomas of Husband Crawly [deleted]
Wheeler, John of Marston
Ward, John of Marston
Wytt, John of Wootton
Warren, Richard of Wilshamstedd

Wheeler, William of Gravenhurst
Wheeler, Richard of Hawnes
Woodcraft, Thomas of Marston

Yorke, John of Over Deane
Young, Thomas of Alcey

Votes for Mr Russell (without Sir Humfry Monax)

Arnald, Thomas of Ampthill, Esq.
Appleston, John of Harrold
Awsten, James of Westoning

Bell, Richard of Bedford, gentleman
Banforth, Paul of the same, gentleman
Beckett, William of the same, gentleman
Dr Bringlehurst [of Toddington *Fasti*]
Briggs, George of Dunstable
Burr, John of Stanbridge
Brisco, Thomas of Keysho, Clerk
Blott, William of Harrold
Bell, Edward of Over Deane
Bread, Bernard of Westoning
Barrenger, Thomas of Steventon
Bett, Lewis of Ampthill
Bethray, Thomas of Pertenhall
Bridgeman, William of Luton
Bennett, John of Statfold
Bradly, William of Wilden
Bennett, Henry of Shefford

Cooper, Robert of Bedford
Courtier, Marmaduke of Bedford
Cranfeild, Thomas of Cardington
Carter, John of Keysho [deleted]
Crouch, Thomas of Crawly
Crawly, John of Aspley Guise
Chettle, John of Yevelden
Cheyney, William of Hockliffe
Clarke, Anthony of Harrold
Cooke, Francis of Milton
Carter, Matthew of Turvey
Cooke, William of Ridgement
Cawdwell, John of Chalgrave
Cooks, Robert of Herne
Chawkly, William of Luton
Cocks, Samuell of Luton
Cheyne, Withers of Hockly
Crawly, Thomas of Milton Bryant
Crawly, Abraham of Luton

Duncombe, William of [blank; probably
    Battlesden], Esq.

Darling, John of Chellington
Dillingham, George of Pertenhall
Doggett, William of Hockliffe
Dennis, Thomas of Gravenhurst
Davy, John of Luton
Disny, Thomas of Arlesey

Eston, John of Bedford, gentleman
Edwards, John of Luton

Foster, John of Dunstable
Fisher, William of Hockliffe
Faldo, John of Bedford, gentleman
Farey, William of Great Barford
Fitton, William of Clifton

Groome, John of Dunstable
Gale, Edward of Wooburne
Gilpin, Richard of Hockliffe
Going, George of Houghton R[egis]
Gregory, John of Evershall

Hildersdon, Thomas of Elstow, Esq.
Hall, Edward of Aspley Guise, Clerk
Hobbs, Matthew of Hitchin

Jones, Robert of Litlington

Keeble, Thomas of Hockliffe

Larkin, John of Cardington
Lyon, Henry of Cardington
Lamb, Robert of Milton [Bryan; *Fasti*]
Lucy, John, sen. of Milton
Lawly, William of Leighton

Mountague, Robert of Sharnebrooke, Esq.
Musgrave, William of Risely
Munns, James, sen. of Bedford
Manly, Richard, gentleman
Meager, William of Clifton
Masham, William of Felmersham
Martiall, William of Wooburne, Clerk

Newman, William of Ridgement
Newman, John of Ridgement
Newman, Simon of Ampthill

Pemberton, John of Goldington
Parker, Richard of Thurleigh
Peddar, Richard of Harrold
Pears, Thomas of Bedford
Parnham, John of Evershall
Pepper, William of Westoning
Potts, Thomas of Tuddington
Poulton, John of Hockly
Pearce, Thomas of Great Barford
Peppercorne, Edward of Great Barford

Robins, William of Ridgement
Ruffe, Francis of Kempston
Richards, Thomas of Keysho
Reddall, Ambrose of Bedford

Sadler, Ralph of Aspley Guise
Spencer, Samuell of [blank], gentleman
Scroggs, Richard of Tuddington
Slough, Samuell of Luton

Turner, Françis of [blank], gentleman
Toll, Robert of Pavenham
Toll, John of Chellington
Thorowgood, Henry of Girford
Thomas, Robert of Bedford
Tilcock, Richard of Aspley Guise
Taylor, Simon of Wooburne, gentleman

Willsheire, John of Wilden, gentleman
Whitbread, William of Cardington
Woodward, William of Bedford
Woodward, Henry of Biddenham
Watford, Henry of Thurleigh
Wootton, Robert of Bedford
Wallis, Robert of Potton
Winch, Thomas of Clifton
Wells, John of Leighton
Willymott, John of Harrold
Wrentham, John of Pulloxhill
Wagstaffe, Richard of Sexton
Wylds, Richard of Bedford

Votes for Sir Humfry Monax (without Mr Russell)

Maxfeild, John of Bletsoe
Money, Thomas, sen of Kempston
Whitly, John of Luton

and added later
Hamond, Richard of Bedford
Hubbins, Thomas of Kempstone

Chapter Two

1695 Election

James II and the Glorious Revolution, 1685–94

The next surviving poll book for the County seat dates from 1695.[1] In the intervening years James II squandered his all-powerful position of 1685 by quarrelling with his natural supporters, the Tories. He also failed to win over nonconformists to his attempts to abolish the Test Act, principally in favour of his fellow Roman Catholics. With singular maladroitness, he managed to unite all parties behind William of Orange, who landed at Torbay on 5 November 1688.

The Effect of National Events on Bedfordshire 1685–95

The four newly elected MPs – Boteler, Chernocke, Chester and Christie – were summoned to appear at the new Parliament, which met on 12 March 1684/5. The first session saw James obtain the money he needed to run the government but he faced an initial skirmish over the Church of England, a foretaste of things to come.

Loyalty to the King was strengthened in summer 1685 by the Monmouth and Argyll rebellion, which gave the King the chance to enlarge the army considerably. He used this as an excuse to introduce a number of Roman Catholic officers in defiance of the Test Act. He even had the support of William of Orange, who was husband to Mary, heiress to the throne as James's eldest child. A Monmouth victory would have ended William's hopes.

Monmouth's demise would have been of great interest to people in the Toddington area, because he had hidden at the manor during the aftermath of the Rye House Plot. The daughter of the house, Lady Henrietta Wentworth, was his lover and they behaved as if they were married, despite Monmouth having a wife who was alive. Also of local interest was the death of Lieutenant Monoux of the Wootton family, killed in the fighting with the rebels.[2]

The Tory Parliament, including the Bedfordshire members, would have looked with foreboding at the subsequent Bloody Assize that saw the execution of numerous Protestants.

On 30 July 1685 Lord Ailesbury, Lord Lieutenant of Bedfordshire, was made James II's Lord Chamberlain, as an important sign of the King's appreciation of his unswerving loyalty to the Stuart dynasty. He did not live long to enjoy his position,

---

[1] Lincolnshire Archives, M(G) 6/1/B/4.
[2] A. Fea, *The Loyal Wentworths* (London, 1928), pp. 106–45.

however, as he died on 20 October, aged 59. Bedfordshire lost a highly experienced leader, who had run the county since his appointment as Lord Lieutenant in 1660.[3]

In *Fasti Oxonienses*, Anthony Wood describes Ailesbury as follows: 'He was a learned person, and otherwise well qualified; was well versed in English History and Antiquities, a lover of all such that were professors of those studies, and a curious collector of MSS, especially of those which related to *England* and English antiquities. Besides also he was a lover of the regular Clergy, as those of Bedfordsh [sic] and Bucks know well enough.'[4]

His 29–year-old son, Thomas Bruce, had been a gentleman of the household of Charles II and was quickly confirmed both in that post and as Lord Lieutenant of both Bedfordshire and Huntingdonshire. The Bruces acted fast to prevent the appointment of a less congenial person, such as the Earl of Peterborough. The gentry wanted as their lord lieutenant someone who was a staunch supporter both of the King and the Anglican Church. Thomas Bruce was their ideal choice.

At the meeting of Parliament in November 1685, at the start of the second session, Thomas carried the sword of state. He and his fellow Tories were perturbed to hear that James II had appointed 80 Catholic officers, despite the Test Act. The House of Commons was sensitive on the issue of Roman Catholicism, because on 22 October Louis XIV revoked the Edict of Nantes, which had given considerable freedom to the French Protestant Huguenots. A deputation was sent to James to ask the names of those officers appointed. He brusquely rejected this request, and on 20 November he prorogued Parliament. It was never to meet again. The four Bedford-shire MPs, over whose election such effort had been expended, had sat for just two short sessions. Now they were left to be passive and frustrated spectators as the drama unfolded.

July 1686 saw the King appoint a new High Commission to discipline the Church of England with the unspoken intention of using it to return the country to the Roman Catholic faith. The Bishop of London was suspended and a Roman Catholic was made Dean of Chichester. That James meant business is shown by his encamping a large army at Hounslow Heath, near London, as a sign of his strength.

The following year, 1687, saw quarrels with Oxford University over the appointments of Roman Catholics to academic positions. Parallel with these, James made his first Declaration of Indulgence, suspending all laws against Roman Catholics.[5] James was turning from his family's natural allies, the Tories, to the dissenters/nonconformists in an effort to bring toleration for all.

In November 1687, James dissolved Parliament and set about creating a House of Commons that would vote for these measures. The lord lieutenants, including Thomas Bruce, the new Lord Ailesbury, were summoned to the Cabinet Council with written orders to ask all deputy lieutenants and justices of the peace three questions: (1) whether if any of them were chosen they would support the abolition of the Test Act against Roman Catholics; (2) whether they would give such candidates

3   Earl of Cardigan, *The Life and Loyalties of Thomas Bruce* (London, 1951), pp. 103–5.
4   Anthony Wood, *Athenae Oxonienses . . . to which are added, the Fasti, or Annals, of the said university for the same time* (London, 1691), col. 887.
5   *English Historical Documents*, vol. 8, pp. 395–7.

their support; and (3) whether they would support the King's Declaration of Indulgence.

Ailesbury decided to obey rather than resign and let in the Earl of Peterborough, a recent convert to Roman Catholicism and a man, Ailesbury considered, as 'hot and fiery and giddy'. Ailesbury summoned the leading figures of both Bedfordshire and Huntingdonshire to his new house in Leicester Fields, London. Others he met at his Bedfordshire seat of Houghton House. He said he would not pressurise them but asked those present to write down what they thought 'according to the dictates of honour and conscience, and as good subjects withal'.[6]

The answers have been published in BHRS, vol. 20.[7] The King also wanted to know of names of dissenters and Roman Catholics who could be added to the deputy lieutenants or the commission of the peace. Charles Leigh of the Prebendal House, Leighton Buzzard, expressed the Tory view by saying that he would vote for those 'of the most constant and unshaken Loyalty, which he takes to be those that are the truest sons of the Church of England'. Sir William Gostwick of Willington said he 'cannot part with the Penall laws and tests'. Sir Anthony Chester, the Borough MP, said he would not stand but he 'can not give his support to take away any such laws as doe support the Church of England'. He spoke for a group of other gentry, including Sir Villiers Chernocke, William Boteler, Richard Orlebar and two William Farrers. Others, like Thomas Bromsall, wanted to repeal the Test Acts, which they saw as having been brought in to spite James when he was Duke of York, but keep the penal laws against the 'phanatiques' (nonconformists) so they should not have too much liberty.

Thomas Christie, the Borough MP, did intend to stand again. He said he would comply with the King's inclination as 'farr as he can with a good conscience, and with the safety of the Protestant religion of the Church of England'. He had always been civil to Roman Catholics and dissenters, and argued with the Parliament men, that is, other MPs, in favour of the repeal of the Test Act.

Most of those listed were prepared to live peacefully with their neighbours, no matter what their religious persuasion. Bedford men clearly had strong views but believed in a degree of religious tolerance.

There were few if any Whigs in these lists, showing what a tight control the Ailesburys had kept of the lieutenancy and the magistracy.

Ailesbury submitted the lists to the cabinet to the rage of James II's chief minister, the Earl of Sunderland. He was sent back to Bedfordshire to dismiss all his deputy lieutenants and supply a new list. He was to add to the justices at the same time. As many of those dismissed were Ailesbury's personal friends, it was a great blow to him.

The new list, dated 3 February 1688,[8] however, was still composed mostly of Tory supporters. When they voted in 1685, with only one exception, they gave at least one vote to Boteler and Chernocke, the Tory candidates. The exception was Robert Montagu of Colworth, Sharnbrook, cousin of the powerful Montagu family

---

6   Cardigan, *Thomas Bruce*, pp. 116–17.
7   W.M. Wigfield, ed., *Recusancy and Nonconformity*, BHRS, vol. 20 (Apsley Guise, 1938), pp. 187–202.
8   Ibid., pp. 196–7.

at Boughton House in Northamptonshire. The list was not made up of nonentities, as it included five knights. William Whitbread became a magistrate at this time. Although having an estate confined to Cardington, the family already had important London connections. He and John Eston represented the Bunyan Meeting and nonconformists.

Whether it was to these or subsequent royal suggestions, Ailesbury wrote to the new appointees as follows: 'Sir, I send you by the King's command, and under his signet, a Commission of Deputy Lieutenant; notwithstanding, I desire that we may live together as we have done formerly.' The Earl of Cardigan in his biography of Thomas Bruce comments: 'Since he had usually not spoken to such people before, this meant that he would continue to have nothing to say to them – and thus the contact of the deputies with their Lord Lieutenant existed on paper only.'[9] In view of the political make-up of the new appointees, it is unlikely that this interpretation is correct.

At the same time as James was putting pressure on the country gentry, he was also negotiating with the nonconformists in the Borough of Bedford to get two MPs elected in favour of toleration. John Eston wrote to the Earl of Peterborough on 22 November 1687, telling him that, after conversations with Mr Margetts, Judge Advocate to General Monk in 1660, and John Bunyan, they had recommended Eston himself and Robert Audley esquire, late deputy recorder to the town, who 'when in power was very indulgent to all Dissenters'.[10] They could not fail to get elected 'if the Lord Leiftenant will cordially assist with his influence over the Church-party'. Eston expressed his fervent zeal against the Test Act. Audley in fact did not run and Dr Foster, Doctor of Laws, was the other candidate.

By 6 December, Eston was complaining of the opposition of the clergy and several corporation officials within Bedford. He asked Lord Peterborough to encourage the Lord Lieutenant to send a letter to Mr Christie, the mayor and aldermen and the clergy, 'who are the Leiftenant's voteries'. He commented generally: 'It is the misery of this kingdom that so much Democrasie is mixed up in the Government, that thereby the exercise of the Souveraign power should in any manner limited by the suffrages of the common people, whose humours are allwayes fluctuating, and the most part guided not by reason, but deliberation like mere animals.'[11]

The Borough of Bedford at its meeting of 19 December 1687 told Lord Ailesbury that it could not elect Eston and Foster on its own 'as the Eleccion of this Towne is not in the Corporacon alone but that every Inhabitant (not taking Collection nor being a Sojorner) and noe Freeman hath a Vote, therefore they cannot give assurance how the Majority of Voices will determine'. The Council, however, said it would do its best to ensure the election of MPs of 'undoubted loyalty and shall be serviceable to the King and Kingdome'. This was not good enough. Half of the corporation was removed under the power in the new charter, including Thomas Underwood, the mayor. Then the other half was removed and replaced by a new group, mainly nonconformists, of whom five were not yet burgesses.

9   Cardigan, *Thomas Bruce*, p. 119.
10   Wigfield, *Recusancy and Nonconformity*, p. 199.
11   Ibid., pp. 200–2.

In May 1688, James issued a second Declaration of Indulgence, with the added information that a general election would be held in November to enact it.[12]

The reaction of the Borough of Bedford, purged as it had been, was virtually instant. On 8 May, a resolution was sent 'thankfully acknowledging the goodness of God Almighty in placing you on the Throne of your Royall Ancestors, Do humbly offer our hart felt thanks to your Majestie for your gratious Declaration to all your Lovinge Subjects for liberty of conscience and . . . to have the same established by a law Whereby the Church of England will be secured and all dissenters protected in the free exercise of their Religion and enjoyment of their Civill rights'.[13] The Borough agreed to work to get two MPs to support this in the new House of Commons.

The response of the Church of England was completely different. James had ordered that the clergy read the Indulgence in all churches at stated times in May and June. On 12 May Archbishop Sancroft and six bishops asked that the reading of the Indulgence be not enforced, as they claimed James's use of dispensing power was illegal. Many clergy disobeyed James's order. Instead of compromising, James prosecuted the bishops. This was a fatal error, as it finally alienated the Tories and the Anglican Church. Their acquittal on 29 June led to James suffering a crucial loss of face. If the bishops had been punished, it is likely there would have been an armed rebellion in the West Country. 'And shall Trelawney die . . . 40,000 Cornishmen shall know the reason why' became the popular song of support for the Bishop of Bristol.

Unhappy and brow-beaten, maybe, but, up to this point, the Tories could look forward to the accession of James's daughter Mary and her Protestant, if Calvinist, husband, William of Orange. But even this hope was removed with the birth, on 10 June 1688, of James II's son, also called James. This established the Roman Catholic succession. Whether the baby was smuggled in a warming pan into Mary of Modena's bed to replace a dead child is open to conjecture, but that was the rumour that was spread about by James's enemies.

An invitation was issued on 30 June by a group of Tory and Whig leaders to William of Orange to invade England and depose James. Among what became known as the 'Immortal Seven' was Edward Russell, later Lord Orford, a cousin of the Edward Russell who had been a candidate in the 1685 County election. This Russell was a leading admiral in the navy and therefore a key element in the conspiracy. Since the execution of his cousin, William Lord Russell, he had been biding his time for revenge. His co-conspirator Henry Sidney had the injustice of his own brother's execution at the same time to inspire him.

Despite promises of overwhelming support and, crucially, an opposing army with divided loyalties, William did not act at once. It was Louis XIV's declaration of war on the Habsburg empire in September that finally pushed William into making a bid for the English throne. He saw that an invasion of Holland was inevitable. The prospect of Britain joining the war against him or, at least, being neutral but hostile, meant that inactivity was not an option. He needed to invade quickly so he could return home in time to defend Holland when Louis attacked.

---

[12] *English Historical Documents*, vol. 8, pp. 399–400.
[13] Wigfield, *Recusancy and Nonconformity*, pp. 202–3.

Lord Ailesbury viewed royal policy with increasingly grave misgivings. He used his position as Gentleman of the Bedchamber to try and warn James, but to no avail.

The despair he felt made him decide to resign as lord lieutenant. Sometime in September 1688 he went to Windsor to inform the King. To his great surprise, James told him that William was certain to invade. As a loyal subject, he felt he could not resign. Burdened with this secret information, he returned to Bedfordshire to prepare how best to resist the invader.[14]

Soon afterwards, in a tardy attempt by James to bolster up his regime, Ailesbury was told 'depending on his Judgement' to restore those deputy lieutenants who had been dismissed in 1687. These men were 'all of the prime gentry and what were most valuable, and who were close friends to me'. Ailesbury summoned them to dine with him at Ampthill and told them he had been authorised to reinstate them. At first they refused but, with Charles Leigh as their spokesman, they agreed to do so for 'my sake only'. They said they would never serve under any other lord lieutenant; nor did they. As the time of the likely invasion approached, Ailesbury called out the militia to make sure they were well armed and trained for action.

It was not until 3 November that favourable winds enabled William to sail to England, landing at Torbay in Devon on 5 November. Ailesbury went to the royal camp at Salisbury on 20 November and accompanied the King to London. Alone among James's inner circle, he advised James to continue fighting and head by way of Nottingham and York to Scotland. Remembering the fate of his father, James fled for France on 11 December 1688. However, he only reached Faversham.

Rumours of an Irish papist army about to attack Protestants caused widespread panic. At Ampthill carts were upturned to provide roadblocks in every street.[15] In London, with William approaching, the Privy Council at his instigation sent Ailesbury to bring James to London, which, despite considerable difficulties, he managed to do. William issued an ultimatum forcing James (with Ailesbury in attendance) to withdraw to Rochester. On the news that William would no longer guarantee his safety, James II finally went to France on 23 December 1688. This time, when asked, Ailesbury could not advise him to stay.

William's coup became nicknamed 'The Glorious Revolution'.[16] It was seen throughout the eighteenth century as the triumph of good over evil, of constitutional monarchy over foreign absolutism, of healthy Protestantism over unhealthy Roman Catholicism, and, of course, of British superiority to the hated French. It had moved from history into myth.

Convention Parliament, elected January 1689

William summoned a Convention to establish the way ahead. The four delegates from Bedfordshire were: William Duncombe and Edward Russell for the County, while Thomas Christie and Thomas Hillersden of Elstow represented the Borough. Both political parties were represented, with Russell, a Whig and Christie, a Tory. The other two candidates voted in 1685 for one Whig and one Tory each.

14 Cardigan, *Thomas Bruce*, pp. 126ff.
15 Ibid., p. 140.
16 Speck, *Reluctant Revolutionaries*.

The first decision the Convention had to make was who should be Sovereign. Ailesbury argued and voted in the House of Lords that the throne was not vacant and that it should not be offered to William and Mary. He and his friends were defeated. Ailesbury immediately resigned his position as lord lieutenant, being replaced by the Whig Earl of Bedford, then aged 73. Ailesbury described his successor as 'a graceful old nobleman – and his outside was all'.[17]

March 1690 Election

A new Parliament to replace the Convention was elected at the beginning of 1690.[18] The County elected Edward Russell and Thomas Browne of Arlesey, probably another Whig, who replaced Duncombe, who had not stood as he had already been appointed Ambassador to Sweden and therefore would have been unable to function as an MP.

The Borough was definitely contested. Thomas Hillersden of Elstow and Thomas Christie of Bedford were duly elected. The defeated candidate, Sir William Franklyn of Mavourn in Bolnhurst, petitioned the House of Commons on 29 March 1690,[19] alleging that the under-sheriff had altered the return of the election to put in a name other than Franklyn's. The petition failed but the mayor and under-sheriff and bailiffs of the borough were bound over to report to the House. By an order of 12 April 1690, the right to elect two MPs for the Borough of Bedford was vested in the burgesses, freemen and householders not receiving alms (see Introduction). The power to create burgesses and freemen was susceptible to huge abuse but probably was reasonably controlled until the late 1730s.

The first Parliament of the reign established the new constitutional ground rules. The Bill of Rights asserted the illegality of James II's acts and that he had vacated the throne by abdication. It also established the role of Parliament, curbing royal pretensions in the fields of taxation, church discipline, standing armies and law. It stated that elections to, and debates in, the House of Commons ought to be free.

A specific oath of allegiance and supremacy to the Protestant succession was demanded of all office-holders in church and state. Although Ailesbury still felt that James was the legitimate King by divine right, he could see the practical necessity of the oath in view of the highly volatile political situation, in which plotting by James's supporters was endemic. Some churchmen, led by Sancroft, Archbishop of Canterbury, also believed in divine right and they felt they could not renege on their earlier oath of allegiance to him. No doubt throughout Bedfordshire clergy wrestled with their consciences. Should they give up their livelihoods and their homes to face an uncertain future with poorly paid teaching as the only alternative? Was it wise to do this in support of a man who, when he was King, had been the enemy of the Church of England? Most stayed put. William Berkeley (Clophill) and George Wateson (Millbrook)[20] did not 'abjur' according to the Act and were deprived of

[17] GEC, *Complete Peerage* (London, 1912), vol. II, p. 79, entry for 1st Duke of Bedford.
[18] O'Byrne, *The Representative History of Great Britain and Ireland*, p. 7.
[19] Ibid., pp. 7–8.
[20] BLARS, Fasti.

their livings. Significantly, they had both been appointed by the Earl of Ailesbury, who had died in 1685. There may be more, but it is difficult to gauge whether resignations at this date from Bedfordshire parishes were on the appointment to another living, because of old age or on genuine conscience grounds.

A reissue in 1702 led to James Kirkwood losing the incumbency of Astwick. He had been appointed by Thomas Browne of Arlesey, the defeated candidate in 1695. It is thought that 400 clergy nationally were deprived as a result of 'non-juring'. Its effect was to produce a more low-church episcopate, more Whig in political allegiance. Local clergy would no longer vote automatically for the Tory candidate, as they had done in 1685.

For a prominent supporter of James II, such as the Earl of Ailesbury,[21] the years after the Revolution were very difficult. He was suspected of Jacobitism and thus of supporting the various plots of James II's supporters to reinstate him. In the crisis around the time of the Battle of the Boyne (1 July 1690), he hid in London, avoiding arrest by a whisker. He did the same in 1692 at the time of the attempted invasion, which ended with the defeat of the French fleet at La Hogue by Admiral Edward Russell, cousin of the Duke of Bedford. It seems as if Ailesbury received protection from Queen Mary with whom he had played as a child. Keeping his head down, he concentrated on a successful attempt to get an act of Parliament to give him more powers over his wife's estate, in defiance of his mother-in-law, the Duchess of Beaufort.

Having avoided Jacobite plots, Ailesbury concocted one of his own in 1693. He went to France, meeting up with both James and Louis XIV. He wanted the commanders of William's fleet to take it away on a long expedition, allowing the French to land a force in the south-west and topple William in the same way that William had toppled James. Louis was polite but not prepared to risk his fleet again.

Having failed in his efforts, Ailesbury 'resolved that I would enter no more in what might bring me to my last end – and for nothing'. At the time of the 1695 election, Ailesbury was leading a quiet life, occasionally seeing Jacobite sympathisers. He was a spent force as far as local politics were concerned.

William had governed from 1689 to 1693 with both Whig and Tory ministers, which had led to less intense political strife. From 1693 under the influence of the Whig Junto (including Admiral Edward Russell), an all-Whig Administration was created with the unintended effect of reinvigorating party conflict. Geoffrey Holmes and W.A. Speck have edited a collection of documents, which clearly recount these events.[22]

William Lord Russell's death after the Rye House Plot had made him into a Whig martyr. The powerful position of his cousin, Admiral Russell, ensured that the martyr's father, William Russell, 5th Earl of Bedford, was created 1st Duke on 11 May 1694. This was granted to him as the 'father to Lord Russell, the ornament of his age, whose great merit was not enough to transmit by history to posterity'. The grant of the dukedom immeasurably increased the importance and regard with which the Russells were held in the county. Their political interest in both town and

21 Cardigan, *Thomas Bruce*, pp. 159–212.
22 Geoffrey Holmes and W.A. Speck, *The Divided Society: Party Conflict in England 1694–1716* (London, 1976).

William Russell, 1st Duke of Bedford (1613–1700), 1694. Engraving by Ravenet of an earlier picture. The duke was aged 78 when he was granted the title.
(BLARS, Casebourne Archive)

county became one of the consistent features in the politics of both borough and county until G.W.E. Russell lost North Bedfordshire in the Tory landslide of 1895.

The year 1694 saw two crucial moves by the Whigs that helped strengthen their position. First, the Bank of England was established, firmly linking the Whigs with the monied interest in the City of London. At the same time they forced William to accept triennial Parliaments, ensuring general elections every three years. This favoured the Whigs, who had the longer purses and thus would be able to bankrupt or at least deter the independent country squires, who had only their rural estates to rely on for income.

Locally, the Whig Russells had the estates in the Covent Garden area of London as well as their estates in Bedfordshire, Cambridgeshire, Devon and Northamptonshire to finance their campaigns. To this they added the potential fortune of Elizabeth Howland, based on estates at Rotherhithe and Streatham. She married Wriothsley, later 2nd Duke of Bedford, on 23 May 1695. The independent gentry, both Whigs and Tories, such as the Gostwicks and the Rolts, found the endless and ruinously expensive elections permanently damage their finances. The weakest went to the wall![23]

The 1695 Election

The County seat was contested by three candidates. A poll book covering part of the votes cast has survived in the archives of the Massingberd family at Lincolnshire Archives.[24] William Massingberd, based at Potsgrove, was the sheriff of Bedfordshire with responsibility for administering the election. The three candidates were the two sitting MPs, Edward Russell of Woburn and Thomas Browne of Arlesey, and William Duncombe of Battlesden. Russell, a Whig, was elected by acclamation. Duncombe and Browne stood a poll.

William Duncombe seems to have been a supporter of William III, a placeman without pronounced party views. In this election he took votes from the non-Jacobite Tories and the Whigs. Crucially he received the support of the Russell family in the areas round Woburn Abbey. His brother, Sir John (Chancellor of the Exchequer in 1672), had rebuilt the family home at Battlesden to the plans of the well-known architect, Hugh May. In 1685, William Duncombe had voted for Sir William Boteler (Tory) and Edward Russell (Whig) in favour of a split representation. William only inherited Battlesden in 1687 and so was not even a magistrate until 1688. He was appointed deputy lieutenant and magistrate when James II had insisted on many of the Tory deputy lieutenants and justices of the peace being dismissed. He was clearly in William III's favour and from 1689 to 1692 was Ambassador to Sweden at the Court of Charles XI. When the young Charles XII came to the throne in 1697, an Anglo-Dutch fleet helped him to drive back the Danes, who had invaded his country. Duncombe's diplomacy may well have laid the seeds for Anglo-Swedish friendship. In 1693 he was made one of the Lord Justices

[23]   Gladys Scott Thompson, *Life in a Noble Household 1641–1700* (London, 1937) and her *The Russells in Bloomsbury 1669–1771* (London, 1940).
[24]   Lincolnshire Archives, Massingberd Archive ref. M(G) 6/1/B/4.

of Ireland, a position of great trust. He later became Comptroller to the Army, an important and lucrative post.

His opponent was Thomas Browne, an Arlesey squire, the eldest son of Samuel Browne, MP for both Town and County in the mid-seventeenth century and a Justice of the Court of Common Pleas from 1660 to 1668. As the sitting MP Browne had thought he would be unopposed. Duncombe, the previous MP, had returned from Sweden and thought that Browne would stand aside. It seems as if the election was based on a misunderstanding. It looks as though Browne's campaign was hastily organised and he was handsomely defeated. He had support from both Whig and Tory voters of 1685. His supporters included William Boteler of Biddenham, Sir William Gostwick of Willington, Henry Ashley junior of Eaton Socon (of the Ouse Navigation), Thomas Hillersden of Elstow and Matthew Denis of Kempston. Browne's vote was strong in the east of the county in such places as Henlow, Potton and Shefford. Because the return is only partial, the names of the voters for Arlesey and Stotfold are not included in areas that would be expected to support Browne. Whereas Boteler and Chernocke had the support of 42 clergy, Browne had the votes of only two.

Browne did very badly in Tory strongholds such as Ampthill and Dunstable: he received no votes in either. Duncombe received 27 and 45 votes respectively.

Of those known to vote in both the 1685 and 1695 elections, Duncombe received votes about equally from the former Tory voters, as well as from the Whigs. He straddled the party divide. Among his supporters were prominent Tories such as Sir Robert Chester, Sir Pinsent and Francis Chernocke and John Vaux of Whipsnade. He had the support of 27 gentry and 17 clergy, as against Browne's 13 and 2. He polled well in the Bedford and Leighton Buzzard areas but was more evenly matched in Luton.

What was happening? Duncombe as a member of the Court and sitting MP was clearly a popular candidate with support in all areas, except the east of the county. The Whigs were in the ascendancy and Russell was elected. It seems probable that there was some form of deal between Duncombe and Russell, so that Russell supporters would vote for Duncombe as long as Russell was unopposed. Crucially the Russell supporters went for Duncombe. Both Tories and Whigs were split locally between the two candidates. Most Tories had not taken a non-juring position. Their loyalty had been to the Anglican Church, as much as to the Stuart dynasty. This election took place at a time of war. Loyalty was therefore both natural and essential. William was a Protestant and he was fighting French Roman Catholics, supporters of James II, who had been such an enemy of their Church.

For the Bedford Borough seat, Thomas Hillersden of Elstow and William Farrer were elected. Farrer of Harrold was the son-in-law of William Boteler, MP for the County in 1685. Hillersden and Farrer were both Whigs and both voted for Browne for the County.[25]

Thomas Christie, MP for Bedford since 1685, retired at this election. He was buried on 9 July 1697 at St Paul's, Bedford, where his monument is sited. His alms-houses survive but on a different site to the ones he originally gave. Bishop Burnet

25 O'Byrne, *The Representative History of Great Britain and Ireland*, p. 10.

in the original draft to his *History of my own Times*,[26] records that: 'The elections went generally for men that loved the present constitution. In many places, those who pretended to be chosen put themselves and their competitors likewise to a great charge; and everywhere there was more spent than could have been expected in elections that could not sit above three years.'

Burnet comments that few Jacobites were elected but 'many of the sourer sort of Whigs, who were much alienated from the King, were chosen; generally they were men of estates, but many were young, hot and without experience'. The two MPs for Bedfordshire would not have fitted this description as Duncombe was an experienced diplomat and servant of William III. Russell had been MP since 1689. Farrer became ultimately a long-serving Chairman of Ways and Means in the House of Commons. Hillersden had been first elected in 1689.

Despite not having to contest the election, Lord Edward Russell had to spend money freely as his surviving accounts show.[27]

The generall Accompt of all the charges att Bedford at my Lord Russell's Election, October 31 1695

To Stephen Taylor for three jornys to Bedford	6s
To two bakers at Woburne for 40 dozen of bread	£2
To Mr Yonger for 5 dozen of Cannary	£6
To Mrs Lowins a Bill of charges at the Swan at Bedford the day of the Election	£36 14s 6d
Payd to severall people for 20 Hogsheads of Ale for the Freeholders to drinke with Tobaco	£53
To the poore of the 5 parishes of Bedford	£10
To the fidlers, Pipers and Drumers	£1 10s
To the Watchmen at the Booth	5s
To the Cryer of the Court	5s
To the Bayliffs of the Nine Hundreds	£1
To the Ringers of the five Churches	£1 10s
To the Watch in the Swan Yard	2s
To the Sword Barer	5s
To the Chearmen	£1
To the Cooke	10s
For a hogshead of Ale and a pound of Tobaco, given to the Rable after the proclamation	£2 13s 6d
In wine after the proclamation was made	£1 5s
My own expences in three days till the pole was ended and the Wrightings signd	15s
To the under shrieffe his Fees for the Indentures etc	£4 10s
To the Ringers of Marson, Lidlington and Rigment	15s

---

[26] Gilbert Burnet, *History of my own Times*, vol. liv, pp. 287–8 and draft original, quoted in Holmes and Speck, *The Divided Society*, p. 17.

[27] BLARS, Russell Box 770, which contains other election bills from 1688 onwards.

To your Grace's servants to Drinke at Bedford	12s
To 8 men to hold the horses at Woburne Abby till the freeholders went in	4s
Total Summe is	£125 2s

Examined and allowd by me this 13th day of November 1695, the summe being one Hundred and twenty five pounds, two shillings. Bedford

The hogsheads for the nine hundreds were accompanied with a note signed by Ambrose Reddall on behalf of Lord Russell. The one for Willey hundred went as follows:

Mr Bamford, You are desired to deliver unto the freeholders of Willey Hundred two hogsheads of Ale and two Pounds of Tobaccoe upon the account of the honourable Lord Russell. Ambrose Reddall.
[PS] You are to deliver each [of the] freeholders as Ralphael Mills shall direct.[28]

Margaret Lowen sent a bill for the £36 14s spent at the Swan, which was being used as the Russell campaign headquarters:[29]

The Bill att the Swan in Bedford October 31 1695

For 113 Gentellsmens Ordennarys	£12 11s
For 78 servants orderings	£3 18s
For Strong bear and Alle	£1 14s
For Fierring	5s
For the fashioning of Vensn pastays	£5 10s
The Bill for the horses	15s
To the Sarvants	£1
For 4 dossens of cannary and 32 Bottels of Cannary	£5 10s
For 5 dossens and 4 Bottells of Port	£4 16s
3 Bottles of Port	4s
	£36 14s 6d

31 Oct.   Received in full of this bill and all Accounts the sum of Thurty six pounds, fourteen shillings and six pence per me, Margaret Lowen

28 BLARS, Russell Box 770.
29 Ibid.

Poll for the County of Bedfordshire 1695

Source: manuscript in Lincolnshire Archives Massingberd Archive ref. M(G) 6/1/B/4.

It was kept by William Massingberd who was high sheriff of the county. The poll book appears to be only part of the voters (875 names). To make use of the document easier, where the original text uses 'of the same' to describe where a person came from, the actual place has been given in this transcript. The original was arranged with two columns, one for each candidate. In this transcript, voters for each candidate are listed separately.

Mr William Duncomb of Battlesden and Mr Brown of Alzy, both yeilding upon View in the field to the Lord Edward Russell as duely elected Knight of the Shire to serve for the County of Bedford in the Parliament to meet at Westminster the [blank] of November next. The Poll between them two for the other Knight's place began on thursday the 31th October 1695 at the Assize house in the Town of Bedford and was closed there the Saturday following in the afternoon and was taken by John Goodhall [original signature], as is within written

    for Mr Duncomb   1108
         Mr Brown   906

Duncomb

John Whitley of Dunstable
John Groome of Dunstable
Daniel Fossey of Dunstable
John Hebbs of Hockliffe
William Newman of Luton
William Ironmonger of Harlington
Ambrose Reddall of Ridgmont
Francis Turner of Wooburne
Edward Stone Esq. of Ridgmont
Sir Pinsent Chernock of Hulcott Bart
Robert Chester Bart of Litlington
Nehemiah Brandrith of Houghton Regis, Esq.
Sir James Astry of Harlington
Thomas Johnson of Milton Brian, Esq.
Thomas Franke, Clerk of Cranfield
William Norcliff of Aspley Guise, Esq.
Francis Chernock, of Hulcott, Esq.
Henry Dearmer of Elstowe
William Cawne of Wilshamsted
Francis Padman of Wilshamsted

John Osborne of Wilshamsted
John Willis of Tuddington
Robert Cooper of Clipson
Thomas Veary of Laighton
George Gurny of Tuddington
William Pryor of Clifton, Bucks
William Barber of Farndish
William Woodward of Harlington
Thomas Palmer of Houghton Regis
Thomas Arnold, jun. of Ampthill
Francis Cooke of Milton Brian
John Marks of Chicheley
Thomas Follett of Chicheley
Samuel Osborne of Tebworth
John Hawkins of Houghton Regis
Robert Bland of Cockain Hatley, Clerk
Thomas Groome of Dunstable
Robert Lamb of Milton Brian, Clerk
Dr Isaac Bringhurst of Tuddington
Thomas Snagg of Ridgmont, Esq.
John Vaux of Whipsnade, Esq.

Joshua Pulford of Laighton, clerk

Thomas Sims of Laighton

Thomas Walker of Laighton

Richard Leach of Laighton

John Ashwell, jun. of Laighton

Simon Taylor of Wooburn, gentleman

Joseph Margetts of Kempston, clerk

John Gale of Dunstable

William Newman jun. of Houghton Regis

Thomas Turney of Wooburne

Edward Hall of Asply, clerk

John Edge of Laighton

William Walker of Tingridy, clerke

Thomas Hubbins of Kempston

Robert Smith of Wooburne

John Cumberland of Oakley

Abraham Sanders of Sundon

Thomas Willis of Herne

Henry Buckingham of Houghton Regis

John Norris of Houghton Regis

William Drury of Tempsford, gent.

Richard Tuly of Laighton

Thomas Molton of Wooburne

James Line of Thurley

Edward Burr of Westoning, gent.

John Tiffin of Souldrop, Clerk

Thomas Crawley of Milton Brian

John King of Sundon

William Pedder of Caddington

William Duncomb of Sundon

Henry Tompkins of Houghton Regis

Henry Osborne of Tebworth

Richard Gibbs of Litlington

John Lucy jun. of Milton Brian

Francis Rands of Flittwick

Thomas Huggins of Dunstable

Thomas Carter of Stanbridge

Thomas Vize of Totternhoe

Edward Holt of Dunstable

St John Thomson of Husborn Crawley, Esq.

John Warner of Dunstable

John Mayes of Milton Brian

William Legg of Westoning

William Fossey of Dunstable

Ambrose Whitmore of Husborn Crawly

William Robbins of Ridgmont

Edward Cooper of Stanbridge

John Birchmore of Whipsnade

William Wells of Egginton

John Ginger of Totternhoe

Edward Barnes of Dunstable

Laurence Crawly of Asply Guise

Samuel Billingham of Dunstable

Wythers Cheney of Chalgrave

Richard Cooke of Ridgmont

John Gregory jun. of Evershalt

William Barker of Evershalt

Joseph Monk of Heath and Reach

Thomas Franklin, jun. of Marston

Robert Costin of Wooburne

James Ambridge of Asply Guise

James Franklin of Evershalt

William Tearle of Stanbridge

Robert Ridle of Milton Briant

Daniel Ellingham of Stanbridge

Edward Polton of Hockliffe

John Smith of Hockliffe

John Snoxall of Stanbridge

Christopher Perry of Hockliffe

George Richardson of Ridgmont

Benedict Coles of Laighton

Richard Northcott of Billington

William Beadle of Wilshamsted, gent.

John Hill of Marston

Francis Fenn of Billington

John Alloway of Wooburne

Thomas Chamberlin of Westoning

John Elsome of Thurley

William Whitmore of Silsoe

David Sutton of Sandey

William Fossey of Tebworth

John Jeffs of Tebworth

John Herbert of Milton Briant

Simon Wood [deleted]

John Odell of Tebworth

John Purratt of Tebworth

Joseph Cooper of Tebworth

Henry Honner of Stanbridge

Nathaniel Cooke of Milton Briant

Edward Higgs of Milton Briant

Thomas Franklin, sen. of Marston

Robert Barrington of Thurley

Thomas Lane of Westoning

Anthony Wilcocks of Marston

Robert Wallis of Potton

Joseph Pudifant of Sundon

William How of Houghton Regis

Stephen Apthorp of Gamlingay, query

George Sole of Flittwick

Thomas Olney of Tebworth

William Fisher of Hockliffe

William Russell of Husborn Crawly

Michael Mouse of Totternhoe

Richard Everitt of Totternhoe

Thomas Potts of Tuddington

John Birt of Litlington

John Bushby of Litlington

John Berry of Husborn Crawley

Thomas Skilliter of Sandy

John Ashbolt of Keysoe

Thomas Prentis of Tilsworth

William Coates of Husborn Crawly

Thomas Luke of Everton

John Newman, sen. of Ridgmont

John Newman, jun. of Ridgmont

Thomas Cooke, jun. of Ridgmont

Richard Burton of Eyworth

Nathaniel Wimpey of Dunstable

John Searle of Potton

Joseph Norman of Northill

Henry Wallis of Potton

George Reeve, sen. of Tuddington

John Hopkins of Husborn Crawly

Edmund Slingsby of Husborn Crawly

Thomas Kefford of Wrestlingworth

Robert White of Riseley

Thomas Martin of Totternhoe

John Mouse of Totternhoe

Thomas Cooper of Silsoe

Joseph Tillcock of Tilsworth

William Crawly of Cardington

William King of Wilden

Henry Thurrowgood of Girtford

George Walker of Wootton

John Foulkes of Wootton

Richard Foulks of Wootton

William Morgan of Tebworth

William Dearman of Wilshamsted

John Higgins of Astwood, query

John Lucy of Milton Briant, sen.

Thomas Keble of Hockliffe

John Caudwell of Tebworth

Henry Honer, sen. of Stanbridge

John Chapman of Potton, query

Thomas Millard of Northill

Stephen Taylor of Marston

Thomas Pearce of Marston

William Marshall of Wooburn, clerk

Henry Smith of Hockliffe

James Ashwell of Eaton Bray

John Crow of Wilden

John Wagstaff of Wilden

John Tearle of Stanbridge

John Balls of Hockliffe

Robert Fitzhugh of Wilden

Humphry Thomas of Mogerhanger

William Stevens of Tuddington

James Allen of Statchden

Edward Sibley of Studham

Henry Peirson of Egginton

John Hill of Wootton

John Sibly of Bidwell

John Ableston of Harrold

Thomas Maxey of Knotting

William Stevens of Egginton

John Man of Eggington

Jeptha Hawkins of Eaton Bray

Edmund Roberts of Billington

Richard Rands of Turvey, clerke

James Reynolds of Cranfield

John Ashwell of Eaton Bray

Roger Bunker of Laighton Buzzard

Nicholas Cooke, jun. of Kempston
John Hipwell of Sharnbrook
Thomas Gurney of Goldington
Henry Hill, jun. of Wootton
Thomas Ireland of Wooburne
Richard Man of Clipson
Thomas Higgs of Wilshamsted
Edward Ashwell of Laighton Buzzard
Joseph Gregory of Laighton Buzzard
John Capon of Laighton Buzzard
Oliver Taylor of Laighton Buzzard
William Faldo of Bedford, Draper
William Tiffin of Sharnbrook, clerk
Robert Richards of Souldrop
Robert Hanger of Souldrop
Joseph Eden of Souldrop
William Chichely of Bedford
James Goods of Bedford
John Negus of Clapham
Oliver Dixon of Milton Ernys
Edward Brockis of Asply Guise
William Manley of Bedford, gent.
Ralph Doggett of Laighton Buzzard
Thomas Coles of Laighton Buzzard
Thomas Foster of Laighton Buzzard
Jeremiah Bonnick of Laighton Buzzard
James Gregory of Laighton Buzzard
John Street of Cardington
Richard Stone of Ridgmont, Esq.
William King, jun. of Colmworth
Thomas Timberlake of Houghton Regis
John Tearle of Stanbridge, son of Thomas
Joseph Read of Eaton Bray
Josias Sanders of Dunstable
George Ward of Asply Guise
Henry Browne of Asply Guise
Richard Maynard of Asply Guise
Richard Bumsted of Asply Guise
Thomas Harden of Cranfeild
William Lucy of Milton Briant
Thomas Knight of Harrold
William Blatt of Statchden
John Hartwell of Harrold

John Dillingham of Deane
Richard Chichely of Bedford, Mayor
  [Esq. deleted]
William Lockwood of Bedford
Thomas Cheney of Sundon, Esq.
Francis Fry of Wooburne
William Griffin of Husborn Crawly
Richard Divitt of Bedford
John Gale of Bedford
John Carter of Northill
John Kidd of Bedford
Thomas Marks of Bedford
George Maddy of Bedford
John Austin of Bedford
John Rogers of Wootton
John Rose of Bedford
William Fairman of Batlesden
John Carvill of Tuddington
Thomas Roe of Tuddington
William Morris of Harlington
Richard Reddall of Potsgrave, clerk
Edward Bourne of Bedford, clerk
William Slingsby of Wrestlingworth, clerk
Thomas Fells of Harlington
William Lanford of Tuddington
Michael Chambers of Bedford
Francis Spufford of Tuddington
Henry Fensham of Tuddington
George Brooks of Tuddington
Robert Whitridge of Houghton Conquest
Edward Veale of Bedford
Simon Beckett of Bedford
William Paradine of Bedford
Henry Morly of Batlesden
William Jetherill of Clapham
John Elson of Bedford
John Hillersden of Stoak Hammond, query
Henry White of Bedford
John Fountaine of Millbrooke
Thomas Carr of Westoning
William Adams of Harlington
Abell Harris of Tilsworth
Henry Empson of Thurley

Thomas Pointer of Houghton Conquest, clerk

John Riseley of Houghton Conquest

Jeremia Peirce of Houghton Conquest

William Webb of Houghton Conquest

John Constable of Houghton Conquest

William Toogood of Houghton Conquest

William Webb of Houghton Conquest

Thomas Willimott of Houghton Conquest

Robert Whitfield of Sandey

Edward Childs of Houghton Conquest

Thomas Purser of Wilshamsted

Henry Hill of Wootton

John Finch of Houghton Conquest

John Hawes of Bedford, gent.

John Bunn of Wootton

Edward Gibbs of Milton Briant

William Faldo of Bedford, gent.

Mathew Witt of Wootton

Praise Noell of Woottton

Thomas Hill of Wootton

Robert Roebuck of Kempston

Robert Potton of Bedford

John Pycroft of Bedford

Edmund Webb of Houghton Conquest

The Hon. Charles Lee of Laighton Buzzard, Esq.

William Theed of Lebbon, gentleman, query

Thomas Farnell of Ridgmont

Thomas Cooke of Ridgmont

Richard Smith of Wilden

William Crow of Wilden

Edward Kippis of Wilden

Abraham King of Colmworth

Stephen King of Colmworth

Thomas Wootton of Colmworth

Thomas King of Wilden

John Witt of Wootton

John Willson of Cardington

Thomas Millard of Wootton

George Farey of Bedford

James Albright of Wooburn, quaker, query

Henry Hunt of Westoning, clerk

Abraham Dix of Westoning

James Farmer of Harlington

Thomas Gregory of Sundon

William Randall of Sundon

Richard Roe of Sundon

Robert Hanscomb of Westoning

John Warren of Westoning

William Wright of Sundon

Thomas Crouch of Husborn Crawly

John Shaw of Wootton

William Roe of Sundon

John Cook of Sundon

Thomas Cooke of Sundon

William Gresham of Husborn Crawly

George Smith of Husborn Crawly

John Wells of Husborn Crawly

Foster Greene of Flitwick

John Maddam of Flitwick

Edmund Farey of Flitwick

John Bur of Flitwick

Thomas Hutson of Flitwick

William Abbott of Husborn Crawly

Mathew Allin of Flitwick

John Tinsly of Statchden

Robert Jones of Litlington

Thomas Clarke of Litlington

Thomas Bonner of Litlington

Edward Stratton of Wilshamsted

Robert Crouch of Cranfield

John Asleton of Marston

William Carr of Litlington, clerk

Thomas Brotherton of Husborn Crawly

William Roff of Husborn Crawly

Francis Howes of Husborn Crawly

Richard Greene of Husborn Crawly

Thomas Money, sen. of Kempston

Philip Negus of Bedford

Edward Marks of Bedford

William Menard of Bedford

Thomas Ward of Bedford

George Lawson of Houghton Conquest, Gent.

John Davie of Houghton Conquest

Thomas Bassingham of Thurley

Richard Whitbread of Ridgmont

William Gregory of Thurley

John Gregory of Thurley

James Eldershaw of Wooburne

Mathew Watts of Cople

Mathew Skevington of Turvey

George Favell of Wilshamsted

Nathaniel Peirce of Wilshamsted

Samuel Richardson of Wilshamsted, clerk

Thomas Favell of Wilshamsted

John Crouch of Litlington

Jesper Webb of Ampthill

George Webb, sen. of Ampthill

Richard Pedder of Harlington

Henry Webb of Ampthill

John Dewbery of Harlington

John Farmer of Steppingley

Thomas Brace of Milbrooke

Joseph Pennyfather of Milbrooke

Robert Read of Houghton Conquest

John Peach of Milbrooke

Thomas Hamerston of Houghton Conquest

Thomas Bushby of Milbrooke

Simon Gale of Oakly, clerk

William Lovell of Salford

Michael Mitchell of Wooburne

John West of Wooburne

Isaac Savage of Wooburne

Robert Martin of Wooburne

Henry Peck of Bedford

Edward Youle of Wooburn

Giles Smith of Ravensden

William Warner of Wilshamsted

John Fessant of Tuddington

John Truelove of Laighton Buzzard

Thomas Valentine of Egginton

William Broxton of Heath and Reach

John Bedcott of Laighton Buzzard

Thomas Reeve of Laighton Buzzard

John Illin of Laighton Buzzard

John Melchburn of Beeston

Thomas Baines of Bedford, gent.

Henry Walker of Beeston

John Richardson of Bedford

Ralph Jeffs of Laighton Buzzard

Richard Warren of Bedford

Thomas Edmonds of Heath and Reach

John Edmonds of Wooburne

Richard Clayton of Litlington

John Tilcock of Asply Guise

Henry Greene of Ridgmont

Thomas Tilcock of Ridgmont

William Jarvis of Ridgmont

Thomas Birdsey of Ridgmont

William Boteler of Ridgmont

Thomas King of Litlington

William Dennell of Tudington

William Whitmore of Laighton

John Butler of Litlington

John Odell of Wootton

Thomas Astin of Asply Guise

John Weston of Sundon

Mathew Watts of Sundon

George Gregory of Evershalt

Henry Goldsmith of Evershalt

George Stevens of Tuddington

William Whitbread of Evershalt

Henry Beaumont of Flitton

Benjamin Whitbread of Evershalt

George Groome of Harlington

William Rainbow of Litlington

George Shaw of Tuddington

William Coles of Houghton Regis

Richard Gregory of Evershalt

Richard Morgan of Chalgrave

John Cox of Marston

Thomas Hull of Marston

Ralph Whitmore of Laighton

Henry Prisly of Tuddington

Henry Butcher of Litlington

John Proctor of Laighton

James Leach of Evershalt

James Broughton of Cranfield

Richard Spufford of Tudington

William Staire of Laighton

Robert Spicer of Sundon
John Johnson of Ampthill
Thomas Greene of Tuddington
Henry Purratt of Evershalt
Robert Byworth of Asply Guise
George Wileman of Tudington
Edward London of Hockliffe
William Goldsmith of Tudington
Abraham Buckingham of Tilsworth
Thomas Tompkins of Totternhoe
Edward Adams of Statchden
Paul Limby of Ampthill
Ambrose Keenes of Ampthill
Barnard Holt of Sundon
Moses Allen of Ampthill
William Franklin of Chaulton
Richard Mouse of Totternhoe
Michael Messinger of Houghton Regis
Barnard Staniford of Tudington
Luke Smith of Laighton
John Myers of Totternhoe
Thomas Hawkins of Houghton Regis
Edward Dod of Totternhoe
John Impey of Houghton Regis
Henry Norris of Houghton Regis
Edward Cox of Totternhoe
Christopher Hinkly of Maulden
William Tilcock of Asply
John Wells of Litlington
William Collins of Totternhoe
Richard Day of Marston
Henry Peddr of Totternhoe
William Cooke of Tilsworth
Thomas Bennett of Wilshamsted
Vincent Mattock of Wilden
Richard Impey of Marston
Richard Woodward of Roxton
John Hanger of Souldrop
Thomas Ward of Totternhoe
Thomas Pratt of Totternhoe
Richard Mouse of Totternhoe
Edward Gurney of Egginton
John Cuttler of Chalton

William Ashburn of Pavenham
Thomas Morris of Pavenham
Richard Cooke of Billington
Thomas Money, jun. of Kempston
George Spufford of Tudington
Thomas Chase of Ampthill
John Brittain of Houghton Regis
John Leader of Kempston
Abraham Feild of Kempston
Thomas Kent of Ridgmont
Johnathan Whitechurch of Girtford
Thomas Bedcott of Ampthill
George Lettin of Asply Guise
Thomas Edwards of Clophill
John Hind of Clophill
Robert Ball of Ampthill
John Kidd of Clophill
John Kimpton of Ampthill
Thomas Denis of Kempston
Robert Clare of Pavenham
John Piggott of Flitton
William Westly of Ampthill
Richard Evans of Ampthill
John Dolton of Kempston
Thomas Norman of Harrold
Thomas Harbert of Kempston
Mathew Woodward of Westoning
William Stoakes of Oakley
John Betts of Maulden
John Bedcott of Marston, gentleman
Richard Sanders of Marston
Thomas Sherman of Sandey
William Russell of Oakley
John Hollinworth of Laighton
John Peirson of Ampthill
Jeremy Sanders of Ampthill
Edmund Lane of Ampthill
John Tenant of Sundon
Ralph Herbert of Totternhoe
John Bayly of Flittwick
Cornelius Chapman of Dunstable
Thomas Huckle of Ampthill
Nathaniel Huggins of Dunstable

Richard Ruff of Oakly

John Hookam of Renhold

William Males of Chalton

Robert Stretch of Dunstable

Roger Fur of Marston

John Whitbread of Elstowe

Nicholas Cooke, sen. of Kempston

Robert Gale of Oakly

John Thomas of Girtford

John Gardner of Kempston

Samuel Spencer of Bedford

John Evans of Ampthill

Richard Upton of Ampthill

Thomas Taylor of Milton Ernys

Nicholas Hopkins of Tudington

Henry Reeve of Tudington

Joseph Feild of Cranfield

Francis Cooke of Marston

Henry Hebbs of Dunstable

Thomas Hervey of Ampthill

Thomas Tearle of Stanbridge

John Davey of Tudington

William Allin of Tudington

Thomas Feild of Maulden

Thomas Ravensden of Clophill

William Linford of Clophill

John Radwell of Clophill

John Bull of Pavenham

Richard Gilbert of Pavenham

John Rentham of Pulloxhill

Richard Winch of Solebury, query

John Gregory, sen. of Evershalt

Robert Thomas of Bedford

Thomas Briant of Harlington

William Hornbuckle of Bedford

Michael Olney of Chalgrave

Charles Dymoke, sen. of Cranfield

Charles Dymoke, jun. of Cranfield

Thomas Turney of Cranfield

Thomas Jackson of North Crawly, query

Thomas Partridge of Cranfield

Isaac Dix of Cranfield

John Seaman of Cranfield

William Grumant of Cranfield

Thomas Grumant of Cranfield

Barnard Turney of Cranfield

Francis Bush of Marston

Stephen Barratt of Cranfield

John Girton of Cranfield

Laurence Sparkes of Cranfield

Thomas Sugar of Marston

William Olney of Cranfield

Jonathan Leabatt of Cranfield

William Chaukly of Luton

William Spencer of Luton

John Pitkin of Kempston

James Marriott of Kempston

James Yarway of Kempston

William Carter of Kempston

Thomas Cooper of Kempston

William Sharpe of Kempston

Stephen Jarvis of Kempston

Nicholas Tompson of Kempston

Charles Wright of Luton

Thomas Baker of Maulden

Thomas Giddins of Silsoe

Edmund Botsford of Batlesden

Thomas Dossiter of Silsoe

Charles Francis of Harlington

Daniel Knight of Luton

John Parker of Sandey

William Bland of Bedford

William Canfield of Luton

Samuel Cox of Luton

Samuel Slow of Luton

William Baxter of Cranfield

Thomas Walsome of Bedford

Thomas Skevington of Turvey

Adam Haughton of Hockliffe, clerk

William Cawne of Wilshamsted

John Pateman of Hardmead, clerk, query

Richard Jones of Laighton

William Maucott of Laighton

John Fauson of Dunstable

Richard Groome of Dunstable

John Laurence of Dunstable

Thomas Foxon of Dunstable

Richard Martin of Dunstable

Edward Cooper of Wilshamsted

Robert Osborne of Chalgrave

John White of Tilsworth

John Kempston of Tebworth

William Pratt of Dunstable

Daniel Groome of Totternhoe

George Catherall of Luton

Richard Smith of Bedford

John Allen of Silsoe

John Bass of Dunstable

Thomas Odell of Dunstable

John Beard of Laighton Buzzard

William Bowler of Laighton Buzzard

Thomas Lawly of Laighton Buzzard

Benedict Worrall of Laighton Buzzard

Francis Dell of Laighton Buzzard

Francis Beckett of Bedford

Thomas Battison of Bedford

Robert Crofts of Bedford

Thomas Cooper of Thurley

John Crouch of Flitton

James Grant of Dunstable

Walter Edmonds of Dunstable

William Crawly of Luton

Thomas Knight of Luton

John Tompson of Bedford

Thomas Rogers of Bedford

Francis Walker of Bedford

John Flint of Bedford

Francis Browne of Milton Briant

Henry Howes of Houghton Regis

William Messider of Eaton Bray

Francis Crawly of Milton Briant

Humphrey Crawly of Milton Briant

John Odell of Salford

William Phillips of Salford

Richard Chittam of Hulcott

John Cartwright of Litlington

Richard Scrivener of Laighton Buzzard

John Herbert, sen. of Milton Briant

Stephen Cox of Kempston

Richard Manley of Wilshamsted, gent.

William Gregory of Wavendon, query

Mathew Franklin of Litlington

George Amps of Sundon

William Purratt of Tuddington

Thomas Arnold, sen. of Ampthill, Esq.

John Richardson of Marston

George Snagg of Marston, clerk

John Digby of Harlington, clerk

John Bur of Harlington

Richard Gilpin of Hockliffe

Thomas Harway of Laighton

Hugh Smith of Sharpenhoe

William Burr of Sharpenhoe

John Stanbridge of Dunstable

William Crawly of Houghton Regis

Thomas Buckmaster of Chalgrave

Thomas Hobbs of Eaton Bray

George Robbins of Ridgmont

John Pedder of Chalgrave

William Gutteridge of Chalgrave

Richard Fowler of Dunstable

William Kirfey of Litlington

Thomas Ashton of Stevington

John Higgins of Kempston

Zachary Man of Kempston

Samuel Browne of Eaton Bray

James Cressy of Eaton Bray

Richard Jackson of Stanbridge

Alexander Leith of Bedford, clerk

Thomas Hawkins of Stanbridge

Edward Hannell of Litlington

Robert Pedder of Marston

Henry Roberts of Litlington [deleted] of
    Ligrave

John Hill of Limbry

Henry Ambross of Limbry

William Blott of Limbry

Thomas Gardner of Lygrave

John Edwards of Limbry

Thomas Sam of Sundon

John Robinson of Sundon

Francis Smith of Milton Briant

Ralph Atwell of Sundon

William Crawly of Limbry

Robert Man of Dunstable

Edward Riley of Dunstable

Mathew Franklin of Marston

John Sheffeild of Dunstable

William Far of Asply Guise

Roger Roe of Marston

William Harden of Marston

John Burt of Marston

John Guest of Marston

Edward Ashwell of Laighton

Thomas Bayly of Flitwicke

John Brigg of Dunstable

Daniel Mash of Dunstable

John Mash of Dunstable

Francis Hoight of Statchden

William Rayner of Dunstable

Henry Reynolds of Flitwick

Clement Waddam of Sundon

Francis King of Laighton

John Impey of Milton Briant

John Long of Houghton Regis

William Elliment of Dunstable

Edward Foxon of Tuddington

William Astry of Maulden, gent.

George Roe of Dunstable

John Sammon, sen. of Cranfield

William Haines of Cranfield

William Gregory of Evershalt

Stephen Whitbread of Evershalt

Thomas Houghton of Evershalt

Thomas King of Dunstable

Edward Fossey of Chaulton

John Pitkin of Houghton Regis

Richard Atkins of Eaton Bray

George Stephens of Dunstable

Henry Rogers of Eaton Bray

Simon Wood of Eaton Bray

Abraham Bigg of Litlington

John Carter of Eaton Bray

Robert Feild of Litlington

Thomas Dawburn of Litlington

William Duncomb of Ivinghoe, query

Thomas Seare of Edgborow, query

Thomas Partridge of Bedford

Joseph Bletsoe of Ravensden

Richard Cooke of Eaton Bray

Thomas Carter, sen. of Stanbridge

Nathaniel Andrews of Stanbridge

John Carpenter of Houghton Regis

Thomas Turney of Husborn Crawly

Thomas Sadler of Husborn Crawly

John Davis of Husborn Crawly

John Bassett of Marston

Thomas Helder of Litlington

Thomas Foskett of Eaton Bray

Henry Lane of Stanbridge

Edmund Greene of Husborn Crawly

Benjamin Breedon of Bedford

John Bayes of Statchden

Robert Man of Egginton

Richard Andrew of Evershalt

Edward Carter of Wrestlingworth

William Barker of Stepingley

William Emerton of Stepingley

Robert Jones of Stepingley

John Hobbs of Marston

John Brotherton of Husborn Crawly

William Roe of Harlington

William Fisher of Milbrooke

Richard Broad of Milbrooke

Peter Yarrell of Evershalt

Humphry Tomlinson of Evershalt

Henry Rogers of Evershalt

John Thredder of Evershalt

Richard Sanders of Ampthill

John Beech of Flamsted, query

George Read of Hockliffe

Joseph Urlin of Evershalt

John Brittnell of Evershalt

Thomas Geary of Evershalt

John Smith, sen. of Evershalt

James Large of Houghton Regis

Thomas Piggott of Stopsley

Stephen Parish of Cranfield

Thomas Lane of Bedford

Mathew Mason of Litlington Quaker, query

John Mathews of Caddington

William Seare of Caddington

John East of Caddington

Edward Bunion of Caddington

William Prentis of Caddington

Richard Peirson of Kingsworth, query

Thomas Daws of Cadington

Richard Odell of Maulden

John Sansome of Maulden

Thomas Hervey, sen. of Ampthill

Thomas Wheeler of Cranfield

Daniel Melmow of Houghton Regis

Henry Rench of Houghton Regis

John Laurence of Harlington

William Groome of Houghton Regis

Thomas Threder of Evershalt

John Dickeson of Harlington

John Harris of Tuddington

William Whitley of Cadington

John Manfield of Flitton

John Sutton of Tuddington

William Prudden of Lygrave

Thomas Males of Limbry

Gregory Tuffnell of Tingrey

William Peirson of Tuddington

James Smith of Caddington

William Bedford of Ampthill

William Bass, sen. of Cranfield

Samuel Buckingham of Houghton Regis

Philip Feild of Barton

William Woodward of Wrestlingworth

Edward Quincey of Harrold

Simon Urlin of Ampthill, gent.

Laurence Richardson of Clophill

John Richardson of Bedford

Henry Savage of Thurley

John Hooton of Thurley

Richard Stringer of Dunstable

John Watts of Kempston

George Reeve, jun. of Tuddington

Henry Chamberlin of Dunstable

John Potts of Chalgrave, gent.

Thomas Olney of Chalgrave

Edwin Denby of Houghton Conquest

John Cooper of Dunstable

John Pearles of Maulden

Richard Maire of Dunstable

Stephen Smith of Pulloxhill

William Lemon of Pulloxhill

William Smart of Pulloxhill

Thomas Woodward of Barton

Thomas Denis of Silsoe

Nicholas Waller of Silsoe

Thomas Philips of Pulloxhill

John Allen of Pulloxhill

William Sumers of Ravensden

William Lake of Flitton

William Carter of Pulloxhill

James Males of Pulloxhill

Thomas Baker, jun. of Cranfield

William Millard of Houghton Regis, Esq.

William Barnwell of Ampthill, clerk

Simon Newman of Ampthill

John Taylor of Cranfield

Richard Craven of Cardington

John Whitmore of Stopsly

William Collins of Stopsly

Peter Edwards of Cranfield

Thomas Edwards of Cranfield

William Mouse of Houghton Regis

John Feild of Cranfield

John Smith, jun. of Evershalt

William Spencer of Batlesden

Thomas Juggins of Marston

Browne

James Folbigg of Stoughton parva
Henry Wheeler of Wilshamsted
William Lewis of Great Barford
Joseph Darmer of Wilshamsted
Pemberton Bedford of Henlowe
Nathaniel Clayton of Risely
John Peacock of Risely
Richard Helder, Esq. of Pulloxhill
William Stephens of Sutton, clerk
John Ashcroft of Bedford, gentleman
James Ball of Turvey
Thomas Feary of Edworth
Thomas Hawkins of Southill
Michael Cole of Clophill
Edward Jennings of Shitlington
Michael Sheldon of Southill, clerk
Matthew Loe of Clifton, gentleman
Henry Ashly of Eaton Socon
Robert Wright of Wyboston
Thomas Joyce of Wyboston
Simon Safford of Eaton Socon
Richard Smith of Litle Staughton
James Browne of Over Staplo
Simon Woodward of Eaton Socon
John Smith of Eaton Socon
William Wagstaffe of Wilden
Jesper Miller of Potton
Robert Thody of Colmworth
William Wagstaffe, jun. of Wilden
Joseph Wood of Cople
Thomas Boston of Colmworth
Richard Easton of Bedford
Thomas Underwood of Henlowe
Richard Lee of Potton, gentleman
George Wheeler of Bedford
William Coomes of Bedford

John Spencer of Cardington
John Higgs of Bedford
John Astin of Shefford
George Chapman of Shefford
William Rowell of Shefford
John Taylor of Eaton Socon
John Barnett of Roxton
Richard Kefford of Roxton
William Wheeler of Bedford
Thomas Dockrill of Roxton
John Childs of Roxton
James Muns, sen. of Bedford
William Boteler of Biddenham, Esq.
Sir William Gostwick of Willington, Bart
Samuel Bedford of Henlow, Esq.
Henry Ashley, jun. of Eaton Socon, Esq.
John Hervey of Thurley
Robert Mountague of Thurley, Esq.
William Spencer of Cople, Esq.
Thomas Hillersden of Elstowe, Esq.
Mathew Denis of Kempston, Esq.
Jeremia Oakly of Luton
Richard Titford of Willington
Robert Richardson of Willington
Walter Hancock of Willington
Edward Day of Roxton
Richard Sexton of Roxton
John Moores of Felmersham
John Bass of Melchburn
William Fowler of Luton
Abraham Crawly of Luton
Daniel Gutteridge of Luton
Francis Smith of Potton
George Nodes, jun. of Southill, gent.
Richard Blunt of Kempston

Chapter Three

1698 to 1705 Elections

From 1685 to 1698: the eclipse of Ailesbury

Thomas Bruce, 2nd Earl of Ailesbury, had been the all-powerful figure in Bedford-shire politics at the time of the 1685 election. By 1695, with his power gone, he was under suspicion because of his social contacts with known Jacobites.[1] He was arrested by the Privy Council in March 1696 when a plot was discovered to assassi-nate William III. Although he vigorously protested his innocence, he was accused of high treason and sent to the Tower of London. The Duke of Bedford, although a political opponent, saw that Ailesbury was visited by a doctor and that Lady Ailesbury was able to stay in the Tower with him. Ailesbury kept his mouth shut but the conspirators in panic tried to implicate him.

As habeas corpus had been suspended, Ailesbury was likely to stay indefinitely in the Tower without trial. It was only on 12 February 1697 that he was let out on bail. Against him at the trial was the Attorney General, Thomas Trevor, later owner of the Bromham Hall estate. On his side was Sir Creswell Levinz, later owner of the Oakley estate. Public demonstrations in his favour in London made him try to slip incognito to Bedfordshire, so as not to irritate the King. Some graziers recognised him on the road and hurried back to Bedfordshire to alert his friends of his return.

Ailesbury wrote: 'I was met by great numbers on horseback on Luton Downs. The bells of that town rung out, and (the same) at all the villages on the right and left until I came home. Others met from distance to distance, and at the bridge above one mile from my house there were upwards of three thousand on horses and on foot, cutting down branches from the trees . . . and strewing rushes and flags with all acclamation and joy.'[2]

At Houghton House, his country seat, many of the gentry waited to offer him congratulations, including a number of his loyal deputy lieutenants and magistrates. The demonstration annoyed the government, so Ailesbury crept back to London and led a restricted life. He was even allowed back to Ampthill for a visit and in May 1697 he was released from his bail.

He recounts: 'Towards the latter end of this summer, going by turns to dine at my neighbours, I met at Sir William Gostwick's, at dinner, many of these gentlemen that I had never seen at my house, nor in my father's time, and they congratulated me for my happy deliverance, and in all respects were highly obliging. And towards my going away, they took Sir William Gostwick aside and made it their request to him

---

[1]   Cardigan, *The Life and Loyalties of Thomas Bruce* (London 1951), pp. 184ff.
[2]   Ibid., p. 209.

that I would permit them to come to my house; that they were heartily sorry for what had passed between them and my family for so many years.'[3]

However, his time of peace from government persecution was short-lived, as, in the same year, William made peace with France. In the Treaty of Ryswick, dated 20 September 1697, Louis XIV recognised William as King of England and both countries agreed not to help disaffected subjects of the other. In other words, Louis would not help the Jacobites, and William the Huguenots.

William and the Whigs saw this as a golden opportunity to destroy the Jacobite sympathisers once and for all. Reconciliation of disaffected Jacobites might have seemed a wise move in the long term. The government, however, considered that Louis did not see the treaty as a lasting peace and was merely intending to 'recouper pour resauter'. It was always likely that there would be war over Louis's family claims to the Spanish throne on the imminent death of their King Charles II without heirs.

A bill to become law on 16 February 1698 stated that all people who had been to France in the years 1689 to 1697 without the royal permission were guilty of high treason. Once again Ailesbury was at high risk of being rearrested and probably executed this time. On the future Duke of Marlborough's advice he decided to leave the country. On 29 January he set out from London for Brussels, where he died in exile on 16 December 1741.

Election of 1698

The County election in 1698 was contested but unfortunately no poll book survives.[4] There were four candidates: Lord Edward Russell and Sir William Gostwick (Whig) against William Duncombe and Thomas Bromsall (Tory). Sir William Gostwick stood for the first time.[5] In 1685 he had voted for Chernocke and Boteler. In 1688 he had favoured the retention of the Test Acts. He voted for Browne in 1695, and in 1697 he had hosted a meeting of Whig gentry to congratulate Ailesbury on his return to Bedfordshire from prison. Next year he emerged as Russell's fellow candidate.

In the years 1695 to 1698 there was clearly some rift between Duncombe and the Russells. The closeness of Battlesden to Woburn Abbey may have affected the relationship. Correspondingly Gostwick seems to have moved toward the Russells. Perhaps they recruited him because of his strong support within Bedford (shown in 1705) and his living in east Bedfordshire, where he could perhaps carry a Russell candidate in an area where they were weak. Whatever the causes of the two-way shift, Russell and Gostwick were fellow candidates in seven elections for the Whigs. Duncombe stood against the Russells in 1698 and his son and heir, Edward, voted against Lord Edward Russell and for a split representation in 1705.

Thomas Bromsall of Biggleswade had voted for Boteler and Chernocke in 1685. His relations were based in Blunham and Moggerhanger and were powerful in this

3   H.P.R. Finberg, *The Gostwicks of Willington*, BHRS. vol. 36 (Streatley, 1956), pp. 109–10.
4   O'Byrne, *The Representative History of Great Britain and Ireland*, pp. 10–11.
5   Finberg, *The Gostwicks of Willington*, pp. 46–146.

central Bedfordshire area. His close neighbours were the Harveys of Ickwell Bury, who were to be successful standard bearers of the Tory cause in later elections. The Duncombe/Bromsall combination therefore hoped to pick up votes in both west and central/east Bedfordshire. Against this was the strong influence of Gostwick in Bromsall's area of strength and the Russells' in Duncombe's.

In 1695 an Act had been introduced to check bribery, and therefore any treating or any other undue influence was likely to be closely scrutinised. The 1698 County election was clearly a dirty one.[6] In consequence a petition was presented to the House of Commons by the defeated candidates, William Duncombe and Thomas Bromsall, on 12 December 1698. It claimed: 'at the last election of knights of the shire for the county of Bedfordshire, Edward, Lord Russell, and Sir William Gostwick, were returned by reason that votes were procured by entertainments and other illegal means, and by reason that many freeholders, who offered to poll for the petitioners, were prevented by the sheriff and his officers; all of which proceedings were to the injury of the petitioners, who were candidates at the said election, and ought to have been returned.' The petition was rejected.

In his 1956 study of the Gostwicks Finberg gives a clue as to what was going on.[7] Mr Tidford, Sir William's bailiff, took control of the arrangements. He told local innholders in Bedford that he would recommend electors to stay at their inns but guests must pay their own bills as Lord Edward and Sir William would not do so. This was said in the presence of two witnesses, who would acknowledge Tidford's statement in the likely event of a Parliamentary enquiry. On the first day of polling, the inns were full to overflowing. At the Half Moon, fewer than half those dining there had paid their bills. The landlord, John Richards, indicated to Tidford that unless these were paid, he might vote for Bromsall. Tidford told him all would be well once Sir William was 'settled' (elected). At the Bell refunds would be made to those who presented themselves in Squire Cater's name. Cater came from Kempston and was a leading supporter of Gostwick's. The Falcon was the centre for the Gostwick campaign. Here Gostwick's servant was told to instruct the landlord to get what he could and then Sir William would pay the rest. When the landlord applied for his money, Sir William denied all knowledge of the deal but said that he would see if there were some among them, who would find him his money. At the White Horse, William Clerk, Gostwick's collar maker, paid for 16 or 17 voters out of his own money, Sir William again publicly denying liability.

In 1774, Samuel Whitbread (1720–96, the famous brewer) looked up the case in the House of Commons Library and added a note on the bottom of a portrait of Edward Gostwick. Gostwick adds this remarkable anecdote to support the charge: 'John Green who kept The Falcon, deposed that of 140 voters, whose reckoning came to 12d each, some paid 2d and some nothing, that the charge of the House that day came to £16 and J. Shaw deposed that at The Bell the charge was for one night and the next day £15.'

At Bedford Borough, Thomas Hillersden, one of the sitting members, had died in 1697. He had been replaced by William Spencer of Cople, who was the widower of Catherine, daughter of Thomas Wentworth of Toddington Manor. Spencer had

6   O'Byrne, *The Representative History of Great Britain and Ireland*, pp. 10–11.
7   Finberg, *The Gostwicks of Willington*, pp. 110–12.

voted for Duncombe in 1695. The 1698 election saw him being returned again, but William Farrer was replaced by Sir Thomas Alston of Odell, probably after a contested election. His brother, Rowland, was later a supporter of Sir Robert Walpole, so Thomas may also have been a Whig.

Nationally the election was seen as more a contest between Court and Country than between Whig and Tory. Lord Somers wrote to the Duke of Shrewsbury: 'The Elections were made on an ill foot; uneasiness at taxes, and the most dangerous division of a Court and Country party.' Robert Harley commented that 'others fancy fewer of the Country are left out than the Court'. Bedfordshire County at least voted in one country gentleman, Gostwick, at the expense of Duncombe, a Court man.[8]

The policies and ambitions of the Country party were well summarised by F. Bonet in a letter to the Elector of Brandenburg on 17 December 1700. It would have found sympathetic nods of approval from many of the Bedfordshire gentry, both Whig and Tory. Bonet wrote: 'Though the English are nearly all divided into Whigs and Tories, there are many country members in Parliament who have never joined with these parties to the extent of closely espousing either. . . . The principles that govern their reasoning are their care for 1. the religion of this country 2. the liberty of the individual 3. the trade which enhances the volume of their produce, and 4. the cultivation of their lands. No matter which is the party in power, and no matter how eloquent its appeal may be, it will never win over these members unless it can convince them that one of these four points is under attack.'[9]

1698 to 1701

William's fourth Parliament saw unprecedented divisions in the Whig government. William III made two secret Partition Treaties of the Spanish Empire with France, not telling all his ministers. Russell's cousin, Edward Lord Orford, was attacked in 1699 for his conduct of the navy.

In 1699 to offset the cost of past wars and pay for future ones, the land tax was introduced, levied initially at the high rate of 4 shillings in the pound. The window tax on houses was also imposed at the same date.[10]

The next year, 1700, saw Tories being introduced into the ministry to offset the quarrelling Whig factions. The death of Charles II meant that Louis XIV's grandson, Philip, was to be King of Spain. Louis's aggressive policy on his eastern frontier was likely to lead to a major European war.

---

8   Holmes and Speck, *The Divided Society*, p. 18.
9   Ibid., p. 19, quoting British Library Add. MSS 30,000 D, fol. 363.
10   W.R. Ward, *English Land Taxes in the Eighteenth Century* (Oxford, 1953); W.R. Ward, *The Administration of the Window and Assessed Taxes 1695–1798* (Chichester, 1963).

General Election of January/February 1701

In February 1701, the general election took place under the shadow of what was to become the War of the Spanish Succession, while England was concerned about the succession after the death of the Duke of Gloucester, the future Queen Anne's final surviving child. What was to happen to the throne on her death? Should it be entailed to James II's son or passed to their distant cousins, the Electors of Hanover? These issues dominated the election.

For the County, Russell and Gostwick were elected. Russell was acting as Lord Lieutenant of Middlesex, following his father, the Duke of Bedford's death, on 7 September 1700. He held this important post for just over a year until the twenty-first birthday of his nephew Wriothesley, the 2nd Duke of Bedford, on 1 November 1701. Wriothesley then became Lord Lieutenant of Bedfordshire, Middlesex and Cambridgeshire until his death in 1711.[11]

At the Borough, William Spencer was returned with Samuel Rolt of Milton Ernest, who replaced Sir Thomas Alston – a Tory probably replacing a Whig.

The Parliament lasted from 2 February to 24 June 1701 and was dominated by the Tories. The Act of Settlement[12] entailed the succession ultimately on the House of Hanover but added in various Country inspired clauses, such as no place-holder could sit in the House of Commons and insisting that the sovereign must be a member of the Church of England. The architects of British involvement in the partition treaties, including Orford, were impeached. The final straw for William was when the bearers of a petition from Kent in favour of his policies were imprisoned by the House of Commons.

Before the election, William had countered the seizing by the French of forts in the Spanish Netherlands by joining a Grand Alliance against them. The War of the Spanish Succession was begun, and was to provide the background for local and national politics for twelve years. Protestant antagonism to Louis was further intensified by his declaring James the Old Pretender to be the rightful King of England.

General Election of December 1701

In this election, William got what he had hoped for: a House of Commons with a small Whig majority, committed to the war and willing to provide the finance William would need. For the County seat there was no change, but at the Borough Rolt was replaced by William Farrer of Harrold. A Whig replaced a Tory. William Spencer was his fellow MP.

Just before William III's death, on 8 March 1702, Parliament passed an act ordering all place-holders to renounce the Old Pretender. This was a dig at any traditional Tories who might still support Jacobitism.

---

[11] O'Byrne, *The Representative History of Great Britain and Ireland*, pp. 50–1. GEC, *Complete Peerage*, vol. II, pp. 79–83 for Dukes of Bedford.
[12] Act of Settlement 1700, 12 & 13 Will. III, c. 2.

General Election of November 1702

The accession of the new monarch, Queen Anne, necessitated a new general election. Her accession was especially welcomed by the Tories, who saw her as a member of the rightful ruling dynasty of Britain, the Stuarts, and as a staunch supporter of the Church of England.

Her opening speech on 11 March 1702 – 'of the true concern I have for our religion, for the laws and liberties of England, for the maintaining the succession to the Crown in the Protestant line and The Government in Church and State as by law established'[13] – was meat and drink to Tory ears. Initially Anne's ministers came from both parties with Marlborough as Commander in Chief. Subsequently her reign was to be dominated by the war and the consequent high taxes.

At this election, Farrer was replaced by Henry Edward Carteret of Hawnes Park. William Spencer was returned yet again as were the two County members, Russell and Gostwick. Nationally the Tories won over 300 seats, dominating their opponents by the margin, it is estimated, of three to two.[14]

Parliament of 1702 to 1705

The two main issues facing this Parliament, which met in December 1702, were the abjuration oath and the Occasional Conformity Bill. The Tories brought in a bill to extend by one year the time that an office-holder had for swearing this oath renouncing James Stuart, the Old Pretender. The Whig majority in the House of Lords sent the bill back in a mangled state. In February 1703, the Tories forced a division on a Lords' amendment that no office-holder could be reinstated once he had refused to take the oath. The amendment was accepted by one vote, including local MPs Lord Edward Russell, Sir William Gostwick and William Spencer. Carteret's vote is not known.

Tories had long disapproved of the practice of nonconformist office-holders occasionally attending the Church of England, so as to be able to keep their offices lawfully. Attempts to tighten up on this were, of course, designed at weakening their opponents, the Whigs. In 1704, local MPs Lord Edward Russell, William Gostwick and Carteret all took the Whig line and voted against attempts to add the occasional conformity clauses to a money bill. The Tories had done this to make it harder for the Whigs to throw it out, as there was a convention that generally finance bills should be passed. Spencer does not seem to have voted. In the Lords, Wriothesley 2nd Duke of Bedford, although a Whig, voted against occasional conformity in support of the interests of the Church of England.

Of greater importance to Bedfordshire was the setting-up of Queen Anne's Bounty, initially funded by the annates or first pennies that clergy had had to subscribe to the crown since 1534. The Bounty was to be given to help support the poorer Anglican clergy, a move approved of by the Tories. The high cost of the land

---

13   Holmes and Speck, *The Divided Society*, pp. 25–6.
14   Ibid., p. 27.

tax at 4 shillings in the pound was a major source of complaint but was paid, helping to provide the financial backing for Marlborough's famous victories, the greatest of which was Blenheim on 2 August 1704.

General Election of 1705

The general election of 1705 saw contests for both the Borough and the County seats. For the first time poll books have survived for both Bedfordshire seats.[15] A significant number of people voted in both constituencies, so that patterns can be detected of voters taking a party line or voting for the individual candidates that they preferred. The Borough election took place first, on 11 May 1705. Two partnerships were opposed: Sir Philip Monoux of Wootton and William Farrer of Brayfield against William Spencer of Cople and Samuel Rolt of Milton Ernest. Farrer was the long-standing MP, who had been unseated in 1702. William Spencer was the sitting MP, and Samuel Rolt had represented the Borough in 1700. Sir Philip Monoux was the son of Russell's fellow candidate in 1685. Farrer was undoubtedly a Whig as he was the successful Whig candidate for the chairmanship of the Committee of Ways and Means in the House of Commons in November 1708. Monoux kept faith with his father's party. Rolt voted for the two Tory candidates in 1705, so was probably a Tory. Spencer's party loyalty is less clear. He had voted with the Whigs over the Lords' amendments to the abjuration oath. Perhaps he was a Tory, who saw that further struggle on the issue might be counter-productive.[16]

The election was won by the two Whigs by a substantial majority with Spencer, the sitting member, doing particularly badly. However, all was not quite as it seemed; perhaps it was not quite such a glorious vindication of the principles of the Glorious Revolution.

On 2 November 1705, a petition was made to the House of Commons by Samuel Rolt that 'by bribery and other indirect methods, Sir Philip Monoux and William Farrer, esquire procured a considerable majority of votes'. Despite referring to the Committee of Privileges, no determination was entered in the journals of the House of Commons.[17]

Nationally the election was very close. Mr Eyles wrote to the Earl of Portland on 27 July 1705 that: 'the lists of the members of the ensuing Parliament are not yet authentically printed . . . but the nearest computation [is] . . . the Whigs and Tories are equal, so that the Placemen will turn the balance'.[18] This nearly equal division, nationally, was closely followed by the County election, which had taken place on 23 May 1705. Sir Pinsent Chernocke of Hulcote headed the poll with 1408 votes. He was the son of Sir Villiers, the MP for the County in 1685. His fellow candidate, John Harvey, was not carried by Chernocke voters and trailed in 475 votes behind the lowest of the Whigs' votes. Sir William Gostwick held his seat, 37 ahead of Lord Edward Russell, the two Whigs tending to receive equal support.

[15] BLARS, Borough election GY 8/3, manuscript; County election OR 1823, printed.
[16] O'Byrne, *The Representative History of Great Britain and Ireland*, pp. 24–5.
[17] Ibid., p. 11.
[18] Holmes and Speck, *The Divided Society*, p. 29.

Outside Bedford, the two Tories Chernocke and Harvey did well in Ampthill, Barton, Biggleswade, Campton, Clophill, Gravenhurst, Luton, Maulden, Meppershall, Millbrook, Northill, Potton, Sandy, Shefford, Shillington, Silsoe, Streatley, Sundon and Wrestlingworth, all of which had supported the Tories in 1685. They did well in Caddington, but there are no figures to indicate how the electors voted there in 1685. Their vote had increased since 1685 in Dunton, Eggington, Flitton and Marston Moretaine.

Chernocke polled heavily in Aspley Guise, Cranfield, Dunstable, Eaton Bray, Flitwick, Harlington, Hockliffe, Leighton Buzzard, Toddington and Totternhoe without being able to take Harvey with him. These parishes are close to Chernocke's seat at Hulcote and felt loyalty to him.

Gostwick and Russell did well in Arlesey, Great Barford, Cardington, Carlton, Colmworth, Dean, Elstow, Eversholt, Felmersham, Goldington, Houghton Regis, Kempston, Keysoe, Langford, Ridgmont, Sharnbrook, Shelton, Stanbridge, Stevington, Stondon, Stotfold, Tilbrook, Wilden, Woburn and Wootton, all of which had supported Russell and Monoux in 1685.

Their vote increased, since 1685, in Clifton, Cople, Eaton Socon (where there was a huge swing), Haynes, Pertenhall, Roxton, Thurleigh, Turvey, Willington and Yielden. A number of these parishes were close to Gostwick's home at Willington manor, and the Whigs were clearly helped by his candidature in this area. Russell narrowed the gap in Aspley Guise and surged ahead in Husborne Crawley, close to the family home at Woburn Abbey. Gostwick in his turn surged ahead in Pavenham and Little Staughton.

However the election was decided in Bedford. Chernocke polled 68 votes (compared with his father's 43 in 1685). This, with his good showing in the market towns such as Ampthill, Leighton Buzzard and Luton, was enough to make him top the poll. Harvey's meagre 25 ensured that he was bottom. The Bedford votes decided which of the two Whigs should be elected as MP with Chernocke. Gostwick gained 97 to Russell's 59, almost exactly the difference between them at the end of the poll. Bedfordshire therefore had three Whigs and one Tory as its MPs.

Poll for the Borough of Bedford 1705

Source: manuscript poll book held at BLARS, GY 8/3. Abbreviations of candidates' names in the transcription:

M   Monoux   F   Farrer   S   Spencer   R   Rolt

The Poll for the Town of Bedford taken the 11th Day of May 1705

	Numbers upon the Poll
Sir Phillip Monoux, Bart	340
William Farrer, Esq.	385
William Spencer	151
Samuel Rolt, Esq.	225
	573 Votes in all

Christian name	Surname	Occupation	Place of abode	M	F	S	R
William	Abbis						1
Simon	Abbott			1	1		
William	Allen			1	1		
John	Alsop			1	1		
Robert	Alsop					1	1
William	Arnold			1			1
William	Arthur						1
Thomas	Arthur				1	1	
Robert	Arthur				1	1	
Richard	Ashburnham			1	1		
John	Ashcroft	Gent.		1	1		
Nicholas	Aspinall	Clerk					1
Samuel	Astwood			1	1		
John	Austin						1
Robert	Awberry			1			
Thomas	Baines	Gent.			1		1
James	Baines		Warden	1	1		
Samuel	Baker			1	1		
Hugh	Baldock			1	1		
John	Bamford			1	1		
James	Barber			1	1		
Richard	Barber			1	1		
Thomas	Basterville			1	1		
John	Basterville	Currier		1	1		
John	Basterville	Shoomaker		1	1		
Nathaniel	Bardolph			1	1	1	
Thomas	Battison jun.				1		

Christian name	Surname	Occupation	Place of abode	M	F	S	R
Thomas	Battison	Alderman			1		1
William	[illegible]			1		1	
William	[illegible]				1		
Thomas	[illegible]				1		
Nicholas	Beachampt			1	1		
Thomas	Beachmpt			1	1		
James	Beachamp				1		1
Thomas	Beckett			1	1		
William	Beckett	Alderman		1	1		
Francis	Beckett			1	1		
Robert	Beckett			1	1		
William	Becher	Esq.		1	1		
Simon	Beckett	Gent.			1		1
Thomas	Bedles			1			1
Robert	Bell	Esq.		1	1		
Robert	Berry sen.			1	1		
John	Berry				1		1
William	Berry jun.					1	1
William	Bentley			1	1		
Daniel	Bings			1			1
John	Blewitt			1	1		
Richard	Bletsoe				1	1	
William	Blanes						1
Edward	Bourne	Clerk		1	1		
John	Bolesby			1	1		
Thomas	Boswell					1	1
Robert	Bonfield				1		1
William	Bonfield						1
John	Bolton	Clerk		1	1		
John	Brace			1	1		
Francis	Brace	Gent.		1	1		
James	Brancklin					1	1
George	Brancklin			1	1		
Jonathan	Branson				1		1
James	Bray				1		1
John	Breadsall			1	1		
George	Breadsall				1	1	
William	Browne			1	1		
Jonas	Browne			1	1		
William	Browne						1
James	Browne					1	1

Christian name	Surname	Occupation	Place of abode	M	F	S	R
Edward	Ball					1	1
John	Bunyon				1	1	
Thomas	Burrowes sen.			1	1		
Thomas	Burrowes jun.					1	1
Thomas	Button			1	1		
Valentine	Calton	Clerk			1		1
John	Cayson					1	1
Thomas	Carter			1	1		
Michael	Chambers			1	1		
John	Chamberlin			1	1		
James	Chamberlin					1	1
George	Chapman						1
William	Chapman				1		1
Thomas	Chaplin	Gent.			1		1
Thomas	Chicheley			1	1		
Ebenezer	Chandler			1		1	
Sir Pinsent	Charnock	Bart			1		1
James	Christie					1	1
Thomas	Church				1		1
Henry	Clarke sen.			1			1
Richard	Clarke			1	1		
Henry	Clarke jun.			1	1		
Oliver	Clarke			1	1		
John	Clarke			1	1		
Lawrence	Clarke			1	1		
Robert	Clare					1	1
John	Clayton jun.			1	1		
John	Coe					1	1
William	Coles			1			1
John	Coleback			1	1		
William	Conquest					1	1
Richard	Confield			1	1		
John	Cooch			1	1		
Thomas	Cook					1	1
Thomas	Cook			1		1	
Luke	Cook					1	1
Robert	Cooper			1	1		
Francis	Cooper			1	1		
Robert	Cooper jun.			1	1		
William	Cooper			1	1		
Thomas	Cooper			1		1	

Christian name	Surname	Occupation	Place of abode	M	F	S	R
Thomas	Corley			1		1	
John	Covington sen.			1	1		
Simon	Covington sen.				1		1
Simon	Covington jun.						1
Robert	Courtman	Gent.		1	1		
Edward	Cox			1		1	
Henry	Crann sen.			1	1		
Henry	Crann jun.			1	1		
William	Cranfield				1		1
Robert	Crawley			1	1		
John	Crawley	Alderman				1	1
Richard	Crofts						1
John	Crofts						1
Thomas	Crockett			1			1
William	Croote					1	1
John	Crouch			1	1		
Richard	Cumberland			1	1		
William	Cupis			1	1		
Miles	Curtis			1	1		
John	Dant			1	1		
John	Daniel		Olney	1	1		
George	Darling sen.			1	1		
George	Darling jun.			1	1		
John	Darling				1		1
John	Day	Labourer		1	1		
William	Day					1	1
John	Day	Tayler					1
John	Day	Baskett maker				1	1
Thomas	Day				1		1
John	Davidson			1			1
Mathew	Dennis	Esq.		1	1		
Thomas	Dew			1	1		
Thomas	Dicks			1	1		
William	Dillingham			1	1		
William	Dimock			1	1		
Richard	Divitt					1	1
William	Dodson			1	1		
James	Dockerille sen.				1		1
Richard	Dotterille					1	
William	Dove			1	1		
Thomas	Edwards				1		1

Christian name	Surname	Occupation	Place of abode	M	F	S	R
William	Edwards	Gentleman		1	1		
William	Edwards			1			1
John	Ellison					1	1
Thomas	Ellis			1	1		
John	Elliott						1
John	Elson					1	1
Bartholomew	Enterduce			1	1		
John	Eston			1	1		
Richard	Eston			1	1		
Hatton	Eston			1	1		
David	Esling					1	1
John	Faldo				1		1
William	Faldo	Gent.			1		1
George	Fairey			1	1		
William	Farrer	Esq.		1			
John	Favell				1	1	
Benjamin	Feild					1	1
Thomas	Feild	Gent.					1
John	Fenn sen.			1	1		
Thomas	Fenn			1	1		
John	Fenn	Hatter			1		1
Samuell	Fenn			1	1		
Humphrey	Finch			1	1		
Richard	Flint		Riseley	1	1		
Richard	Flint	Barber		1	1		
Edward	Flint			1	1		
John	Flint jun.			1	1		
William	Flint						1
William	Foster	Dr of Laws			1		1
Samuel	Fox			1	1		
Samuel	Foxcraft			1	1		
Thomas	Francklin		Harrold	1	1		
William	Francklin					1	1
John	Francklin			1		1	
John	Francklin sen.			1		1	
John	Francklin jun.					1	1
Richard	Freeboarne			1	1		
William	Freelove			1			1
William	Frisbey			1	1		
Richard	Gale			1	1		
John	Gale sen.					1	1

Christian name	Surname	Occupation	Place of abode	M	F	S	R
John	Gale jun.					1	1
Simon	Gascoigne			1	1		
Stephen	Gascoigne					1	1
Thomas	Gascoigne					1	1
George	Gascoigne			1	1		
Marke	Gascoigne					1	1
William	Gascoigne					1	1
William	Gates	Clerk			1		1
Thomas	Gery				1		1
John	Gideons			1	1		
Thomas	Gifford						1
William	Gilliflower					1	1
John	Gooboy					1	1
Noah	Gooboy			1	1		
James	Goodes				1		1
John	Goode				1		1
John	Goodall	Gentleman		1	1		
William	Goodyeare			1	1		
Robert	Grey			1	1		
Edward	Grey			1	1	1	
Joseph	Grey				1		1
John	Grey			1	1		
Edward	Griffin			1		1	
Lewis	Grimsditch			1	1		
John	Groves			1	1		
William	Groves			1	1		
Robert	Groves					1	1
Thomas	Gurney		Hitchin	1	1		
Thomas	Gurney jun.			1	1		
Leonard	Gurney			1	1		
Edward	Haithwaite			1	1		
William	Haggis					1	1
Thomas	Hancock			1			1
John	Hancock			1	1		
Edward	Harrison			1	1		
William	Harrison			1	1		
John	Henceman sen.				1	1	
John	Henderson						1
David	Henderson			1	1		
Stephen	Herne			1	1		
John	Higgs sen.			1	1		

Christian name	Surname	Occupation	Place of abode	M	F	S	R
John	Higgs jun.					1	1
Roger	Hills			1	1		
William	Hills					1	1
Michael	Hills			1	1		
William	Hillersdon	Esq.		1	1		
John	Hillersdon	Esq.		1	1		
Lewis	Hillyard			1	1		
Thomas	Hind					1	1
Sebastian	Hind					1	1
John	Holloway					1	1
William	Hornebuckle				1	1	
John	Hornebuckle						1
Joseph	Holdstock					1	1
Thomas	Honylove			1	1		
William	Howard	Labourer		1			1
John	Howard			1			1
William	Howard	Butcher					1
Joseph	Howard					1	1
Simon	Howard			1	1		
Thomas	Hawes	Gent.				1	
Nicholas	Hawkins					1	1
Thomas	Hayes				1	1	
Robert	James			1	1		
Thomas	James			1	1		
John	Johnson					1	1
Shadrack	Johnson				1	1	
Richard	Jones						1
Thomas	Jones			1	1		
William	Jones			1	1		
David	Jones				1		1
Samuel	Jones			1	1		
John	Infield				1		1
John	Ireland sen.			1	1		
John	Ireland jun.			1	1		
Thomas	Ireland					1	1
Francis	Ireland					1	1
Ralph	Keale			1	1		
John	Keale				1	1	
Walter	Kemp						1
William	Kemp			1	1		
John	Kidd	Alderman		1	1		

Christian name	Surname	Occupation	Place of abode	Candidates voted for			
				M	F	S	R
Thomas	King sen.			1			1
Thomas	King jun.			1	1		
James	Kirbey					1	1
Valentine	Kirbey sen.			1			1
Valentine	Kirbey jun.			1	1		
John	Knight			1	1		
Henry	Knight			1			1
Thomas	Lane				1		1
Samuel	Lane sen.					1	1
Samuel	Lane jun.					1	1
William	Lake				1	1	
Robert	Langford			1	1		
John	Langford			1	1		
John	Lavinder				1		1
William	Leeds				1		1
Thomas	Lee			1	1		
William	Leighton				1		1
Alexander	Leith	Clerk		1	1		
William	Linford						1
William	Livitt			1	1		
Thomas	Lodgsdon					1	1
Henry	Lowen sen.			1	1		
Henry	Lowen jun.			1	1		
William	Lovelidge					1	1
Nicholas	Luke	Esq.				1	1
James	Lyon			1		1	
Joseph	Margetts	Clerk		1	1		
Thomas	Markes			1			1
Edward	Markes			1	1		
Edward	Marvill				1	1	
Robert	Martin				1		1
Nicholas	Martin			1	1		
William	Mascall			1	1		
William	Mathews				1	1	
James	Mathewes				1	1	
William	Mathers				1		1
George	Maddy	Alderman		1			1
John	Maybe			1	1		
John	Mayes			1	1		
George	Meadbury			1	1		
William	Meynard			1		1	

Christian name	Surname	Occupation	Place of abode	Candidates voted for			
				M	F	S	R
George	Meynard			1		1	
Robert	Mehew jun.			1			1
Robert	Mehew sen.			1	1		
Thomas	Merchant			1	1		
James	Mobbs			1	1		
Sir Phillip	Monoux	Bart		1			
Christopher	Munns			1	1		
John	Munns			1	1		
James	Munns			1			1
Thomas	Musgrave					1	1
Ruben	Nash			1	1		
William	Negus			1	1		
Phillip	Negus			1	1		
Gilbert	Negus			1	1		
William	Negus	Victualler			1		1
Robert	Nelson				1		1
Samuel	Nelson			1	1		
Thomas	Newman sen.					1	1
William	Newman			1	1		
William	Newman	Weaver					1
William	Nicholls			1	1		
Phillip	Nicholls	Gent.		1	1		
Thomas	Norman				1	1	
John	Newman jun.					1	1
John	Newman sen.					1	1
James	Norman					1	1
John	Oakeley			1	1		
Richard	Orlebar	Esq.		1	1		
Thomas	Palmer				1		1
John	Palmer			1	1		
Thomas	Pancrost			1	1		
Richard	Pass	Gent.		1	1		
Anthony	Peacock	Gent.		1	1		
Richard	Pearles			1	1		
John	Peck	Mayor		1	1		
Henry	Peck	Bayleiffe			1	1	
John	Peere					1	1
Thomas	Peeres					1	1
Morgan	Peere				1		1
Thomas	Peare					1	1
Thomas	Peirce			1	1		

Christian name	Surname	Occupation	Place of abode	Candidates voted for			
				M	**F**	**S**	**R**
George	Peirson			1	1		
Solomon	Pennyfather			1	1		
John	Peppiat			1	1		
Thomas	Perrin				1	1	
William	Petch jun.					1	
William	Petch sen.			1			1
John	Phillipps sen.			1	1		
John	Phillpps jun.			1	1		
William	Phillips			1	1		
Benjamin	Poole			1	1		
William	Poole			1	1		
John	Poole sen.				1		1
John	Poole jun.			1			1
Lewis	Poole						1
John	Pooley sen.			1	1		
John	Pooley jun.			1	1		
Robert	Potton			1	1		
Simon	Prant			1	1		
Josias	Prigmore			1	1		
Richard	Propp sen.					1	1
Jonathan	Pullford						1
William	Pullford					1	1
Charles	Purser				1	1	
Edward	Purton			1	1		
Evans	Quick			1	1		
Richard	Rabbitt			1	1		
John	Randall jun.			1	1		
John	Randall	Farmer		1	1		
Henry	Read			1			1
Joseph	Reeve			1	1		
William	Reynolds sen.			1	1		
William	Reynolds jun.			1			1
Thomas	Reynolds				1		1
John	Reynolds			1	1		
Thomas	Reynolds	Cordwayner		1	1		
Richard	Rickett					1	1
George	Richardson			1	1		
John	Richardson	Gaoler			1		1
Lawrence	Richardson					1	1
John	Richardson		Shefford	1	1		
Thomas	Richards			1	1		

Christian name	Surname	Occupation	Place of abode	M	F	S	R
Daniel	Rich				1		1
William	Riseley			1	1		
John	Robins			1	1		
Thomas	Robinson				1		1
John	Robinson			1	1		
John	Roberts			1	1		
Edward	Rogers						1
Thomas	Rogers					1	1
Samuel	Rogers					1	1
John	Rogers			1	1		
Tobias	Rogers				1	1	
John	Roe	Butcher		1	1		
Stephen	Rolt					1	1
Thomas	Rose			1	1		
John	Rose jun.			1			1
John	Rose sen.				1		1
Josiah	Ruffhead jun.					1	1
Josiah	Ruffhead	Shoomaker			1	1	
Anthony	Rush				1	1	
John	Rush			1	1		
Thomas	Rutter			1	1		
John	Saunders			1	1		
John	Saville					1	1
John	Scott			1	1		
William	Scott						1
Henry	Scarborough					1	1
Thomas	Seeley						1
William	Sharpe						1
Francis	Sheard					1	1
Richard	Sheriffe			1	1		
Spencer	Sheriffe			1	1		
John	Shellard					1	1
William	Shellard			1		1	
Richard	Shellard			1	1		
Edward	Simms				1		1
John	Simms			1	1		
Thomas	Simms			1	1		
Samuel	Simons			1	1		
Joseph	Simons			1			1
William	Simons			1			1
Samuel	Simpson			1	1		

Christian name	Surname	Occupation	Place of abode	Candidates voted for			
				M	F	S	R
Thomas	Simpson					1	1
John	Sindry	Gent.		1	1		
John	Skelton				1		1
William	Smyth	Glover		1	1		
Thomas	Smyth	Tayler					1
Thomas	Smyth	Gardiner		1	1		
Thomas	Smyth		Cople		1	1	
Robert	Smyth jun.				1	1	
John	Smyth alias Lyon			1	1		
James	Smyth						1
Joseph	Smyth			1	1		
Robert	Smyth sen.			1	1		
John	Smyth	Baylieffe			1		1
Arthur	Smythy			1	1		
John	Smyth		Eaton		1	1	
Robert	Smyth alias Lyon			1			1
Thomas	Smyth	Tanner			1		1
John	Spencer jun.				1	1	
Samuel	Spencer				1	1	
John	Spencer		Pavenham		1	1	
John	Spencer	Esq.			1	1	
Hockett	Spenceley			1	1		
Thomas	Spenceley			1	1		
William	Spenceley				1	1	
John	Sperrey					1	1
Thomas	Stapleton			1	1		
Thomas	Stevenson			1	1		
Thomas	Stoakes			1	1		
William	Stratton			1	1		
Richard	Stratton			1	1		
Hugh	Stringer			1			1
Lewis	Sulch			1			1
Christopher	Tall			1			1
Gilbert	Tall sen.			1	1		
Thomas	Tansley		Hawnes	1	1		
Jonathan	Tansley			1	1		
Thomas	Tansley				1		1
William	Tansley						1
Randolph	Taylor			1	1		

Christian name	Surname	Occupation	Place of abode	Candidates voted for			
				M	**F**	**S**	**R**
John	Taylor jun.			1	1		
John	Taylor sen.					1	1
George	Tayler			1	1		
John	Tayler jun.			1	1		
Samuel	Tayler			1		1	
John	Teedon						1
Robert	Thomas					1	1
John	Thompson			1	1		
Robert	Tilley sen.			1	1		
John	Tilley	Maulster		1	1		
William	Tilley			1	1		
John	Tilley	Blacksmith		1	1		
Richard	Tilley						1
William	Tilley	Weaver		1		1	
Thomas	Tilley				1	1	
Robert	Tilley			1		1	
John	Truelove				1	1	
Edward	Veale			1		1	
Thomas	Vincent			1		1	
Thomas	Ule				1		1
Thomas	Underwood	Alderman		1	1		
Robert	Upton						1
Robert	Wagstaffe			1	1		
John	Wagstaffe	Esq.		1	1		
George	Wagstaffe	Alderman		1	1		
Thomas	Wagstaffe			1	1		
Robert	Wales				1		1
John	Wales	Serjeant			1	1	
Edward	Wales			1	1		
George	W[alker?]			1	1		
Francis	Walker sen.				1		1
Francis	Walker jun.					1	1
Thomas	Waller			1	1		
John	Wallis			1	1		
Thomas	Ward				1	1	
John	Ward				1		1
Ralph	Warren			1	1		
Francis	Warren			1	1		
Richard	Warren			1	1		
John	Watts		Cauldwell		1	1	
Thomas	Watts					1	1

Christian name	Surname	Occupation	Place of abode	Candidates voted for			
				M	F	S	R
Henry	Watts					1	1
John	Watmough			1		1	
John	Wavin					1	1
William	Weale	Gent.			1		1
Benjamin	Wells			1			1
Matthew	West jun.			1	1		
Matthew	West sen.					1	1
Sander	West						1
Robert	West			1	1		
William	West					1	1
William	West		St Cuthbert's	1			1
William	West	Drummer				1	1
John	West		St Cuthbert's	1	1		
John	West				1	1	
John	West		Thurleigh				1
Stephen	West				1		1
Robert	West	Labourer				1	1
Robert	West	Drummer		1	1		
Marmaduke	West					1	1
Richard	Wheeler			1		1	
George	Wheeler			1	1		
John	Whish			1	1		
William	Whish				1		1
Henry	White	Alderman		1	1		
John	White jun.					1	1
John	White sen.					1	1
Stephen	White			1	1		
William	White					1	1
Robert	Whitmore					1	1
James	Wiffin			1	1		
William	Wiffin			1	1		
John	Wiffin			1	1		
Thomas	Wiffin			1	1		
Joseph	Wiffin			1	1		
John	Wiggins					1	1
John	Wileman					1	1
Joseph	Wileman					1	1
Richard	Wiles			1	1		
John	Willmott			1	1		
Richard	Willis						1
Thomas	Wilkes	Alderman		1	1		

Christian name	Surname	Occupation	Place of abode	Candidates voted for			
				M	F	S	R
John	Wilsheire			1	1		
William	Wilsheire			1	1		
Thomas	Witt			1	1		
Joseph	Woods					1	1
John	Woods jun.			1	1		
John	Woods sen.					1	1
William	Woodward sen.			1	1		
William	Woodward jun.			1	1		
Thomas	Wootton			1	1		
William	Wootton	labourer					1
William	Wootton			1			1
William	Yarnton			1	1		
Richard	Yarnton			1	1		

Copy of poll, County election 1705. From 1695 the printing of poll books became more common. (BLARS, Orlebar Archive)

Poll for the County of Bedfordshire 1705

Source: printed poll book held at BLARS, OR 1823. Abbreviations used for candidates' names in the transcription:

R   Russell   G   Gostwick   C   Chernock   H   Hervey

A Copy of the Poll for the Knights of the Shire for the County of Bedford. Taken at the Town of Bedford, the 23rd day of May, Anno Dom. 1705

Edward Duncombe, Esq: High-Sheriff

Candidates	Numbers upon the poll
The Right Honourable Lord Edward Russell	1239
Sir William Gostwick, Bart	1276
Sir Pinsent Chernock, Bart	1408
John Hervey, Esq.	764
	2563 Votes in all

Christian name	Surname	Occupation	Place of abode	R	G	C	H
			Ampthill				
Robert	Sybkins					1	
John	Corley					1	1
Thomas	Bedcott					1	1
Edward	Waite					1	1
William	Westley					1	1
William	Bolton					1	1
Thomas	Vincent					1	1
John	Best					1	1
John	Watson					1	1
Thomas	Hawes					1	1
Henry	Browne					1	
John	Pierson					1	1
Thomas	Evans					1	1
Thomas	Arnold	Gent.				1	1
Arthur	Boone					1	1
John	Warner					1	1
Thomas	Hervey					1	1
Richard	Hervey					1	1
Richard	Evans					1	1
Jeremiah	Saunders					1	1
John	Kempton					1	
Jeremiah	Grey					1	1
Thomas	Hervey	Jun.				1	1
John	Simpkins					1	

Christian name	Surname	Occupation	Place of abode	R	G	C	H
John	Simpkins					1	1
Jeremiah	Grey					1	
Robert	Balls					1	1
John	Johnson					1	1
Robert	Peake			1	1		
Edmund	Green			1	1		
Robert	Pedder			1		1	
Joseph	Barber			1	1		
Ambrose	Heynes					1	1
John	Minns					1	1
Simon	Newman					1	1
Thomas	Hollingsworth			1		1	
Thomas	Copperwheate					1	1
Charles	Dymock	Gent.				1	1
			Arlesey				
Robert	Lee	Gent.				1	
Edward	Jones					1	1
Richard	Border			1	1		
Thomas	Cane			1	1		
Thomas	Cane			1	1		
Myles	Sam			1	1		
Henry	Hinton			1	1		
Thomas	Copper			1	1		
John	Kirby			1	1		
Robert	Tayler			1	1		
Jacob	Lee			1	1		
Vincent	Rice	Clerk		1	1		
Thomas	Young			1	1		
Thomas	Browne	Esq.		1	1		
			Aspley				
Edward	Hall	Clerk		1		1	
James	Selbey	Esq.				1	1
Thomas	Worcester					1	1
Robert	Byworth					1	
John	Crawley			1		1	
Stephen	Chicemore					1	
Joseph	Tillcock					1	
Richard	Myles			1		1	
Simon	Clark					1	1
Richard	Gazeley					1	
John	Worlidge					1	

Christian name	Surname	Occupation	Place of abode	R	G	C	H
William	Worcliff	Esq.		1		1	
Samuel	Palmer					1	1
William	Turkey					1	
Richard	Bumstead			1		1	
Lawrence	Crawley					1	1
Thomas	Austin					1	
William	Far					1	1
Richard	Saunders					1	1
William	Russel			1	1		
William	Tilcock					1	1
George	Lettin					1	1
Joseph	Brooks			1		1	
George	Wells	Esq.				1	
Henry	Browne					1	1
William	Seabrooke					1	1
Thomas	Herman			1		1	
Thomas	How			1	1		
Ralph	Far			1	1		
Joseph	Tillcock			1		1	
William	Church			1	1		
Francis	Coleman			1	1		
Robert	Burrowes			1	1		
George	Ward			1	1		
Richard	King			1	1		
Astwick							
John	Cockaine	Gent.				1	1
John	Squire			1	1		
John	Squire	Jun.		1	1		
Thomas	Garden	Clerk		1	1		
Barford Magna							
John	Williamson					1	1
Richard	Willis	Jun.				1	1
Thomas	Pierce			1	1		
William	Ward				1	1	
Joseph	Watford					1	1
William	Bass				1		
Edward	Ward			1	1		
William	Lewis					1	1
Thomas	Palmer					1	1
John	Spring			1	1		
Thomas	Lenton			1	1		

Christian name	Surname	Occupation	Place of abode	R	G	C	H
John	Harding			1	1		
John	Harding				1		
John	Hart			1	1		
John	Harwood			1	1		
Samuel	Browning			1	1		
Edmund	Ward			1	1		
Robert	Wooten			1	1		
John	Farey			1	1		
Benjamin	Ward			1	1		
Thomas	Pierce			1	1		
Joseph	Huckle				1	1	
John	Sudbury			1	1		
William	Titford			1	1		
Walter	Hancock			1	1		
George	Favell				1		1
			Barford Parva				
William	Berry					1	1
Samuel	Berry					1	
Thomas	Tingry			1	1		
Thomas	Sayer	Clerk				1	1
			Barton				
Arthur	Humphreys	Clerk				1	1
Thomas	Woodward					1	1
Robert	Draper	Gent.				1	1
Samuel	Hopkins	Gent.				1	1
Jeremiah	Rogers					1	1
John	Hale					1	1
Richard	Crouch			1		1	
Matthew	Woodward			1	1		
			Battlesden				
Edward	Duncombe	Esq.				1	1
			Bedford				
Thomas	Gurney					1	1
John	Robins				1	1	
Henry	Newman					1	1
William	Pateton					1	1
William	Staines				1	1	
William	Foster	Dr of Law				1	1
Thomas	Bedles				1	1	
William	Mathers				1		
Robert	Grey				1	1	

Christian name	Surname	Occupation	Place of abode	Candidates voted for			
				R	G	C	H
Robert	Thomas				1	1	
Henry	Peck				1	1	
Michael	Chambers				1	1	
William	Gilliflower				1	1	
Edward	Sculthorp	Clerk				1	1
Robert	Potton				1	1	
John	Shelton					1	1
Benjamin	Wells				1	1	
Shadrack	Johnson					1	1
Thomas	Rogers					1	1
Thomas	Lane					1	
Francis	Walter	Jun.				1	
Nicholas	Aspinal	Clerk				1	1
Nathaniel	Bardolph			1	1		
William	Hornbuckle				1	1	
John	Bamford				1	1	
Edward	Markes				1	1	
John	Smith				1	1	
James	Goodes					1	
Francis	Walker	Sen.				1	
John	Crawley					1	
Thomas	Partridge					1	1
William	Bonfield					1	1
Alexander	Leith	Clerk			1	1	
Robert	Crofts				1	1	
Richard	Divitt				1	1	
George	Gascoigne				1	1	
William	Faldoe				1	1	
John	Berry				1	1	
John	Truelove					1	
William	Flint					1	1
Francis	Brace	Jun. Gent.		1	1		
Thomas	Impey					1	
Ruben	Nash					1	
Samuel	Spencer			1	1		
William	Smyth			1	1		
William	Pierce			1	1		
Thomas	Honylove			1	1		
Richard	Flint			1	1		
John	Peck	Gent.		1	1		
John	Phillipps				1	1	

Christian name	Surname	Occupation	Place of abode	Candidates voted for			
				R	G	C	H
John	Ivory					1	1
John	Austin					1	
John	Fenn	Jun.				1	1
Thomas	Battisson					1	
George	Maddy					1	1
Thomas	Battison	Jun.				1	1
Thomas	Smyth					1	1
John	Pepiatt			1	1		
Thomas	Robinson				1	1	
William	Petch				1	1	
John	Richardson					1	1
Richard	Propp	Jun.				1	1
Myles	Curtis					1	1
James	Munns					1	1
John	Elson					1	1
John	Rose					1	
Robert	Propp					1	1
Thomas	Markes					1	1
Francis	Brace	Gent.		1	1		
John	Pycroft			1	1		
William	Faldoe	Sen.			1	1	
Robert	Upton					1	1
Nicholas	Thompson			1	1		
Thomas	Reynolds			1	1		
George	Darling	Sen.		1	1		
Thomas	Cooper			1	1		
Thomas	Hays				1		
John	Spencer	Esq.		1	1		
George	Wheeler			1	1		
Richard	Wyles			1	1		
Lewis	Norman			1	1		
William	Becket	Gent.		1	1		
William	Jones				1	1	
Gilbert	Tall	Sen.		1	1		
Daniel	Rich			1	1		
Charles	West			1	1		
John	Daniel			1	1		
John	Taylor	Sen.		1	1		
Robert	Bamford	Clerk		1	1		
John	Faldoe				1	1	
Thomas	Wilkes			1	1		

Christian name	Surname	Occupation	Place of abode	R	G	C	H
Edward	Veale			1	1		
Randolph	Tayler			1	1		
George	Wagstaffe				1		
Benjamin	Coleson			1	1		
William	Reynolds			1	1		
Edward	Bourne	Clerk			1	1	
John	Tayler	Jun.		1	1		
John	Henceman			1	1		
Thomas	Banes	Gent.			1	1	
Thomas	Hawes	Gent.			1	1	
George	Richardson			1	1		
John	Higgs			1	1		
Christopher	Munns			1	1		
Phillip	Negus			1	1		
Evans	Quick			1	1		
William	Riseley			1	1		
George	Darling	Jun.		1	1		
John	West			1	1		
John	Bunyon			1	1		
Edward	Wales			1	1		
John	Wartmough			1	1		
Henry	Lowen			1	1		
Richard	Eston			1	1		
John	Oakely			1	1		
William	Iley			1	1		
William	Wilsheire			1	1		
Henry	White			1	1		
John	Smyth			1	1		
Samuel	Tayler			1	1		
Lawrence	Clarke				1		
William	Nicholls			1	1		
Gilbert	Tall	Jun.		1	1		
Thomas	Pancroft				1		
Thomas	Ashfeild	Gent.		1	1		
Robert	Bell	Esq.		1	1		
Josias	Prigmore			1	1		
Thomas	Arthur			1	1		
James	Matthewes			1	1		
William	Weale	Gent.			1	1	
William	Brown				1		
William	Arthur	Jun.			1	1	

Christian name	Surname	Occupation	Place of abode	R	G	C	H
William	Yarnton					1	
William	Coombs					1	
			Beeston				
George	Croote					1	1
John	Green					1	1
William	Walker					1	1
Thomas	Walker					1	1
Edward	Walker			1	1		
John	Christmas					1	1
			Biddenham				
Henry	Haines					1	1
Robert	Chester	Esq.				1	1
Thomas	Faldoe	Clerk				1	1
William	Woodward				1	1	
Robert	Leeder					1	
George	Battisson			1	1		
Samuel	Fenn			1	1		
			Bidwell				
William	Elmoth			1	1		
			Bigleswade				
John	Keeling	Esq.				1	1
Edward	Laundy	Gent.				1	1
William	Beaumont			1	1		
Anthony	Reynolds				1	1	
Robert	Moreton					1	1
William	Rud					1	
Sir John	Cotton	Bart				1	1
Henry	Mitchell					1	1
			Billington				
Robert	Atterbury					1	1
Edward	Simons					1	1
William	Heed					1	1
Henry	Kidgell					1	1
John	Lee			1	1		
Thomas	Cook			1			
			Bletsoe				
Joseph	Eden					1	
John	Gyles					1	
Valentine	Caulton	Clerk			1	1	
Joseph	Wilson					1	1
Henry	Savidge					1	

Christian name	Surname	Occupation	Place of abode	R	G	C	H
Thomas	Rider			1	1		
Robert	Ashburne			1	1		
John	Maxey			1	1		
Luke	Adington				1	1	
Blonham							
Richard	Burrough					1	1
William	Thickpenny					1	1
William	Harrowden					1	1
John	Bave				1	1	
John	Sollis					1	1
Matthew	Harding						1
James	Ravens			1	1		
Joseph	Ravens			1	1		
Humphrey	Thomas				1		1
John	Ravens			1	1		
Bolnehurst							
Willian	Gates	Clerk				1	1
Richard	Helder					1	1
Nathaniel	Acock			1	1		
Samuel	Gurry			1	1		
Broome							
John	Abbott			1	1		
Thomas	Collop			1			1
Bromham							
Thomas	Vincent					1	
Thomas	Skevington				1		
Caddington							
John	Ryley					1	1
John	Beale					1	1
James	Smyth					1	1
William	Seare					1	1
Thomas	Langford					1	1
John	Coppin	Esq.				1	1
William	Whitley			1	1		
Campton							
Anitmanell	Keeling	Clerk				1	1
Joseph	Francklin					1	1
William	Noddings					1	1
William	Rutney	Dr of Law				1	
William	Raddius	Sen.				1	1
John	Goodship					1	1

Christian name	Surname	Occupation	Place of abode	R	G	C	H
John	Ventris	Esq.				1	1
William	Rowell					1	1
			Cardington				
Joseph	Hodgskins	Clerk				1	1
Thomas	Daw					1	
William	Careless			1	1		
Thomas	Huckle					1	1
Jonathan	Cranfield				1	1	
Richard	Barmster					1	
Symon	Thomas				1	1	
William	Hall					1	1
William	Scarlet			1	1		
Edward	Tayler					1	
Thomas	Howard					1	1
Thomas	Smyth			1	1		
Charles	Hare	Clerk			1	1	
Oliver	Peck				1		1
Humphrey	Geare			1	1		
Edward	Bonner					1	
John	Thody			1	1		
John	Mace			1	1		
Oliver	Pymore			1	1		
Robert	Arthur			1	1		
Edward	Honyborn			1	1		
John	Wilson			1	1		
John	Howard			1	1		
Richard	Houseman			1	1		
Henry	Whitbread	Gent.		1	1		
John	Lorkins			1	1		
Thomas	Redman			1	1		
John	Austin				1	1	
William	Chaulton			1	1		
George	Huckle				1		1
George	Element			1	1		
James	Mell			1	1		
Zachary	Neale			1	1		
John	Whitbread			1	1		
Samuel	Course			1	1		
Samuel	Larkins			1	1		
Henry	Green			1	1		
George	Huckle			1	1		

Christian name	Surname	Occupation	Place of abode	Candidates voted for			
				R	G	C	H
Henry	Chapman			1	1		
William	Cockaine	Gent.		1	1		
Thomas	Bigrave			1	1		
Richard	Thody			1	1		
William	Bull			1	1		
Thomas	Cranfield			1	1		

Carleton

Christian name	Surname	Occupation	Place of abode	R	G	C	H
William	Massome					1	1
Joseph	Chaderton	Clerk				1	1
Thomas	Bithwray			1	1		
William	Steffe			1	1		
William	Wootton			1	1		
William	Welhorne					1	1
John	Marshal			1	1		
Jonas	Barret			1	1		
Uriah	Ray			1	1		
Robert	Whish			1	1		
William	Franklin			1	1		
Gideon	Rud			1	1		
Thomas	Lucas			1	1		
William	Warner			1		1	
John	Warner				1		
John	Steffe			1	1		
Thomas	Harper			1	1		
William	Smyth					1	1
Thomas	Barringham			1	1		
John	Toll			1	1		

Chalgrave

Christian name	Surname	Occupation	Place of abode	R	G	C	H
William	Barloe				1		
Richard	Morgan				1		
Thomas	Buckmaster				1		
John	Bell				1		
Michael	Olney				1		
Thomas	Olney				1		
Thomas	Willis				1		1
Henry	Osborne				1		1
John	Jeffes				1		1
John	Morgan				1		
Gabriel	Snoxall				1		
John	Wilson				1		
Thomas	Dogget				1		

Christian name	Surname	Occupation	Place of abode	R	G	C	H
John	Cadwell					1	1
John	Odell	Jun.				1	
Thomas	Bunker			1	1		
John	London					1	
Robert	Hawkins			1	1		
Benjamin	Groome			1	1		
Thomas	Ligoe			1	1		
Thomas	Olney			1	1		
William	Olney			1		1	
			Chaulton				
Thomas	Goldsmith			1			
John	Davis			1	1		
William	Mayles			1	1		
John	Wotton			1		1	
William	Davidson			1	1		
William	Knight				1	1	
Richard	Coleson			1	1		
John	Bithwray			1	1		
Roger	Nicholls			1	1		
Richard	Rud			1	1		
Henry	Browne			1	1		
			Chellington				
Thomas	Unyon					1	1
William	Fowler					1	1
John	Warner					1	
John	Killworth					1	
Richard	Hood			1			
Thomas	Green			1	1		
Thomas	Brittain			1	1		
			Clapham				
Thomas	Halsey	Esq.				1	
John	Negus			1	1		
			Clifton				
Richard	Fletcher				1	1	
Matthew	Lee					1	1
Matthew	Rogers					1	1
Matthew	Umberstone					1	1
John	Pedley					1	1
William	Lake					1	1
John	Cuckow			1	1		
John	Rowson			1	1		

Christian name	Surname	Occupation	Place of abode	R	G	C	H
Thomas	Gamble			1	1		
Thomas	Sniglehurst			1	1		
William	Baker			1	1		
Richard	Endersbey			1	1		
John	Matthewes			1	1		
John	Tingey			1	1		
Thomas	Whish			1	1		
John	Sam			1	1		
John	Fitten			1	1		
			Clipson				
Richard	Man					1	
			Clophill				
Michael	Cole			1		1	
William	Linford					1	1
Arthur	Topney			1	1		
William	Peck					1	1
Ralph	Pulley					1	1
John	Hive					1	
John	Wilshire					1	1
Edward	Peck					1	1
Thomas	Hawkins				1	1	
William	Bothage					1	1
Samuel	Austin					1	1
Thomas	Waters					1	1
Thomas	Linford					1	1
Richard	Read					1	1
Charles	Fletcher	Clerk				1	1
Nehemiah	Stratton					1	1
Richard	Waters					1	1
Samuel	Fowler	Gent.			1	1	
Richard	Poynton					1	1
Richard	Stevens			1	1		
Henry	Gascoigne					1	
			Cockaine Hatley				
William	Sterne					1	
Richard	Cockaine	Gent.			1	1	
			Colmorth				
Isaack	Clerk			1	1		
Richard	Fisher			1	1		
John	Newcombe			1	1		
William	Fortune			1	1		

Christian name	Surname	Occupation	Place of abode	Candidates voted for			
				R	G	C	H
William	King					1	1
Thomas	Judd					1	1
Henry	Underwood					1	1
William	Willis					1	1
Robert	Newman			1	1		
Richard	Stringer			1	1		
George	Boston			1	1		
Robert	Ives			1	1		
William	Wootton			1	1		
Thomas	Cooper			1	1		
John	Phillipps			1	1		
Joseph	Mayes			1	1		
John	Robinson	Clerk		1	1		
John	Tayler			1	1		
			Cople				
Samuel	Holloway				1	1	
Richard	Thorowgood				1	1	
Matthew	Watts				1	1	
Thomas	Palmer			1	1		
Stephen	Harding			1	1		
Nicholas	Luke	Esq.		1	1		
William	Griggs			1	1		
Thomas	Atwell				1	1	
Joseph	Cotton			1	1		
Edward	Marsh			1	1		
Robert	Joy			1	1		
David	Jones			1	1		
Edward	Marsh			1	1		
Thomas	Copperwheate				1		
			Cranfield				
John	Scott					1	
Robert	Crouch					1	1
Francis	Duncombe	Esq.				1	
John	Higgins					1	
William	Carter					1	1
Lawrence	Parkes					1	1
Thomas	Partridge	Gent.				1	1
Thomas	Francks	Clerk		1		1	
Richard	Partridge					1	1
George	Osborne					1	
Joseph	Field	Gent.				1	1

Christian name	Surname	Occupation	Place of abode	Candidates voted for			
				R	G	C	H
William	Pancost					1	1
Thomas	Turney					1	1
Joseph	Greenwood					1	1
Richard	Vaus					1	1
William	Olney					1	1
Timothy	Field					1	
Charles	Ellis					1	1
John	Sammon	Sen.				1	1
Francis	Tayler					1	1
Charles	Dymock	Sen. Gent.				1	1
George	Collins					1	
Thomas	Harris					1	1
William	Gruminant					1	1
Thomas	Baker			1	1		
Peter	Edwards			1	1		
John	Mead			1	1		
John	Sammon			1		1	
Henry	Wheeler			1	1		
William	Foskett			1	1		
Jonathan	Lebatt			1		1	
Thomas	Baker	Sen.		1		1	
James	Broughton			1		1	
Jacob	Odell			1		1	
William	Bass			1	1		
Isaac	Dix			1		1	
Thomas	Field			1	1		
Thomas	Coote			1		1	
William	Aspin	D.D		1	1		
Charles	Dymock	Jun. Gent.			1	1	
Thomas	Dymock				1	1	

Crawley

Christian name	Surname	Occupation	Place of abode	R	G	C	H
Thomas	Crouch					1	
Stephen	Emerton					1	1
Symon	Wynes			1			
Thomas	Graffham			1	1		
Valentine	Clarke			1		1	
John	Hopkins					1	1
Henry	Sinfield					1	
Randall	Tayler					1	1
Francis	Green			1	1		
William	Grassham			1		1	

Christian name	Surname	Occupation	Place of abode	Candidates voted for			
				R	G	C	H
Roberth	Smyth			1	1		
Richard	Folkes					1	
Edmund	Slingsbey			1		1	
Richard	Major					1	1
John	Rutley					1	1
John	Launder			1	1		
Richard	Crouch					1	
John	Abraham			1	1		
James	Harding			1	1		
William	Griffith			1			
Thomas	Turney			1	1		
Edward	Cook			1	1		
Samuel	Browne			1	1		
Robert	Costin			1	1		
William	Paine			1	1		
Richard	Coates			1		1	
William	Ralph			1	1		
Thomas	Sadler			1	1		
John	Davyes			1		1	
William	Berry			1	1		
John	Wells			1	1		
Richard	Berry			1	1		
John	Brotherton			1		1	
Anthony	Rutley			1		1	
John	Sutton			1	1		
Thomas	Gurney			1	1		
St. John	Thomson	Esq.		1		1	

Deane

Christian name	Surname	Occupation	Place of abode	R	G	C	H
John	King	Clerk				1	1
Richard	Wagstaffe			1	1		
John	Mason			1	1		
Thomas	Mayes			1	1		
Thomas	Eaton			1	1		
John	Marryot			1	1		
John	Yorke			1	1		
Peter	Boundey	Clerk		1	1		
Phillip	Sykes			1	1		
Robert	Savage			1	1		
Thomas	Fennel			1	1		
Joseph	Seare			1	1		
Gyles	Leakes			1	1		

Christian name	Surname	Occupation	Place of abode	Candidates voted for			
				R	G	C	H
John	Berry			1	1		
Samuel	Fairey			1	1		
Simon	Buckland			1	1		
John	Kiteley			1	1		
Maurice	Carey			1	1		
William	Goare			1	1		
John	Kiteley			1	1		
Theophilus	Leach			1	1		
William	Norton			1	1		
Robert	Fox			1	1		
Thomas	Fox			1	1		
Thomas	Boswel			1	1		
			Dunstable				
Nathaniel	Groome					1	
William	Green					1	
Henry	Cooper					1	
John	Fassome					1	
Richard	Groome					1	
Peter	Carville					1	
James	Grant					1	
Thomas	Groome					1	
Edward	Hallton					1	
Richard	Maine					1	
Edward	Cooke					1	
John	Bass					1	
Henry	Tyler					1	
Thomas	Vaux					1	
John	Woodfield					1	
Thomas	Moreton					1	
John	Sheffeild					1	
Nathaniel	Wympey					1	
Edward	Cecill					1	
John	Lawrence					1	
Richard	Fowler					1	
John	Pomfrett					1	
William	Ramer					1	
William	Partridge					1	
Richard	Rogers					1	
John	Groome					1	
John	Foxton					1	1
John	Crawley					1	

Christian name	Surname	Occupation	Place of abode	R	G	C	H
Daniel	Marsh	Gent.				1	1
William	Chew	Esq.				1	1
William	Ashton					1	1
John	Tombes				1	1	
John	Laud					1	1
Thomas	Toolers			1		1	
Josiah	Saunders					1	
William	Simpson					1	1
Thomas	Foxon					1	1
Edward	Hillow					1	
Francis	Fry	Gent.		1		1	
John	Gale			1	1		
Richard	Stringer			1	1		
Henry	Chamberlin			1		1	
Henry	Chamberlin			1		1	
Daniel	Fossey			1	1		
William	Fossey			1	1		
Richard	Clarke					1	
John	Briggs			1	1		
John	Stanbridge			1	1		
Thomas	King			1	1		
Richard	Moreton			1	1		
John	Cooke			1	1		
William	Chapman			1	1		
William	Element			1	1		
Henry	Heyward					1	
Thomas	Odell					1	
Walter	Edmunds			1	1		
Edward	Chester			1	1		
Thomas	Palmer			1	1		
Robert	Chapman			1	1		
Thomas	Squire			1	1		
John	Chester			1	1		
Daniel	Finch			1	1		
Daniel	Fossey			1	1		
			Dunton				
John	Keeling			1	1		
William	Searle					1	1
William	Sheppard			1	1		
John	Chapman					1	1
Edmund	Rudd					1	1

Christian name	Surname	Occupation	Place of abode	R	G	C	H
John	Flemming					1	1
Zachariah	Cleare					1	1
John	Whetstone					1	1
William	Phillips				1		1
John	Moreton					1	
Michael	Phillipps					1	1
Michael	Philipps					1	1
John	Mitchell					1	1
Thomas	Fairey					1	1
John	Banks			1	1		
Henry	Monk			1	1		
Thomas	Arnold			1	1		
John	Issard			1	1		
			Eaton Bray				
John	Sandon			1		1	
Richard	Wood					1	
William	Wells					1	
Samuel	Brown					1	
Henry	Rogers					1	
George	Cooper					1	1
John	Pudifant					1	
Symon	Woods					1	
Thomas	Prentice					1	
Thomas	Fasket					1	
Thomas	Kidgell					1	
John	Sybley			1		1	
Thomas	Watts			1			
William	Hawkins					1	
Henry	Stonestreet	Clerk				1	
Edwin	Buckmaster					1	
John	Dimock					1	
James	Ashwell					1	
Richard	Robins					1	
James	Cressey			1		1	
William	Eltwick			1	1		
William	Astwick			1	1		
Daniel	Atkins					1	
Richard	Bird					1	
John	Ashwell					1	
John	George					1	
Joseph	Read			1	1		

Christian name	Surname	Occupation	Place of abode	R	G	C	H
John	Hillyar			1	1		
Ralph	Thomkins			1	1		
George	Cressey			1	1		
Henry	Atkins			1	1		
Richard	Ashwell			1	1		
Richard	Atkins			1	1		
John	Carter			1	1		
Jeffrey	Hawkins			1		1	
Joseph	Cook			1	1		
Thomas	Bridges			1	1		
			Eaton Socan				
Robert	Pattisson			1	1		
Thomas	Berry			1	1		
Thomas	Joyce				1	1	
Carolina	Smyth				1	1	
John	Wright				1	1	
John	Lovell				1		
Francis	Atwod				1		
John	Boston			1	1		
John	Topham					1	1
John	Moakes					1	1
James	Astrey				1		
Henry	Ashley	Esq.		1	1		
Joseph	Waller			1	1		
Thomas	Atwood					1	1
Phillip	Dixey				1	1	
James	Wyon					1	1
John	Topham			1	1		
James	Hewett			1	1		
Joseph	Basset					1	1
Thomas	Foster					1	1
Richard	Stocker				1		
Maunasty	Green			1	1		
Thomas	Tyler			1	1		
Silvester	Edmunds			1	1		
John	Gery			1	1		
Thomas	Hewett			1	1		
Isaac	Cleve					1	1
Samuel	Luff					1	1
Samuel	Grey				1	1	
John	Wright					1	1

Christian name	Surname	Occupation	Place of abode	Candidates voted for			
				R	G	C	H
Robert	Grey					1	1
Richard	Smyth				1	1	
William	Wright			1	1		
William	Frank			1	1		
William	Radwell					1	1
William	Crow					1	1
James	Creare					1	1
John	Peete					1	1
George	Williams			1	1		
Francis	Studhouse			1	1		
William	Ibbot			1	1		
Richard	Boston			1	1		
Owen	Dixey			1	1		
Samuel	Eden			1	1		
John	Emery			1	1		
William	Cotton			1	1		
James	Hills			1	1		
Thomas	Stocker			1	1		
James	Cozens			1	1		
John	Stocker			1	1		
James	Sparrow			1	1		
Jonathan	Stocker			1	1		
John	Oakley			1	1		
John	Edmunds			1	1		
Henry	Negus			1	1		
Samuel	Boston			1	1		
William	Brown			1	1		
Henry	Tingry			1	1		
John	Quinton			1	1		
John	Emery			1	1		
Richard	Worland			1	1		
Matthew	Sybley			1	1		
Robert	Robinson			1	1		
John	Wright			1	1		
Thomas	West			1	1		
Richard	Harper			1	1		
John	Negus			1	1		
John	West			1	1		
Phillip	Chapman			1	1		
John	Goreham			1	1		
William	Sammon			1	1		

Christian name	Surname	Occupation	Place of abode	Candidates voted for			
				R	G	C	H
Gilbert	Sibley			1	1		
Thomas	Sibley			1	1		
Henry	Boston			1	1		
Robert	Hewett				1		
Thomas	Lindsey				1		
John	Franck			1	1		
John	Boote			1	1		
Robert	Wright			1	1		
George	Boston			1	1		
Robert	Sibley			1	1		
Edward	Flowers			1	1		
Thomas	Chesham			1	1		
Thomas	Yarrow			1	1		
Mark	Stanbridge			1	1		
Stephen	Wiles			1		1	
Matthew	Sibley			1	1		
John	Gowler			1	1		
Benjamin	Skinner			1	1		
Thomas	Bosterne			1	1		
George	Wright			1	1		
William	Messinger			1	1		
John	Ekins			1	1		
Thomas	Devereux			1	1		
Thomas	Frank			1	1		
William	Cooper			1		1	
Thomas	Sheppardson			1	1		
Thomas	Willison			1	1		
William	Hewett					1	1
John	Wright			1	1		
Thomas	Wyles			1	1		
John	Emery			1	1		
Thomas	Atkins			1	1		
James	Whisson			1	1		
Thomas	Whitchutch			1	1		
Richard	Emery			1	1		
Joseph	Bell			1	1		
Edward	Palladine			1	1		
James	Banks			1	1		
John	Goodwin			1	1		
Charles	Gery	Esq.		1	1		
Simon	Safford			1	1		

Christian name	Surname	Occupation	Place of abode	R	G	C	H
Samuel	Wright				1		
James	Hewett			1	1		
Mark	Stanbridge				1		
			Eggington				
Jeremiah	Stoakes					1	1
Edward	Robins					1	1
John	Mann					1	
Richard	Andrewes	Esq.				1	1
Richard	Andrewes	Gent.				1	1
William	Stephens					1	
John	Andrewes					1	1
			Elvestoe				
John	Osborne					1	
John	Newold			1	1		
Ralph	Warren			1	1		
John	Berry			1	1		
William	Foukes			1	1		
William	Hillersdon	Esq.		1	1		
Thomas	Cranfield			1	1		
John	Osmond			1	1		
George	Green			1	1		
Robert	Wilshire			1	1		
John	Saville			1	1		
John	Cox			1	1		
John	Crockett			1	1		
Thomas	Stoakes			1	1		
Richard	Andrewes					1	
			Eversholt				
Richard	Gregory					1	
William	Parker	Gent.		1		1	
William	Wainwright					1	
John	Simons			1	1		
James	Leach					1	
William	Whitewell			1	1		
Humphrey	Thomalin			1	1		
Thomas	Mussle					1	1
John	Riseson			1	1		
Robert	Tilcock			1	1		
Thomas	Theed			1	1		
Henry	Rogers			1			
Samuel	Butler			1	1		

Christian name	Surname	Occupation	Place of abode	R	G	C	H
			Candidates voted for				
Ambrose	Reddall	Sen.		1		1	
John	Edmonds			1	1		
William	Wenwright			1			
William	Deacon			1		1	
John	Barton			1		1	
Andrew	Lambert			1	1		
Peter	Yarwell			1	1		
John	Smyth			1	1		
Benjamin	Whitbread			1	1		
William	Houghton			1	1		
Thomas	Hawthorne			1	1		
John	Franklin			1	1		
Henry	Ford			1	1		
William	Hawkins			1	1		
Stephen	Whitbread			1	1		
Robert	Fuller			1	1		
James	Leach			1			
John	Thredder			1	1		
John	Reddall			1	1		
James	White			1	1		
John	Morris			1	1		
George	Wotton			1	1		
William	Roberts			1	1		
Edward	Gibbs			1		1	
John	Gregory			1	1		
Henry	Goldsmith			1		1	
James	Gregory			1	1		
			Everton				
William	Green			1		1	
Francis	Merryweather					1	1
George	Dennis					1	1
William	Hale					1	1
John	Jennings				1		
William	Hale					1	1
Phillip	Lewis					1	1
Walter	Carey	Esq.			1	1	
			Eyworth				
Henry	Burgis					1	1
Paul	Chissall	Clerk		1			1
John	Cullick			1	1		

Christian name	Surname	Occupation	Place of abode	R	G	C	H
				Candidates voted for			
			Farneditch				
George	Alderman					1	1
William	Lamb					1	1
Thomas	Islip					1	1
William	Barber	Clerk				1	1
			Felmersham				
Richard	Paine			1	1		
Thomas	Davey					1	1
Thomas	Clarke					1	1
John	Berry				1	1	
William	Warner					1	1
Joseph	Bletsoe				1	1	
John	Beale			1	1		
William	Leach	Gent.		1	1		
John	Berry			1	1		
John	Farey			1	1		
William	Smyth			1	1		
Thomas	Boddington					1	1
Matthew	Essex			1	1		
John	Bolton	Clerk		1	1		
Thomas	Allen			1	1		
Henry	Amps			1	1		
Thomas	Henceman			1	1		
Robert	Warner			1	1		
William	Aspin	Esq.		1	1		
William	Ashburne			1	1		
William	Warner				1	1	
Francis	Iffod				1		
William	Carter	Gent.			1		
James	Gregory			1	1		
			Fenlake				
Henry	Goss			1	1		
			Flitton				
John	Tidd					1	1
Thomas	Lawrence					1	
John	Bonner					1	1
Lawrence	Smyth					1	1
John	Piggot					1	1
Thomas	Cooper					1	1
John	Piggot	Jun.				1	1
Thomas	Beaumont					1	1

Christian name	Surname	Occupation	Place of abode	R	G	C	H
John	Crouch			1	1		
William	Clandwell	Clerk				1	1
Thomas	Freeman			1	1		
Henry	Bonner					1	1
John	Wheeler					1	1
Nicholas	Wheeler					1	
William	Beaumont					1	1
Thomas	Freeman					1	
John	Allen					1	1
Samuel	Purnel					1	1
John	Manfield					1	
Thomas	Borrowes					1	1
John	Stevens					1	1
John	Pennyfather			1	1		
William	Tilcock			1	1		
Richard	Gutteridge			1	1		
Flitwick							
Foster	Green	Jun.		1		1	
Richard	Loe			1		1	
John	Howson					1	1
John	Madam			1		1	
Matthew	Allen			1		1	
James	Franklin					1	1
Benjamin	Rhodes	Gent.				1	1
George	Sole			1		1	
Thomas	Hudson					1	
Thomas	Howsen					1	
Matthew	Freelove					1	
Edmond	Fairey					1	
John	Feasant					1	
John	Coliop					1	1
Thomas	Smyth			1	1		
John	Collop			1		1	
Henry	Webb					1	1
Foster	Green	Sen.				1	1
Samuel	Rhodes	Esq.				1	1
Michael	Arnold	Gent.		1		1	
Thomas	Lilbourne					1	
Thomas	Freelove			1	1		
Thomas	Deacon			1	1		

Christian name	Surname	Occupation	Place of abode	R	G	C	H
Matthew	Brazier			1	1		
Kendall	Mayne			1	1		
			Girtford				
John	Chaulkley					1	1
William	Halfhead					1	1
John	Parker					1	1
Henry	Thorowgood				1		1
			Goldington				
John	Sheppard				1	1	
John	Haseldine	Gent.				1	1
John	Forrest			1	1		
Richard	Watford			1	1		
Edward	Nelthorp	Esq.		1	1		
John	Haseldine	Gent.		1	1		
William	Cranfield			1	1		
Thomas	Watford			1	1		
William	Riseley			1	1		
John	Whitbread			1	1		
Thomas	Clayton			1	1		
Roberr	Clayton			1	1		
Thomas	Wiffin				1		
James	Wiffin			1	1		
William	Wiffin			1	1		
Henry	Watson				1		
			Gravenhurst				
John	Symth					1	1
Thomas	Berwick					1	1
John	Dennis					1	1
Morgan	Hind			1	1		
Peter	d' Aranda	Clerk				1	1
			Hardwick				
Nathaniel	Taylor					1	1
			Harlington				
Sir James	Astry	Kt			1		
Richard	Carter					1	1
Joseph	Ironmonger			1	1		
William	Ironmonger			1	1		
James	Farmer			1		1	
John	Burr				1		
Thomas	Chamberlaine					1	1

Christian name	Surname	Occupation	Place of abode	R	G	C	H
Robert	Morris					1	
Robert	Fells					1	
William	Woodward					1	1
Charles	Francis					1	
John	Dewburry					1	1
William	Morris			1		1	
John	Digby	Clerk				1	1
William	Bowyer	Esq.				1	1
James	Astry	Esq.			1	1	
James	Farmer					1	1
John	Odell					1	
James	Sudbury					1	
Edward	Handscomb			1	1		
John	Lawrence					1	
William	Roe			1		1	
Richard	Pedder			1	1		
John	Punter			1	1		
Harrold							
Alexander	Dawson			1	1		
Richard	Wootton					1	1
Edward	Edwards					1	1
William	Soames					1	1
Robert	Abraham					1	
John	Ableston			1	1		
John	King	Clerk				1	1
Stephen	Thomas					1	1
John	Dunckley					1	1
Thomas	Knight	Sen.				1	1
Robert	Reynolds					1	1
Samuel	More					1	1
Thomas	Knight					1	1
Richard	Narrar					1	1
Thomas	Bletsoe					1	1
John	Bletsoe				1	1	
Robert	Bletsoe					1	1
John	Matthew			1	1		
Richard	Loe			1	1		
George	Wells			1	1		
Thomas	Hartwell			1	1		
Anthony	Clarke			1	1		
Thomas	Norman			1	1		

Christian name	Surname	Occupation	Place of abode	R	G	C	H
William	Reynolds			1	1		
William	Brewer			1	1		
Thomas	Mabbot			1	1		
Oliver	Fairey			1	1		
John	Pratt			1	1		
John	Woolstone			1	1		
Robert	Grey					1	
John	Fairey				1		
Edward	Quincey			1	1		
Francis	Bletsoe			1	1		
			Harrowden				
John	Wilson					1	1
			Hawnes				
John	Cross					1	1
William	Woodcock					1	
John	Warren					1	1
Edward	Gibson	Clerk				1	1
John	Cook			1	1		
Thomas	Vincent					1	1
Samuel	Cotton					1	1
Samuel	Maxey			1	1		
William	Layton			1	1		
William	Warren			1	1		
William	Costin			1	1		
Thomas	Berry			1	1		
Richard	Wheeler			1	1		
Richard	Wheeler	Jun.		1	1		
Richard	Barrett			1	1		
John	Osmond			1	1		
John	Whitteridge			1	1		
			Heath and Reach				
Edward	Hanwell			1	1		
			Henlow				
John	Hobbs			1	1		
Edward	Sams			1	1		
Robert	Hanscombe					1	1
Francis	Clare					1	
Pemberton	Bedford					1	1
John	Bonfield					1	1
John	Sam					1	1
John	Cooper				1		

Christian name	Surname	Occupation	Place of abode	R	G	C	H
Thomas	Underwood			1		1	
John	Hobbs			1	1		
John	Hurst			1	1		
Thomas	Cooper			1	1		
Samuel	Sandon			1	1		
			Henwick				
Adam	Sturges					1	1
Richard	Turland					1	1
Robert	Caton					1	1
Thomas	Edmonds					1	
William	Seares					1	1
Paradine	Livesey	Esq.				1	1
Richard	Marsh ['shall' added in a mss hand]					1	1
Joseph	Norman					1	1
			Higham Gobian				
John	Cross					1	1
Thomas	Pauper				1	1	
John	Field					1	1
Henry	Fuller			1	1		
Richard	Goldsmith			1	1		
			Hockley				
Benjamin	Cross					1	
Edward	Poulton					1	
Withers	Cheyney					1	
Adam	Horton	Clerk				1	
John	Hebbs					1	
Henry	Smyth					1	
Thomas	Gladman					1	
Christopher	Perry					1	1
John	Fowler					1	
Nathaniel	Peirson					1	
Robert	Gilpin			1	1		
John	Smyth			1	1		
Edward	Poulton					1	1
James	Read					1	
Thomas	Kibble					1	1
Joseph	Smyth					1	
John	Hillersdon	Esq.		1	1		
John	Beech					1	

Christian name	Surname	Occupation	Place of abode	Candidates voted for			
				R	G	C	H
Robert	Dogget					1	
			Hollcott				
John	Littlejohn	Jun. Clerk				1	1
Sir Pinsent	Charnock	Bart			1		
			Hollowell				
William	Watts			1	1		
Edward	Glemster					1	1
George	Nodes	Gent.				1	1
Thomas	Heatson	Clerk		1	1		
			Houghton Conquest				
John	Elevent					1	1
Henry	Southers					1	1
Robert	Webb					1	1
Thomas	Hamerston					1	1
John	Maxey					1	1
Ezekiel	Rouse	Clerk				1	1
Joseph	Satton			1	1		
William	Webb			1	1		
Edwin	Denby	Gent.		1		1	
George	Bird			1		1	
John	Davey			1	1		
Jeramiah	Pearce			1	1		
William	Bonner			1	1		
John	Stone	Clerk		1		1	
John	Tompion			1	1		
			Houghton Regis				
John	Pitkin					1	1
Francis	Barnewell					1	
John	Wallis			1	1		
Valentine	Cressey	Clerk				1	
William	Andrew					1	
John	Partridge					1	
William	Newman			1		1	
Henry	Newman			1	1		
Andrew	Peacock					1	1
William	Gillman					1	1
Edward	Fossey					1	1
William	How					1	1
Thomas	Timberlake			1	1		
William	Valentine			1	1		

Christian name	Surname	Occupation	Place of abode	R	G	C	H
John	Brittaine			1	1		
Richard	Gosbey			1	1		
William	Rickson			1	1		
Michael	Messider			1	1		
William	Groome			1	1		
John	Groome			1	1		
John	Carpenter			1	1		
Joseph	Brittaine			1	1		
George	Goring			1	1		
William	Francis			1	1		
James	Large			1	1		
Edward	Bright			1	1		
Sir William	Millard	Kt		1	1		
John	Cooper			1	1		
Thomas	Hawkins			1	1		
John	Norris			1	1		
William	Line			1	1		
Richard	Buckingham			1	1		
Henry	Strait			1	1		
John	Hawkins			1	1		
Michael	Cook			1	1		
Thomas	Buckingham			1	1		
Thomas	Hawkins			1	1		
Henry	Tomkins			1	1		
John	Baudry			1	1		
Thomas	Fox			1	1		
Henry	How			1	1		
Robert	Hawkins			1	1		
Richard	Martin			1	1		
Edward	How					1	
William	Brittaine			1	1		
Simon	Merry			1	1		
Nehemiah	Brandith	Gent.		1		1	
Samuel	Buckingham					1	1
			Ickwell				
Humphrey	Fish	Esq.				1	1
John	Hervey	Esq.			1	1	
James	Tompion				1		1
			Kempston				
Robert	Butcher					1	
Samuel	Wheeler					1	1

Christian name	Surname	Occupation	Place of abode	Candidates voted for			
				R	G	C	H
James	Yarway					1	
John	Pierce					1	
Robert	Roebuck			1	1		
William	Sheppard			1	1		
Samuel	Burroughes			1		1	
Henry	Purton					1	1
Edward	Litchfield					1	
Joseph	Pennyfather					1	
Jacob	Clarke			1	1		
John	Barber			1	1		
Henry	Higgins					1	
William	Allen			1	1		
Nicholas	Cook			1	1		
Jeremiah	Stoakes			1	1		
Henry	Clarke			1	1		
John	Green			1	1		
Thomas	Gurney			1	1		
John	Purton			1	1		
William	Jetherell			1	1		
William	Sharpe			1	1		
John	Lyder			1	1		
Willam	Carter			1	1		
Matthew	Carew			1	1		
John	Pitkin			1	1		
Stephen	Jarvis			1	1		
Jonas	Gibson			1	1		
Thomas	Hubbins			1	1		
John	Reynolds			1	1		
Robert	Davidson			1	1		
John	Higgins			1	1		
William	Holmes			1	1		
John	Pierson			1	1		
George	Green			1	1		
John	Haines			1	1		
Robert	Hind			1	1		
John	Sheppard			1	1		
Thomas	Bolton			1	1		
Edward	Marshall			1	1		
Zachariah	Mann			1	1		
Thomas	Money	Gent.		1	1		
John	Bullmer			1	1		

Christian name	Surname	Occupation	Place of abode	R	G	C	H
Joseph	Barber			1	1		
John	Emes			1	1		
James	Sharpe			1	1		
Lewis	Haines			1	1		
Henry	Woodward			1	1		
Thomas	Cooper			1	1		
Thomas	Saunders			1	1		
Peter	Shrowsberry			1	1		
Joseph	Margetts	Clerk		1	1		
Michael	Hootton			1	1		
Thomas	Pierce			1	1		
Abraham	Field			1	1		
John	White			1	1		
Thomas	White			1	1		
Mathew	Denis	Esq.		1	1		
John	Watts			1	1		
John	Cater	Esq.		1	1		
Thomas	Johnson				1	1	
Guy	Hillersden				1	1	
Robert	Courtman	M.D.			1		

Keyshoe

Christian name	Surname	Occupation	Place of abode	R	G	C	H
John	Cunningham			1	1		
John	Folbigg			1	1		
Joseph	Northfield					1	
George	Neale			1	1		
Richard	Stapleton			1	1		
George	Tuley	Clerk			1		
John	Lettice	Clerk				1	1
Thomas	Ruffes					1	1
Thomas	Shaler			1	1		
Thomas	Hall					1	1
John	Rutter			1	1		
Gilbert	Jackson			1	1		
Henry	Haines			1	1		
William	Hills			1	1		
John	Newold			1	1		
Thomas	Halseby			1	1		
William	Henseman			1	1		
John	Money			1	1		
Thomas	Mayes			1	1		
Henry	Watford			1	1		

Christian name	Surname	Occupation	Place of abode	R	G	C	H
				Candidates voted for			
Samuel	Carver			1	1		
Thomas	Hawkins			1	1		
John	Bassett			1	1		
John	Coles			1	1		
John	Coles	Jun.		1	1		
John	Carter			1	1		
Thomas	Rutland			1	1		
Thomas	Feobigg			1	1		
			Knotting				
John	Sharpe	Clerk				1	1
			Langford				
William	Cooper			1	1		
Edward	Bentley			1	1		
William	Moreton			1	1		
John	Draper					1	1
George	Deane			1	1		
Thomas	Lunbrey					1	1
John	Lunbury					1	1
Robert	Skegg					1	1
Thomas	Osborne					1	1
John	Wright					1	1
Joseph	Cheshire			1	1		
William	Moreton			1	1		
John	Young			1	1		
Edward	Griffin			1	1		
John	Hill			1	1		
Richard	Ravens			1	1		
			Leighton				
John	Porter					1	1
John	Ashwell					1	
Samuel	Maulden					1	1
Joseph	Cooper					1	
Thomas	Butfield					1	
Thomas	Porter					1	
Jonas	Verey			1	1		
Francis	Dell					1	
William	Brockton					1	
John	Johnson					1	
Edward	Stayre					1	
William	Stayre					1	
William	Whitmore					1	

Christian name	Surname	Occupation	Place of abode	Candidates voted for			
				R	G	C	H
Henry	Honner					1	
George	Whittamore					1	
William	Spencer					1	
George	Elliot					1	
Henry	Deane					1	
John	Marsh	Gent.				1	1
Ralph	Jeffes					1	
William	Chaddock					1	
Thomas	Gurney					1	1
Matthew	Disley	Clerk				1	1
Emery	Forth			1		1	
Thomas	Lawley				1		1
Thomas	Simms					1	
Thomas	Skettlethorpe					1	
William	Freeman					1	
Benidict	Worrall					1	
Robert	Parrat					1	
Richard	Tuley					1	
Henry	Collin					1	
John	Vaux					1	1
George	Pratt					1	1
John	Deane			1	1		
Edward	Ashwell					1	1
Richard	Poynter					1	1
Thomas	Walker					1	1
Richard	Leach	Jun.		1		1	
Thomas	Tristram					1	1
William	Whipham					1	1
Michael	Lisbey					1	1
Richard	Ashwell					1	1
Thomas	Cole					1	1
Arthur	Tarsey					1	1
Peircesey	Chandler					1	1
John	Ely			1		1	
John	Marshal			1	1		
Thomas	Procter					1	
Thomas	Ward			1	1		
Thomas	Ward	Sen.		1	1		
John	Leach			1	1		
Thomas	Valentine					1	
John	Hollinsworth			1		1	

Christian name	Surname	Occupation	Place of abode	R	G	C	H
John	Bowick			1	1		
John	Capon					1	
Thomas	Stanford			1	1		
Oliver	Tayler					1	
John	Plummer					1	
Robert	Hale			1		1	
John	Edge			1	1		
Joseph	Jeffes			1	1		
Richard	Scrivener					1	
Richard	Smyth			1		1	
Edward	Ashwell			1		1	
Joshuah	Pulson	Clerk				1	
Richard	Leach	Sen.				1	
Edmond	Roberts					1	1
Richard	Norcott					1	1
John	Gregory			1	1		
Edward	Seare					1	
John	Deane					1	
Robert	Bawdry			1	1		
James	Kingham			1	1		
James	Gregory					1	1
			Ligrave				
Abraham	Lee					1	1
Thomas	Truddon			1		1	
Edward	Broughton			1		1	
John	East				1		1
			Limbury				
Henry	Albury					1	
			Litlington				
John	Wright			1	1		
John	Boteler			1		1	
William	Alder					1	
William	Crouch					1	
John	Lane					1	1
Thomas	Dickings					1	1
Sir John	Chester	Bart				1	1
Henry	Sibthorpe					1	
Nathaniel	Sam					1	1
Thomas	Catwright					1	1
John	Clarke			1	1		
Thomas	King					1	

Christian name	Surname	Occupation	Place of abode	Candidates voted for			
				R	G	C	H
Thomas	Clarke					1	
John	Knight			1		1	
William	Cartwright					1	
Thomas	Bonner			1		1	
John	Seabrooke					1	1
Richard	Clayton					1	
Francis	Bushby					1	1
Thomas	Dawborne			1		1	
John	Bedcott					1	1
Francis	Bedcott	Jun.				1	1
Thomas	Hunt			1	1		
John	Bandy			1	1		
John	Bushby			1	1		
Richard	Gibbs			1		1	
John	Wells			1	1		
William	Bushbey			1	1		
William	Richardson			1	1		
Robert	Cooke			1	1		
Robert	Field			1		1	
Thomas	Stanbridge			1	1		
William	Hanwell			1	1		
Mathias	Fraucklin			1	1		
Abraham	Bigg			1	1		
Nicholas	Crouch			1		1	
Humphrey	Hickman			1		1	
William	Hickson					1	
William	Cartwright			1			
Charles	Jones					1	1
			Luton				
Abraham	Chapman			1		1	
John	Richards					1	
William	Calkley					1	
John	Sherlock					1	1
Richard	Moores			1	1		
James	Marlin			1	1		
Anthony	Etterick	Esq.				1	1
Jonathan	Chaulkey					1	1
Robert	Jenkins	Gent.				1	1
John	Roberts					1	1
William	Stratton					1	1
Richard	Harlow					1	

Christian name	Surname	Occupation	Place of abode	Candidates voted for			
				R	G	C	H
John	Dillham			1		1	
Thomas	George					1	1
William	How					1	
John	Olney					1	
Richard	Hill					1	
John	Knight					1	
James	Crawley					1	1
Thomas	Aldbright					1	1
Nicholas	Clarke					1	1
Jeremiah	Barker					1	1
Henry	Keene					1	1
John	Tayler					1	1
Henry	Roberts					1	
William	Crawley					1	1
Roger	Weeden					1	1
Thomas	Davyes					1	1
Joseph	Burt					1	1
Isaac	Canfield					1	1
Robert	Browne					1	1
John	Hill					1	1
Thomas	Beale					1	
Edward	Cursey					1	1
Richard	Whitley					1	1
Thomas	Chapman					1	1
William	Cotton					1	1
Richard	Trustill					1	1
John	Chambers			1	1		
John	Toomes					1	1
James	Freem					1	1
Samuel	Bull	Gent.				1	1
William	Millard			1	1		
Jacob	Derby					1	1
Archibald	Napier	Esq.				1	1
Theophilus	Napier	Esq.				1	1
Thomas	Weekes					1	
Joseph	Humphreys					1	1
George	Caterell			1	1		
Thomas	Sam					1	1
Edward	Collins					1	1
John	Cane					1	1
Thomas	Goodgin					1	1

Christian name	Surname	Occupation	Place of abode	Candidates voted for			
				R	G	C	H
Thomas	Day					1	1
Samuel	Syve					1	1
John	Piggot					1	1
Thomas	North					1	1
Thomas	Cheyney					1	1
William	Hyorne			1	1		
Michal	Hooden			1		1	
William	Blunt					1	1
John	Davyes					1	1
Thomas	Swaine					1	1
Joseph	Jeakes					1	1
William	Day			1	1		
William	George					1	1
Samuel	Cock					1	1
John	Davey					1	1
Phillip	Marshall			1		1	
Joseph	Adams			1	1		
Henry	Pedder			1	1		
Michael	Moss			1	1		
Francis	Young			1	1		
John	Grover			1	1		
Henry	Harris			1	1		
Henry	Harris	Jun.		1	1		
Thomas	Smyth			1	1		
Thomas	Sedman			1	1		
Thomas	Gardiner			1	1		
Thomas	Massome	Jun.		1	1		
Richard	Bigg			1	1		
Jonas	Briggs			1	1		
Thomas	Holmes			1	1		
John	Ewer	Gent.				1	1
Thomas	Smart			1	1		
Francis	Hopkins			1	1		
Nathaniel	Massome			1	1		
Thomas	Massome	Sen.		1	1		
John	Stone			1		1	
William	Olney			1		1	
Thomas	Chaplin	Gent.				1	
John	Bigg			1	1		
John	Crawley			1	1		
Thomas	Seabrooke					1	1

Christian name	Surname	Occupation	Place of abode	R	G	C	H
Josep	Carter			1	1		
John	Silke					1	1
Thomas	Crawley			1	1		
Matthew	Lee					1	
Michael	Coleman			1	1		
Francis	How			1	1		
George	Irons			1	1		
George	Toppin			1	1		
Thomas	Wainwright			1	1		
Matthew	Gutteridge			1	1		
Thomas	Paine			1			
Gregory	Heath					1	1
William	Oakley			1	1		
Joseph	Sheppard			1	1		
John	Whittamore			1	1		
Clement	Sheppard			1	1		
Joseph	Crawley			1	1		
Francis	Stone			1	1		
Samuel	Catlin			1	1		
Thomas	Field			1	1		
Samuel	Chaulton			1	1		
Thomas	Smyth			1	1		
John	Sybley			1	1		
			Market Street				
Edward	Dryden			1	1		
			Marston				
John	Gilbert				1	1	
Thomas	Lane					1	
John	Holcott					1	
William	Rudd					1	
John	Hobbs					1	1
James	Randall					1	1
Thomas	Bennet					1	
John	Cox					1	1
William	Jackson					1	
Roger	Farr					1	1
Anthony	Wilcocks					1	1
Roger	Rowe					1	
John	Howard					1	
John	Denby					1	1
Mathew	Woolhead					1	1

Christian name	Surname	Occupation	Place of abode	R	G	C	H
William	Atwell					1	1
Charles	Champernoon	Clerk				1	1
John	Richardson					1	1
Edward	Snagg	Esq.				1	1
Francis	Bush					1	1
John	Gennoway					1	1
Joseph	Marston			1	1		
Richard	Harding					1	1
Thomas	Bird					1	1
John	Bedcott					1	1
Thomas	Sugar					1	1
Thomas	Franklin					1	1
Michael	Woodward					1	1
Thomas	Warburton	Esq.				1	1
Thomas	Woodcraft			1	1		
John	Barney					1	
Joseph	Thompson			1	1		
John	Baskerville					1	
Thomas	Pierce					1	1
John	Newman					1	1
William	Smyth			1	1		
Robert	West			1	1		
John	Odell			1	1		
John	Woodcroft			1	1		
John	Tuffnaile			1	1		
			Maulden				
Ralph	Kilbey					1	1
Richard	Smyth					1	
Nathaniel	Tompkins					1	1
Francis	Child					1	1
John	Wordall					1	
John	Betts	Jun.				1	1
John	Betts	Sen.				1	1
Nicholas	Voss					1	1
John	Ball					1	
Christopher	Hinckley					1	1
John	Godfrey	Gent.				1	1
Robert	Whittery					1	
George	Wainwright					1	1
Edward	Randall					1	1
Thomas	Field					1	1

Christian name	Surname	Occupation	Place of abode	Candidates voted for			
				R	G	C	H
William	Betts					1	1
John	Hill					1	1
Richard	Odell					1	1
Henry	Bennet					1	1
Thomas	Browne					1	1
William	Jennings					1	1
John	Charles			1	1		
John	Chaulton			1	1		
William	Crawley			1	1		
Richard	Allen	Clerk				1	1
Andrew	Baker			1	1		
Ebenezer	Chandler			1	1		
John	Webb			1	1		
			Metchborne				
Edward	Aspin	Clerk		1	1		
John	Bass			1	1		
			Meppersall				
John	Stringer					1	
Abraham	Stevens					1	1
Thomas	Palmer	Clerk				1	1
William	Fowkes					1	1
Thomas	Wiltshire					1	1
Thomas	Sams			1		1	
William	Blundell					1	1
Robert	Creamer				1	1	
			Milbrooke				
Thomas	Huckle					1	1
William	Wainwright					1	
Henry	Hardacre					1	1
Edward	Favell					1	1
Thomas	Brace					1	1
Robert	Scarborough					1	1
William	Swayne					1	1
William	Fisher					1	1
Edmond	Fowkes	Gent.		1	1		
John	Fountaine			1		1	
William	Brasier			1			
Robert	Squire			1	1		
			Milton Bryan				
John	More					1	1
Edward	Higgs					1	

Christian name	Surname	Occupation	Place of abode	Candidates voted for			
				R	G	C	H
Hugh	Crawley					1	
Francis	Smyth			1	1		
Robert	Harris					1	
Francis	Wheeler					1	
William	Fossey			1	1		
William	Tomlin					1	
William	Bolton					1	
William	Lucey			1		1	
William	Steare			1		1	
Thomas	Backhurst			1		1	
John	Impey			1	1		
Thomas	Blackhurst			1		1	
William	Turner			1			
Edward	Herbert			1	1		
William	Brotsworth			1		1	
William	Herbert			1	1		
Francis	Cooke			1		1	
Francis	Cooke	Jun.		1		1	
John	Lucy			1		1	
John	Mayes			1		1	
John	Herbert			1		1	
John	Lucey			1		1	
Samuel	Lud			1	1		
John	Robinson					1	1
			Milton Earnes				
John	Morgan					1	
John	Hawkins	Clerk				1	1
John	Buraet			1		1	
Douglass	Little					1	1
Oliver	Dicks					1	1
Samuel	Rolt	Esq.				1	1
William	Benton			1	1		
Thomas	Tayler			1	1		
			Mogerhanger				
Stephen	Thomas					1	1
Richard	Lawrence					1	1
Simon	Sperry			1	1		
John	Gregory			1	1		
			Newton				
James	Nash					1	1
William	Chapman					1	1

Christian name	Surname	Occupation	Place of abode	Candidates voted for			
				R	**G**	**C**	**H**
			Northill				
Thomas	Watts					1	1
Thomas	Wells					1	1
Thomas	Millard					1	1
Richard	Stary				1	1	
Isaac	Thomos				1	1	
Thomas	Tompion					1	1
Thomas	Carter					1	1
William	Hulkins					1	1
George	Barnadiston	Clerk				1	1
James	Calamy	Clerk				1	1
Thomas	Hams					1	1
Thomas	Croote					1	1
John	Atterton					1	1
Edward	Sparkes					1	1
John	Merrill					1	1
Thomas	Pierson					1	1
John	Carter						1
Thomas	Impey					1	1
John	Sibthorpe					1	1
William	Thompkins					1	1
John	Cooper					1	1
Edward	Rose					1	1
Peter	Clarke						1
Joseph	Baker					1	1
John	Mordant	Gent.				1	1
William	Ravens			1	1		
John	Ravens			1	1		
William	Clarke				1		
Richard	Ravens			1	1		
Thomas	Perrin			1	1		
Richard	Barr				1	1	
Simon	Kidman				1		1
John	Hitchcock				1		1
			Oakley				
Thomas	Peacock					1	1
William	Stoakes					1	
Richard	Knight					1	
Robert	Stoakes			1		1	
Thomas	Grundon					1	
Robert	Gale					1	

Christian name	Surname	Occupation	Place of abode	Candidates voted for			
				R	G	C	H
Gyles	Smyth					1	
Simon	Gale	Clerk				1	1
Phillip	Grundel			1		1	
Richard	Ruff				1		
Samuel	Negus				1		
William	Harvey			1	1		
Thomas	Smyth			1	1		
John	Sams			1	1		
John	Stoakes			1	1		
William	Paine			1	1		
Giles	Smith			1	1		
James	Fowler			1	1		
Thomas	Higgs				1		
Lawrence	Cumberland			1		1	
			Odell				
Thomas	Toller				1	1	
Robert	Lightfoot	Clerk			1	1	
Stephen	Estwick					1	1
John	Elmer			1		1	
John	Wells			1	1		
William	Ridge					1	
John	Scrivener			1	1		
			Pavenham				
Thomas	Crane					1	
Samuel	Smyth					1	
Thomas	Morris				1	1	
Abraham	Little				1	1	
John	Bull				1	1	
William	Morris				1	1	
Henry	Bull				1	1	
John	Spencer			1	1		
Richard	Lambert			1	1		
Robert	Layer			1	1		
Thomas	Bodington			1	1		
Thomas	Hipwell			1	1		
Thomas	Norris			1	1		
Robert	Toll			1	1		
Lewis	Poole				1		
			Pertenhall				
Thomas	Cheyney	Clerk				1	1
Charles	Merritt					1	1

Christian name	Surname	Occupation	Place of abode	Candidates voted for			
				R	G	C	H
Oliver	Warner			1	1		
John	Ibbot			1	1		
Charles	Gisby			1	1		
Thomas	Hunt			1	1		
Edward	Warner			1	1		
William	Watson			1	1		
James	Oliver			1	1		
Simon	Bass			1	1		
John	Lister			1	1		
Thomas	Arnold			1	1		
Thomas	Pentled			1	1		
John	Foster			1	1		

Potton

Christian name	Surname	Occupation	Place of abode	R	G	C	H
Henry	Finch					1	1
John	Phipp	Gent.				1	1
Richard	Lee	Gent.				1	
George	Pedley				1	1	
John	Smyth					1	
Thomas	Miller					1	1
John	Searle					1	1
Richard	Maulden					1	1
Thomas	Langhorne					1	1
Robert	Burgis					1	1
Thomas	Hawkins					1	1
Richard	Thorle					1	1
Alexander	Atkinson					1	1
John	Pedley					1	1
William	Cloake					1	1
Richard	Atkins					1	1
Robert	Smyth					1	1
George	Rugly					1	1
Samuel	Osmond	Sen.		1	1		
Thomas	Miller				1	1	
John	Langhorne			1			1
John	Banbury				1		1
Richard	Read			1		1	

Puddington

Christian name	Surname	Occupation	Place of abode	R	G	C	H
Jonas	Styles	Clerk				1	
Richard	Wagstaffe					1	1
John	Cook					1	1
Richard	Rands			1	1		

Christian name	Surname	Occupation	Place of abode	Candidates voted for			
				R	G	C	H
Henry	Wagstaffe			1	1		
William	Livesay	Esq.				1	1
John	Mason [added in later hand]					1	1
			Pulloxhill				
Edward	Bishopp					1	
Charles	Nichols	Gent.				1	1
James	Steward					1	1
William	Pearles					1	
Hichard	Helder	Esq.				1	1
John	Rentham			1		1	
Thomas	Hollis			1	1		
John	Allen			1		1	
Thomas	Gamble			1	1		
Stephen	Smyth			1	1		
William	Smyth			1	1		
Bernard	Halfepenny	Esq.		1	1		
George	Chaulkey			1	1		
Joseph	Ravensden				1		1
Thomas	Harrison					1	1
Thomas	Vincent			1	1		
John	Gamble			1	1		
Richard	Cook			1		1	
			Radwell				
John	Molesoe			1		1	
Spencer	Sheriffe			1	1		
James	Paine			1			
John	Battisson			1	1		
Thomas	Norman			1	1		
John	Tapp			1	1		
			Ravensden				
James	Lattimer					1	1
John	Watford			1		1	
Richard	Warren					1	1
John	Kidd				1	1	
Paul	Faldo	Clerk			1		
Thomas	Walker			1	1		
Thomas	Smith			1	1		
Bartholomew	Best			1	1		
Stephen	White			1	1		
			Renhold				
Moses	Price			1	1		

Christian name	Surname	Occupation	Place of abode	R	G	C	H
George	Favell			1	1		
William	Becher	Esq.		1	1		
Richard	Smyth			1	1		

Ridgemont

George	Richards					1	
Thomas	Hollingsworth					1	
Richard	Newman					1	
John	Clarke			1	1		
John	Dorman					1	
Thomas	Farney			1	1		
Richard	Whitebread			1	1		
William	Boteler			1	1		
William	Robbins			1	1		
Richard	Newman			1			
Thomas	Kent			1	1		
John	Emerton			1	1		
George	Robins			1	1		
Thomas	Birdsey			1	1		
William	Jarvis			1	1		
John	Newman			1	1		
Rebert	Morrisson			1	1		
Anthony	Dodsworth	Esq.		1	1		
John	Newman			1	1		
Richard	Cook			1	1		
Thomas	Cook			1	1		

Riseley

William	Allen					1	1
Oliver	Day					1	1
John	Allen				1	1	
John	Aspler					1	
John	Peacock					1	1
Simon	Gurney			1	1		
Edward	Litchfield					1	
John	Hobson					1	1
George	Snagg	Gent.				1	1
Twyfoot	Woodham					1	
Nathaniel	Clayton					1	
Henry	Cowley			1		1	
Daniel	Rowlet					1	1
Hugh	Elstoe			1	1		
Thomas	Bletsoe	Clerk				1	1

Christian name	Surname	Occupation	Place of abode	R	G	C	H
Thomas	Marlin					1	1
Thomas	Dawson			1		1	
Robert	White					1	1
John	Harding	Clerk				1	1
Robert	Thompson					1	1
William	Lord					1	1
Thomas	Marlin	Jun.				1	1
William	Woodward					1	1
Thomas	Rutham					1	1
John	Curtis					1	
John	Henson			1	1		
Thomas	Elliot			1	1		
William	Woodham			1	1		
Richard	Lee			1	1		
Edward	Woodward			1	1		
William	Field			1			
William	Chamberlaine			1	1		
Thomas	Litchfield			1	1		
Thomas	Bourne			1	1		
John	Woodward			1	1		
William	Dickings			1	1		
Richard	Sansome					1	1
John	Risely			1	1		
Daniel	Stoakes			1	1		
Joseph	Barringham			1	1		
John	Wagstaffe			1	1		
		Roxton					
John	Rowse	Clerk				1	1
Henry	Child					1	1
Thomas	Swyft					1	1
Thomas	Robinson					1	1
Robert	Child					1	1
Thomas	Child					1	1
John	Peck					1	1
Richard	Keyford					1	1
Edward	Day					1	1
John	Barnett					1	1
Edward	King					1	1
Richard	Woodward					1	1
John	Child					1	1
Richard	Sexton					1	1

Christian name	Surname	Occupation	Place of abode	R	G	C	H
				Candidates voted for			
William	Aspelland				1	1	
John	Scarborough				1	1	
Edward	Cupis			1	1		
			Salford				
John	Odell					1	1
William	Phillipps					1	1
Ambrose	Raddall					1	1
William	Lovell					1	1
John	Littlejohn	Clerk				1	
Isaac	Odell	Clerk				1	1
			Sandy				
John	Ayres			1	1		
John	Palmer						1
John	Bishop					1	1
John	Pedder					1	1
Richard	Richardson				1	1	
John	Atkins					1	1
Thomas	Longland					1	1
William	Tilcock					1	1
Thomas	Vinter			1	1		
Thomas	Field	Gent.				1	1
Robert	Fuller					1	1
Thomas	Sherman					1	1
Samuel	Sutton					1	1
William	Tilcock					1	1
John	Swynsey					1	1
David	Sutton					1	1
Thomas	Sweatman					1	1
Robert	Whitfield					1	1
William	Bush					1	1
Francis	Bishop					1	1
William	Gayne					1	1
John	Smyth					1	H
Richard	Rux					1	1
Barron	Brittaine					1	1
Robert	Browne					1	
John	Sutton					1	1
Lewis	Monoux	Esq.		1	1		
John	Allen			1	1		
John	Palmer			1	1		
John	Bishop				1		1

Christian name	Surname	Occupation	Place of abode	Candidates voted for			
				R	G	C	H
William	Collins	Clerk				1	1
William	Griggs					1	1
John	Warren					1	1
John	Elliot					1	1
Edward	Hugden					1	1
Thomas	Elmer					1	1
Robert	Kitchenner					1	1
Thomas	Fowler					1	1
Thomas	Beaumont					1	1
George	Fowler					1	1
John	Whitbread					1	1
Thomas	Myles					1	1
John	Burrowes					1	1
William	Hanscombe					1	1
James	Crouch					1	1
Daniel	Carter					1	1
Anthony	Apleby					1	1
James	Hanscombe					1	1
Joseph	Honnor					1	1
Thomas	Elmer					1	1
William	Lucas			1	1		
Thomas	Bonnist					1	
Richard	Sheppard			1	1		
John	Capon			1	1		
Ephraim	White			1	1		
John	Tristhill					1	1
Edward	Tapster			1	1		
Stephen	Constable					1	1
Thamas	Atkins					1	1
John	Darling			1	1		
John	Ireland			1	1		
William	Seeling			1	1		
			Silsoe				
John	Gwyn					1	1
Thomas	Gideons					1	1
Robert	Cooper					1	1
William	Nichols					1	1
Nicholas	Paine					1	1
Charles	Millard					1	1
William	Fowler					1	1
John	Godfrey					1	1

Christian name	Surname	Occupation	Place of abode	Candidates voted for			
				R	G	C	H
Thomas	Sellers					1	1
Thomas	Capon					1	1
Henry	Gwyn					1	1
			Souldrop				
John	Tiffin	Clerk				1	
William	Evans					1	
Robert	Paradine	Clerk				1	1
David	Bedey			1	1		
			Southill				
Thomas	Upwood					1	1
Thomas	Rogers			1	1		
Thomas	Dilley			1			1
John	Bennett			1	1		
George	Nodes	Gent.				1	1
John	Wye				1	1	
Thomas	Hawkins				1		1
Michael	Sheld					1	1
John	Wilsoe					1	1
Thomas	Alcome					1	1
George	Inskipp					1	1
William	Norris					1	1
Thomas	Linton					1	1
Phillip	Randall					1	1
William	Barber			1	1		
Thomas	Hawkins				1		1
William	Mayes			1	1		
Theophilus	Negus			1	1		
John	Anicoe			1	1		
John	Blott			1	1		
Thomas	Rogors			1	1		
Thomas	Inskipp			1	1		
John	Carrington			1	1		
Nicholas	Osborne			1	1		
Robert	Osmond			1	1		
Thomas	Ward			1	1		
			Stachden				
Edward	Adams					1	
James	Allen					1	
Richard	Allen			1	1		
James	Morgan			1	1		

Christian name	Surname	Occupation	Place of abode	R	G	C	H
			Stanbridge				
Edward	Woodward					1	1
Henry	Barnes					1	
Richard	Jackson					1	
John	Titchford					1	
John	Barnes					1	
John	Atwell					1	
Thomas	Ellingham					1	1
Henry	Morley					1	
Thomas	Stale					1	1
Gabriel	Ellingham					1	1
Edward	Cooper					1	1
Ralph	Bauldwin					1	1
Daniel	Ellingham					1	1
Thomas	Carter					1	
Thomas	Johnson					1	1
Nathaniel	Andrewes					1	1
Henry	Lane					1	1
John	Impey			1	1		
Richard	Cooper			1	1		
			Stanford				
Thomas	Fage					1	1
Edward	Jefferson					1	1
Joseph	Randall					1	1
Froncis	Hurdle					1	1
			Stepingley				
Thomas	Hudson			1		1	
Robert	Jones			1		1	
John	Whitebread			1		1	
John	Farmer			1		1	
John	Jones			1	1		
Maurice	Abbot	Esq.		1		1	
Matthew	Dutton			1	1		
Samuel	Bunyon			1		1	
William	Emerton			1	1		
			Steventon				
Thomas	Lawrence			1	1		
Joseph	Barring			1	1		
Thomas	Ashton			1	1		
Thomas	Cox			1	1		
Thomas	Phillips			1	1		

Christian name	Surname	Occupation	Place of abode	R	G	C	H
George	Odell			1	1		
			Stondon				
Samuel	Leach	Clerk				1	1
William	Hanscombe					1	1
			Stopsley				
Thomas	Basterfield					1	1
Thomas	Piggott					1	1
Thomas	Swann					1	1
Francis	Piggott					1	1
John	Ward			1	1		
			Stotfold				
Edward	Crouch					1	1
John	Hearh			1	1		
John	Hunt			1	1		
George	Wiltshire					1	1
John	Price	Clerk				1	1
John	Wright					1	1
William	Gore					1	1
Thomas	Cox					1	1
Nicholas	Reynolds					1	1
John	Ford					1	1
Michael	Freeman			1	1		
William	Bennett			1	1		
George	Baldock			1	1		
William	Kitchener				1	1	
Michael	Deare			1	1		
Edward	Freeman			1	1		
William	Green			1	1		
Henry	Squire			1	1		
Matthew	Bennett			1	1		
John	Plumber			1	1		
John	Cooper			1	1		
Thomas	Tayler			1	1		
Thomas	Bentley			1	1		
Abraham	Tayler			1	1		
John	Bennett			1	1		
William	Eaton			1	1		
John	Freeman			1	1		
Thomas	Pauper			1	1		
Edward	Burton			1	1		

Christian name	Surname	Occupation	Place of abode	Candidates voted for			
				R	G	C	H
			Stoughton parva				
John	Woodhurst					1	1
Thomas	Haines			1	1		
Thomas	Best					1	1
Daniel	Wayman					1	1
John	Smyth					1	1
Thomas	Smyth					1	1
Henry	Fell					1	
Daniel	Eaton			1	1		
Thomas	Paine			1	1		
John	Atwood			1	1		
William	King					1	1
John	Spicer					1	1
Robert	Worland					1	
Thomas	Crow			1	1		
John	Eston			1	1		
William	Disher			1	1		
			Stretley				
William	Prentice					1	1
Hugh	Smith					1	1
Walter	Ryon					1	1
James	Frayle				1	1	
John	Biscoe			1	1		
William	Burr					1	
			Studham				
John	Halsey					1	1
Edward	Sybley			1		1	
Richard	Messenger					1	1
John	Roberts					1	
John	Spencer					1	1
Edward	Walliter					1	1
Thomas	Tratt					1	1
Benjamin	Munn			1	1		
John	Wells			1	1		
George	Seare			1	1		
Richard	Baines			1	1		
Joseph	Muns			1	1		
			Sundon				
William	Randall			1		1	
John	Weston			1		1	
Thomas	Sam					1	

Christian name	Surname	Occupation	Place of abode	R	G	C	H
John	Tyrrell					1	
Robert	Watts					1	
John	Robinson					1	
William	Roe					1	
George	Amps					1	1
Henry	Hodgis	Esq.			1	1	
Edward	Lace					1	1
Thomas	Gregory			1		1	
George	Rawderham					1	1
Thomas	Cheyney	Esq.				1	1
William	Mouse				1		
Clement	Wadham			1	1		
Robert	Baker			1		1	
Daniel	Hobbs			1	1		
William	Duncombe			1	1		
George	Duncombe			1		1	
John	Ashby			1		1	
Richard	Carter				1	1	
Edmond	Buckingham			1	1		
Richard	Randall			1	1		
Abraham	Saunders			1		1	
John	King			1		1	
Richard	Lane			1	1		
Thomas	Tuffin			1	1		
John	Atker			1	1		
William	Crawley			1	1		
			Sutton				
William	Stevens	Clerk		1	1		
			Tebworth				
Robert	Barker					1	1
			Temsford				
John	Whiston				1	1	
Thomas	Chace				1	1	
William	Newam				1	1	
Thomas	Aspley			1	1		
William	Perkins					1	1
Mahalaleel	Windham					1	1
John	Joyce			1	1		
Robert	Hawkins	Clerk				1	
John	Woods				1	1	
Joseph	Rogers				1		

Christian name	Surname	Occupation	Place of abode	Candidates voted for			
				R	G	C	H
Henry	Rich			1	1		
Joseph	Barnes				1		1

Thurleigh

Christian name	Surname	Occupation	Place of abode	R	G	C	H
Edward	Browne					1	1
George	Dickson	Clerk				1	1
Simon	Woodward					1	1
John	Hervey	Esq.		1	1		
Richard	Willimott			1	1		
William	Tale			1	1		
Peter	Gregory			1	1		
John	Hootton			1	1		
John	Power	Clerk		1	1		
Richard	Parker			1	1		
Samuel	Gery			1	1		
Daniel	Arne			1	1		
Christopher	Watford			1	1		
John	Darling			1	1		
John	West			1	1		
Joseph	Mann			1	1		
William	Bradley			1	1		
Francis	Earle			1	1		
James	Line			1	1		
Francis	Clarke			1	1		
John	Gale			1	1		
Samuel	Dudley			1	1		
Robert	Barrington			1	1		
William	Earle			1	1		
Joseph	Hobb	Clerk		1	1		
James	Earle			1	1		
Ralph	Hills				1	1	
Richard	Flint			1	1		

Tilbrooke

Christian name	Surname	Occupation	Place of abode	R	G	C	H
John	Dell	Clerk				1	1
Abell	Harris					1	
John	Allen			1	1		
William	Bass			1	1		
John	Day			1	1		
John	Putrille			1	1		
Robert	Gaylott			1	1		
Simon	Sheppard			1	1		

Christian name	Surname	Occupation	Place of abode	Candidates voted for			
				R	G	C	H
			Tilsworth				
William	Cook					1	1
Thomas	Prentice					1	
			Tingrith				
William	Walker	Clerk				1	1
Richard	Lawson			1	1		
Thomas	Stevens			1		1	
William	Adams			1	1		
			Tottrenhoe				
Thomas	Ward					1	
John	Underwood					1	
Edward	Cox			1		1	
Thomas	Vyes					1	
Richard	Mouse			1	1		
Thomas	Tompkins			1	1		
Richard	Gadbury					1	
Thomas	Martin	Jun.				1	
William	Collins			1	1		
John	Mouse					1	
Robert	Ironmonger					1	1
Richard	Everard					1	1
Thomas	Webb					1	
Michael	Mouse					1	
Thomas	Henceman					1	1
William	Sheriffe					1	
Joseph	Vyes					1	
William	Sheriffe	Jun.				1	
John	Brancklin					1	1
Robert	Thompkins					1	
Bernard	Hone					1	
John	Ginger					1	
Thomas	Martin					1	
Thomas	Pedder					1	1
Henry	Corneforth					1	1
John	Myers			1	1		
Thomas	Dagnell			1	1		
William	Fowler			1	1		
John	Dod			1	1		
Thomas	Pratt			1	1		
Henry	Whitbread			1	1		
William	Hobbs			1	1		

Christian name	Surname	Occupation	Place of abode	R	G	C	H
John	Robins			1	1		
John	Herbert			1	1		
John	Robins			1	1		
Thomas	Herbert			1	1		

Tuddington

Christian name	Surname	Occupation	Place of abode	R	G	C	H
Francis	Pufford					1	
John	Sutton					1	
Edward	Gurney					1	
Hugh	Cook					1	
Thomas	Maine					1	
George	Shaw					1	
George	Wainwright					1	
Thomas	Gregory	Clerk				1	
John	Parsons					1	
George	Pufford					1	
William	Parrat					1	
Edward	Carville					1	
William	Stevens					1	
Jonathan	Norris					1	
Jonas	Porter					1	
George	Shaw					1	
Ralph	Carden					1	1
Thomas	Dearman					1	
Abraham	Light					1	1
Thomas	Potts					1	
William	Fisher					1	
John	Cook					1	
Miles	Odell	Clerk				1	
Richard	Spufford					1	
Thomas	Kidder					1	
Luke	Bush					1	
Benjamin	Scivener					1	
William	Astry					1	1
John	Harris			1		1	
Thomas	Harrisson					1	
Edward	Foxon					1	
Thomas	Gregory					1	
Samuel	Sutton					1	
Thomas	Row					1	
Bernard	Honeyford					1	
John	Strange			1	1		

Christian name	Surname	Occupation	Place of abode	Candidates voted for			
				R	G	C	H
Samuel	Page			1	1		
Thomas	Bull			1	1		
Nicholas	Hopkins			1	1		
Christopher	Bennill			1	1		
Thomas	Goldsmith			1			
Thomas	Wright			1		1	
William	Franklin			1	1		
John	Carvell					1	
George	Catterall			1		1	
George	Gurney			1	1		
Sir Henry	Johnson	Bart				1	

Turvey

Christian name	Surname	Occupation	Place of abode	R	G	C	H
John	Freeman	Gent.				1	1
Thomas	Dicks			1	1		
John	Bodington			1		1	
John	Weeden			1	1		
Robert	Trettey			1	1		
Robert	Grundon			1	1		
Thomas	Skevington			1	1		

Warden

Christian name	Surname	Occupation	Place of abode	R	G	C	H
Charles	Bovey	Esq.				1	1
William	Beane			1		1	
William	Inskipp					1	1
Samuel	Ongley	Esq.				1	1
John	Mardougle	Esq.				1	1
William	King			1	1		

Westoning

Christian name	Surname	Occupation	Place of abode	R	G	C	H
Henry	Hunt	Clerk				1	1
William	Legg					1	1
John	Green					1	1
John	Dickason					1	1
Abraham	Dix					1	1
Hesekiah	Burr					1	1
Edward	Burr					1	1
Thomas	Sheppard			1	1		
Richard	Petty			1	1		
Daniel	Dennis					1	1

Whipsnade

Christian name	Surname	Occupation	Place of abode	R	G	C	H
John	Twydall					1	1
William	Herman					1	
John	Vaux	Esq.				1	1

Christian name	Surname	Occupation	Place of abode	R	G	C	H
John	Clarke	Clerk				1	1

Wilden

Christian name	Surname	Occupation	Place of abode	R	G	C	H
Richard	Smith			1	1		
Richard	Castle					1	1
Thomas	Wagstaffe					1	
Thomas	Holden			1	1		
William	Smith					1	
John	Nodes	Clerk				1	
William	King			1	1		
William	Crow					1	1
Thomas	Favell					1	1
Robert	Fitzhugh	Gent.				1	1
William	Church			1	1		
William	Wagstaffe			1	1		
John	Church			1	1		
Richard	Wagstaffe			1	1		
John	Crow			1	1		
John	Mason			1	1		
Robert	Clarke			1	1		
Thomas	King					1	1

Willington

Christian name	Surname	Occupation	Place of abode	R	G	C	H
Richard	Willis					1	1
Thomas	Smyth			1	1		
John	Gostwick	Esq.		1	1		
Matthew	Jones	Clerk		1	1		

Wilshamstead

Christian name	Surname	Occupation	Place of abode	R	G	C	H
William	Bird					1	
William	Tompkins			1		1	
Samuel	Richardson	Clerk				1	1
John	Woodcroft			1		1	
William	Marlin					1	
Thomas	Favell					1	
William	Bedells	Gent.		1		1	
Richard	Manley	Gent.		1		1	
James	Fisher					1	
George	Lawson					1	
William	Dearmore					1	
William	Cawne			1		1	
Thomas	Smyth					1	1
William	Cawne	Clerk				1	1
John	Markes					1	1

Christian name	Surname	Occupation	Place of abode	Candidates voted for			
				R	G	C	H
John	Fisher					1	
Francis	Padman			1	1		
Edward	Higgins			1			
William	Cook			1	1		
Michael	Bonfield			1		1	
Thomas	Lawrence			1	1		
James	Cox			1	1		
William	Warner			1	1		
Sir Ralph	Ratcliffe	Kt		1	1		
Edward	Stratton			1	1		
Nathaniel	Linford					1	1
John	Cooch			1	1		
Samuel	Ballard			1	1		
Robert	White			1	1		
John	Woodcroft			1	1		
Thomas	Higgs			1	1		
John	Munday					1	1
			Wimington				
John	Serjeant					1	1
John	Purney					1	1
William	Wyles					1	1
John	Slauber					1	
Richard	Newcombe	Clerk				1	1
Stephen	Newcombe					1	1
John	Church					1	1
Robert	Richards					1	1
William	Wyles						1
Thomas	Mason			1	1		
John	Richards					1	1
John	Pearle			1	1		
John	Quenby				1	1	
			Wingfield				
Thomas	Edwards			1	1		
			Woobourne				
Thomas	Walton					1	
John	Holloway					1	
Arthur	Walbank			1	1		
Henry	Clarke					1	1
Thomas	Ireland			1	1		
Nicholas	Sanders			1	1		
Francis	Ireland			1	1		

Christian name	Surname	Occupation	Place of abode	R	G	C	H
James	Eldershaw			1			
Bartholomew	Evans			1	1		
Thomas	Gregory			1	1		
John	Blood			1	1		
Jeremy	Roebert			1	1		
Samuel	Knight			1			
Daniel	Gyles			1	1		
Thomas	Croote			1	1		
John	West			1	1		
Henry	Bullhead			1	1		
Thomas	Hill			1	1		
Simon	Tayler	Gent.		1	1		
			Wootton				
Anthony	Chapman					1	1
Thomas	Fennell			1		1	
Thomas	Hill					1	1
Matthew	Witt					1	1
John	Green			1	1		
John	Rogers			1	1		
William	Whittmore					1	1
Thomas	Mee					1	
Thomas	Juggins					1	1
Thomas	Moss			1	1		
Samuel	White			1	1		
Sir Philip	Monoux	Bart		1	1		
Henry	Cooper			1	1		
John	Fowkes			1	1		
Matthew	Hill			1	1		
John	Hill			1	1		
Joshua	Wheeler			1	1		
Praise	Noell			1	1		
John	Bird			1		1	
Dennis	Cooling	Clerk		1	1		
John	Hill			1	1		
Richard	Ousley			1	1		
Henry	Hill			1	1		
John	Shaw			1	1		
William	Boteler	Esq.		1	1		
John	Goddard			1	1		
George	Walker			1	1		

Christian name	Surname	Occupation	Place of abode	Candidates voted for			
				R	G	C	H
			Wrestlingworth				
George	Sam					1	1
Edward	Burton					1	
James	Blow					1	1
Edward	Rosling					1	
John	Usher					1	1
Nicholas	Rossin					1	1
John	Blow					1	1
James	Ekins					1	
John	Lake					1	1
George	Newall					1	
John	Rossin					1	1
William	Abbis					1	1
William	Turner					1	1
Robert	Hanley					1	1
James	Ekins				1		
William	Edey			1	1		
John	Pierson			1	1		
			Wyboston				
George	Knott					1	1
Henry	Lee					1	1
Thomas	Stocker			1	1		
			Yielden				
John	Goare			1	1		
John	Joyce			1	1		
William	Horseford			1	1		
Matthew	Wyld					1	1
		No place of freehold mentioned					
Thomas	Bauldock			1	1		
Edward	Reason			1	1		
Eastall	Warren			1	1		

Fair Warning.

MADAM, look out, your Title is arraign'd;
Sacheverell saps the Ground whereon you stand.
'Tis Revolution that upholds your Throne.
Let Non-Resistance thrive, and you're undone.
If passive Doctrines boldly are reviv'd,
Your Crown's precarious, and your Reign short-liv'd.
Such Notions with Impunity profest,
Will make the Pow'r of Parliaments a Jest.
Their Acts of Settlement are Ropes of Sand,
And Hannover may rule his native Land.
When Pulpits found no Limitations good,
No Right, but in Proximity of Blood,
Who sees not the Pretender's understood?
Impatient for their darling Chevalier,
You're in their Mercy for another Year:
Tho' Loyalty and Church are their Pretence,
Inherent Birth-right is their secret Sense,
And Restoration is the Consequence.

Enter'd in the Hall-Book of the Company of Stationers, pursuant to Act of
Parliament.

London, Printed for, and Sold by John Baker, at the Black Boy in Pater-
Noster-Row. 1710.   Price One Penny.

Fair Warning 1710. A piece of Whig propaganda connecting the Tory's support for the clergyman Sacheverell with passive resistance and Jacobitism. (BLARS, Orlebar Archive)

Chapter Four

1708–1715 Elections

General Elections of 1708, 1710 and 1713

Election of 1708

The next election under the Triennial Acts was due in 1708. It was held soon after a failed attempt by a French/Jacobite force to invade Scotland. The situation was ideal to produce what Lord Sunderland called 'the most Whig Parliament [there] has been since the Revolution'.[1] Sir John Cope reckoned on 22 June that the Whigs would have 299 and the Tories 214 seats. For the County, Lord Edward Russell and Sir William Gostwick, two Whigs, were elected probably unopposed. For the Borough, two Whigs, William Farrer and William Hillersden, were elected, again probably unopposed.

Election of 1710

By the election of October 1710, there had been a complete turnaround in politics. Electors had become weary of war and the consequent high taxes. The Sacheverell trial gave a platform for the High Church Tories. The Tories, led by Harley, won a majority of 150. The meltdown did not affect Bedfordshire, as Russell and Gostwick were again returned, and again probably unopposed. In the Borough, Farrer was re-elected, with John Cater of Kempston, another Whig, as a fellow MP. He had to be re-elected on his becoming Chairman of Ways and Means in the new Parliament. He does not seem to have been opposed on either occasion.

Election of 1713

Russell fell dangerously ill soon after the election and, within a fortnight of the poll, the efficient Whigs were canvassing for his successor. He recovered and did not die until 1714.[2]

In 1713, the Whigs would have done even worse nationally if the Tories had not been riven with quarrels, principally between Harley and Henry St John, later Lord Bolingbroke. The victory nationally in 1710 had put new heart into the Tories. They put up two candidates for the County, Sir Pinsent Chernocke of Hulcote (son of an earlier MP) and John Harvey of Ickwell Bury. Russell and Gostwick retired from the scene – Russell from illness and Gostwick from poverty.

---

[1] Holmes and Speck, *The Divided Society*, pp. 27–30.
[2] G. Holmes, *British Politics in the Age of Anne* (London, 1987), p. 318. He quotes from British Library, Add. Mss 29599, fol. 121.

The two new Whig candidates were John Cater of Kempston Bury and William Hillersden of Elstow. Hillersden had been a member for Bedford up to 1710, and Cater was standing for both seats. Although the election was very close, no poll book has survived. The votes were given as follows: Harvey (1264) and Chernocke (1261) narrowly defeated the Whigs Cater (1254) and Hillersden (1241). Chernocke only won by 7 votes, and 23 votes separated all four candidates.

For the Borough seats, there was a three-cornered fight between Farrer and Cater and Samuel Rolt. Surprisingly, Farrer was the unlucky candidate. Possibly Cater living closer to the town gave a marginal advantage over Farrer. Rolt seems to have profited from a similar swing to the Tories, which elected Chernocke and Harvey for the County. Farrer protested to the House of Commons 'that Mr Rolt was not qualified according to Act of Parliament, and that the petitioner had the majority'. As no determination was recorded in the Journal of the Committee of Privileges, Rolt remained as MP. His sin was probably a failure to swear the oath of allegiance that was required. Nationally, in the county seats, the Whigs had a majority of 15.[3]

General Election of 1715

The next scheduled election would have been in 1716, but on 1 August 1714 Queen Anne died and George I came to the throne. This meant that the election would have to come earlier. As Anne's end drew near, the danger of a pro-Jacobite invasion in favour of James II's son, James the Old Pretender, became ever greater. In fact the Protestant succession, as laid out in the Act of Settlement of 1701, worked perfectly. As soon as Anne died the country was in the hands of seven regents, including Henry Grey of Wrest Park, created Duke of Kent on 28 April 1710. They held the country for George, Elector of Hanover, until he could make the journey to his new kingdom.

George I's initial speech to the House of Commons went down well in Bedford, where the Borough sent a letter congratulating him on his accession. They added: 'Your Majesties most gracious speech to both Houses of [Parliament] give us the highest satisfaction of Your Majesties good and just Intentions of supporting the National Church with the Protestant Dissenters, whose Consciences are truly scrupulous.'[4]

George was crowned in October in 'pudding time'.[5] The general election took place in the following February. The Tories were badly split between the supporters of the 'King over the water' (James, the Old Pretender) and the 'Hanoverian Tories', who supported George I. The Whigs were in the ascendancy, with George giving them all the most important ministries. The Whigs would therefore seem to be set for a massive victory. Yet Romney Sedgwick has shown that in county seats the Tories were still ahead of the Whigs, although the gap had narrowed significantly as compared with 1713.[6] It was in the boroughs with an electorate of fewer than 500 that the swing to the Whigs was most pronounced.

---

3   O'Byrne, *The Representative History of Great Britain and Ireland*, p. 11.
4   BLARS, BOR B. B13/6.
5   From the song *The Vicar of Bray*.
6   See Colley, *In defiance of oligarchy*, pp. 120–1.

For the County seat the candidates were the same as 1713 and, despite the Hanoverian succession and the Tory splits, the election was again very tight. The money involved in an election and how it was spent is captured by an account of the Tory candidates' expenses for this election. It shows that there was a great deal of treating of electors, giving food and drink on the day of the elections to voters who had often come considerable distances to Bedford. There was also less justifiable treating in parishes outside Bedford, such as Carlton, probably forming part of a liquid canvas. The payments to the messengers show how local support was being galvanised in specific areas. The candidates thought fit to support the appeal for funds for the first organ in St Paul's Bedford. This would help keep Alexander Leith, the vicar, and his Anglican congregation true to the Tories, as the political arm of the Church of England.

Direct bribery, however, is difficult to detect. As the later petition showed, the main question mark over the election related to unqualified voters, rather than over-treating or bribery.

Chernocke and Harvey's Joint Account[7]

Paid on the Joynt Account of Sir Pynsent Chernock and Mr John Harvey Esquire for the County Eleccon 1714

Paid St Neotts Drummer that came with Alderman Carter	£0	7s	6d
Gave a man at Hulcott	£0	1s	0d
Over paid in the Cast bread	£0	4s	6d
Paid Mr Crafts towards his Journeys	£1	0s	0d
Paid Haggis for goeing to Great Barford	£0	1s	0d
Paid Haggis for goeing to Ickwell and Hullcott	£0	3s	0d
Paid a Messenger to Ampthill	£0	1s	6d
Paid a Messenger to Wilstead and Ampthill	£0	1s	6d
Paid Mr Crofts in part to Croxton, Woodford and other places	£0	5s	0d
Paid a Messenger from Eaton	£0	1s	6d
Paid Richard Crofts for his man	£0	5s	0d
Paid a messenger to Lord St John	£0	2s	6d
Paid Crofts more in part of his Journeys	£0	3s	0d
Paid Richard Prox for his Chear and Vote	£0	10s	0d
Paid the Chearman and Messengers to stand in all the Roads the Eleccon day and Court Keeper	£8	15s	0d
Paid the Ringers of the five parishes	£2	0s	6d
Paid the four Drummers and their horses	£1	4s	0d
Paid the Fidlers	£0	10s	0d
Paid Mr Pallmer of Shefford for the Tenders that he sent	£1	10s	0d
Mr Harvey paid all this	£17	6s	6d
Paid Mr Leith the Joynt Subscription to the Organ	£10	0s	0d
Paid James Allen's bill at the Boy and Oar in full	£27	6s	4d
Paid Mr Pedly bill of Potton	£2	14s	0d
Paid in part William Wootton's bill at Bell	£80	0s	0d

7   BLARS, WG 2653.

Paid John Skelton at Ragged Staff in part	£12	0s	0d
Paid the remainder of the Maidenhead bill in full	£32	0s	0d
Paid Francis Hoyl's bill of Stachden	£0	13s	8d
Paid Edward Rogers bill at Raven in full	£22	18s	0d
Paid Mr Walker's bill at Cross Keys in full	£22	3s	0d
Paid John Franklyn' bill at Black Swan in full	£29	14s	0d
Paid the remainder of Mr Beadle's bill in full	£03	0s	0d
Paid Mr Jemmatt's bill of Great Barford	£02	8s	0d
Paid Mr Spell at the Bear his bill in full	£1	7s	6d
Paid James Bray at the Wrestlers in part	£15	0s	0d
Paid John Tayler at Starr the remainder of his bill in full	£3	10s	0d
Paid Timothy Bunker in part at the White Hart	£7	4s	0d

£172 6s, 6d Sir Pynsent paid
£100 0s 0d Mr Harvey paid   Total £272   6s   6d

Paid Mr Tayler's bill of Ampthill	£07	13s	11d
Paid Mr Tuckey's bill of Tillsworth	£11	17s	10d
Paid Mr Partridge's bill of Eggington	£10	11s	2d
Paid Dr Crawly's bill of Dunstable	£02	2s	0d
Paid Mr Thomas Warburton bill	£0	15s	0d
Paid John Lawly of Laighton	£1	16s	2d
Paid the letter founder of Oxford	£0	10s	0d

This paid by Sir Pynsent	£35	6s	1d
Still to clear whole acount	£170	0s	0d

Paid on the separate Account of John Harvey Esquire

Paid Carriage of the Poll to London	£0	1s	0d
Paid horse hire to Holcott	£0	2s	0d
Paid a messenger to Keysoe and Risely	£0	2s	6d
Ditto to Stachden, Turvey and Harrold	£0	2s	6d
Ditto to Eaton Socon	£0	2s	0d
Ditto to Ampthill	£0	1s	6d
Ditto to Shefford etc	£0	2s	0d
Paid Post boy for Carriage of Letters	£0	0s	6d
Paid Messenger to Ampthill, Hulcot, Risely, Keysoe etc	£0	6s	0d
Ditto to Cople, Potton, Creakers, Duloe, Shefford etc	£0	10s	6d
Paid Mr Croft's bill	£0	12s	6d
Paid Jo Grey's bill and Charges in serving Speakers warrant	£1	1s	6d
Paid William Massom's bill of Carlton	£1	1s	6d
Paid William Woodward's bill of Risely	£3	6s	0d
Paid John Dewberry's bill	£0	7s	6d
Paid John Estwick's bill	£1	5s	0d
Paid Mr Pedly's bill	£1	13s	6d
Paid Jo Grey's bill	£3	17s	0d
Paid Francis Hoyl's bill	£0	13s	0d
Paid Thomas Barber's bill	£2	17s	6d
Paid Mr Wright's bill	£1	9s	5d
Paid Mr Topham's bill	£1	10s	0d
Paid horse hire for Mr Crofts to Ampthill, Barton etc	£0	3s	6d
Paid the tender at Bell, the Eleccon day	£0	5s	0d
Paid Mr Crofts more in part	£0	2s	6d
Paid Mr Crofts the remainder of his bill	£0	14s	6d

Paid Mr Thompson in part for takeing the Poll	£0	15s	0d
Paid the Constables of Bedford for keeping the Courts	£1	1s	6d
Paid Mr Willis bill of Wilden	£0	12s	6d
Paid the Drummer of Potton	£0	5s	0d
Paid Mr Jespar Briddell for takeinge the Poll	£3	4s	6d
Paid Spell at the Beare in part of his bill	£10	0s	0d
Paid Tayler at Starr in part of his bill	£20	0s	0d
Paid Mrs Beadles in part of her bill	£20	0s	0d
Paid Timothy Bunker at White Hart in part	£5	7s	6d
Paid Mr Brideoaks bill of Ampthill	£8	0s	0d
Paid the George bill in part	£21	10s	0d
Paid the Maidenhead bill in part	£10	0s	0d
Paid Mr Weal in part for takeinge the Poll	£3	0s	0d
Paid Alderman Negus part of his bill	£0	10s	0d
Paid James Goods in part of his bill	£0	2s	0d
Paid John Richardson in part of his bill	£20	0s	0d
Mr Harvey paid all this	£125	13s	6d
Paid Timothy Bunker in part of his bill	£5	0s	0d
Paid Alderman Negus in part of his bill	£8	0s	0d
Paid John Rose in part of his bill	£12	0s	0d
Paid James Goods in part of his bill	£5	0s	0d
Paid David Eslin in part of his bill	£13	0s	0d
Paid James Bray in part of his bill	£13	0s	0d
Paid John Crouch in part of his bill	£18	0s	0d
Paid Simon Abbott into Mr Willis Senior's hands	£20	0s	0d
Paid John Goods in part into Mr Willis Senior's hands	£10	0s	0d
Paid Hocket Spencely's bill in full	£2	10s	6d
Paid John Skelton in part	£8	0s	0d
Paid Anthony Rush in part per Mr Dymoke	£6	0s	0d
Paid Mr Parker at George in part	£12	0s	0d
Paid Mr Edwards, St Leonards in part	£20	0s	0d
Paid Timothy Bunker more per Mr Rudd	£5	0s	0d
Paid Mr Brazier's bill of Cople	£1	10s	0d
Paid John Skelton per Mr Bedford for Mr Beadles	£3	10s	0d
£100 Sir Pynsent paid	£162	10s	6d
£62 10s 6d Mr Harvey paid			
Paid the Quit Rent to Mr Swaine	£0	19s	0d
Paid to John Ward of Goldington horse hire and Charges	£0	15s	0d
Paid Mr Purton of Kempston	£3	4s	6d
Paid Mr Brasier's bill of Cople	£1	19s	6d
Paid myself the Clarke's Sallary, 1715	£1	0s	0d
Memorandum Mr John Willis is still to pay which I know of	£27	6s	11d
The Total Joynt Charge	£783	3s	7d
The halfe of it	£391	11s	6½d
Mr Harvey's Separate Account	£27	6s	11d
	£418	18s	5½d

Received £21 10s 0d
more £305 2s, 10d
more £53 15s 0d   £418 17s 10d
Rand Taylor's bill £33 10s

The election took place on 16 February 1715. According to the poll books,[8] John Harvey (Tory) and William Hillersden (Whig) were elected with 1264 and 1261 votes respectively, defeating John Cater (Whig) and Sir Pinsent Chernocke (Tory), who had 1254 and 1241 votes each. These figures are so close to the 1713 figures that one wonders whether O'Byrne had not transposed some of the figures in his account of the Bedfordshire constituency. It would seem that Hillersden gained twenty votes at the expense of Chernocke, while Cater and Harvey remained exactly the same. The two surviving poll books differ in the addition of votes recorded on 12 out of 58 pages! None of the figures add up to those quoted in the subsequent petition. The figures, such as they are, show a tiny swing to the Whigs, leading to the Tories losing a seat.

It is useful to see how voting patterns had changed since 1705, the last contested election for which a poll book survives. In 1705 Chernocke had headed the poll, with two Whigs close to one another, and Harvey tailed off badly in last place. Forty votes split Gostwick from Russell, but Chernocke was 644 votes in front of his fellow candidate, Harvey. In 1715 Hillersden was 7 in front of Cater and there were only 21 votes between the first and the last candidates.

Clearly, there was greater cohesion in the Tory voting, with their supporters giving their votes to both candidates and not plumping for one of them. In Bedford, although the Tories continued to trail the Whigs, they received 44 votes in 1715 rather than the 68 for Chernocke and 25 for Harvey that they had gained in 1705. In Leighton Buzzard in 1705, voting was 62 for Chernocke and 21 for Harvey; in 1715 it was 66 and 54. In Luton it had been 75 and 54; in 1715 it was 66 each. In Chalgrave it had been 17 and 4; in 1715 it was 28 and 26. In Dunstable in 1705 the votes were 43 and 7, and in 1715, 34 apiece. They made significant gains in Great Barford, Southill and Studham, where they led the poll. In Cardington they narrowed the gap of the Whigs' majority. While Tory voters in the west of the county in the areas where Chernocke had most influence tended to support Harvey in 1715, in the east, Chernocke lagged behind his fellow candidate just enough to make him lose the election. Crucially in Sandy, the next parish to Harvey's house at Ickwell Bury, in 1715 Harvey polled 55 votes to Chernocke's 40. Chernocke was 5 votes behind in Potton, 4 in Wrestlingworth, 3 in Shillington and 2 in Northill.

With both the sitting Whig members not standing again, the Whigs in 1715 were likely to have new territorial strengths. Both candidates lived near Bedford, at Elstow and Kempston, which would be likely to strengthen their cause in central Bedfordshire. They crushed the Tories in Bedford. In Kempston, Elstow and Goldington, the Whigs were as overwhelming as they had been in 1705. Other Whig strongholds were Houghton Regis, Eversholt, Keysoe and Eaton Socon, though in the latter the Tories were closing the gap. In 1715, the Whigs went top of the poll in Blunham, Harrold, Flitton and Silsoe, where the Duke of Kent was an important

8   BLARS, HY 833 and OR 1825.

landowner. In the west of the county, they went ahead in Totternhoe and Westoning. On the poll, Hillersden had a majority of only seven over his fellow candidate. Minor differences between the votes cast for the two Whigs occur in a number of parishes. Hillersden did better in Eaton Bray, Eaton Socon and Toddington, Southill, Campton and Milton Bryan. Cater was substantially ahead of Hillersden in Sandy and Cranfield.

Cater was not satisfied with the result and successfully appealed to the House of Commons that he be elected in place of Harvey because some of Harvey's voters were not properly qualified. As the House had a Whig majority, it was always likely that Cater would succeed, no matter what the merits of the case were.

Poll for the County of Bedfordshire 1715

After the election a petition was presented by John Cater. Sources: *Journal of the House of Commons*, vol. 18, quoted in R. H. O'Byrne, *The Representative History of Great Britain and Ireland* (London, 1848), p. 4.

1715 Petition

1715, March 31 A petition of John Cater, Esq was read, setting forth, 'that at this election, the petitioners (sic) William Hillersden, Sir Pyncent Chernocke, and John Harvey stood candidates . . ., that the petitioner and Mr Hillersden had a majority of legal votes; but several persons, voting for the said Mr Harvey, though not qualified, and by the illegal practises used by Mr Harvey and agent, there was procured a majority of sixteen for the latter gentleman above the petitioner, who would otherwise have had the majority.' The rights of the petitioner admitted; returned accordingly.

The Poll for the County

Source: BLARS, HY 833 and OR 1825. Both are printed and are almost identical. The differences are that HY 833 begins with the number of votes cast for each candidate and the number the sum of votes recorded differs on 12 out of 58 pages. The poll books are not marked to show which voters were disallowed following Cater's petition.

Abbreviations of candidates' names used in the transcription:

Cher.   Chernock   Har.   Harvey   Hill.   Hillersdon

1715 Poll

Copy of the Poll for Knights of the Shire for the County of Bedford. Taken at the Town of Bedford, February Sixteenth, 1714[1715]. Thomas Bromsall of Blunham, High Sheriff. Candidates, Sir Pynsent Chernock, Bart, John Harvey, Esq; John Cater, Esq; William Hillersdon.

Christian name	Surname	Occupation	Place of abode	Candidates voted for			
				Cher.	Har.	Cater	Hill.
			Ampthill				
Thomas	Hollingworth					1	1
Jeremiah	Grey			1	1		
Nicholas	Read		Islington	1	1		
Thomas	Ivens			1	1		
Richard	Evans			1	1		
John	Emmerton			1	1		
John	Finley			1	1		
Richard	Upton			1	1		
Thomas	Bedcott			1	1		
Thomas	Hawes			1	1		
William	Foulks			1	1		
Robert	Ball			1	1		

Christian name	Surname	Occupation	Place of abode	Cher.	Har.	Cater	Hill.
John	Best			1	1		
Robert	Cooper			1	1		
John	Pearson		Maulden	1	1		
William	Crouch			1			1
William	Stringer			1	1		
Edmund	Greene					1	1
Thomas	Sandey					1	1
William	Love			1	1		
Henry	Browne		Newport BKM	1	1		
Thomas	Copperwheat					1	1
Simon	Lindy					1	
Samuel	Nash	Esq.	St James's Westminster			1	1
Joseph	Barber					1	1
John	Newman					1	1
Edwin	Denbigh					1	1
Jeremiah	Grey			1	1		
Robert	Phillips		Royston			1	1
Edward	Lane			1	1		
Robert	Vincent			1	1		
John	Whatton	Gent.		1	1		
John	Kimpton			1			1
Thomas	Vincent			1	1		
John	Warner			1	1		
Robert	Farnell			1	1		
Charles	Dymoke	Jun. Gent.		1	1		
Andrew	Hickson		Woolidge KEN	1	1		
William	Westly			1	1		
Thomas	Arnold	Gent.		1	1		
Ezekial	Rewce	Clerk		1	1		
William	Bedcott		Bedford	1	1		
George	Webb			1	1		
William	Allen			1	1		
			Arlsey				
Michael	Deare			1	1		
Edward	Jones	Gent.	Watford	1	1		
John	Godfrey		Hitchin	1	1		
Miles	Sands		Letchworth HRT	1	1		
John	Preist		Gravely HRT			1	1
Thomas	Papworth					1	1
Thomas	Rawlings					1	1

Christian name	Surname	Occupation	Place of abode	Cher.	Har.	Cater	Hill.
Henry	Hutton					1	1
William	Deare					1	1
Samuel	Browne	Esq.				1	1
George	Hailey					1	1
Thomas	Cooper					1	1

Aspley Guise

Christian name	Surname	Occupation	Place of abode	Cher.	Har.	Cater	Hill.
Edward	Cope			1	1		
Stephen	Chasemore		Hartley Roe	1	1		
George	Letting		North Crawley	1	1		
Thomas	Dogget		Wavendon BKM	1	1		
Bernard	Gregory		Wavendon	1	1		
Joseph	Wiles			1	1		
Henry	Browne			1	1		
Thomas	Hewes		Hogstie End	1	1		
Samuel	Brook		Newington Butts	1	1		
William	Tuckey		Tillsworth	1	1		
Lawrence	Crawley			1	1		
George	Farr			1	1		
John	Moore		Braughton BKM	1	1		
Stephen	Richardson		Oxford	1	1		
Francis	Doggett			1	1		
Edward	Worster			1	1		
Thomas	Coott		Wavendon BKM	1	1		
Robert	Byworth			1	1		
Thomas	Austin			1		1	
Thomas	Harman			1		1	
John	Crawley			1			1
John	Samm			1			1
James	Ambridge			1			1
Richard	Tillcock			1			1
Thomas	How	Sen.				1	1
George	Ward					1	1
Robert	Burrows					1	1
Edward	Brockett					1	1
Bartholemew	Evans		Hackney MDX			1	1
George	Sadler	Esq.				1	1
William	Rustall					1	1
Thomas	How	Jun.				1	1
William	Church		Wooburne			1	1

Christian name	Surname	Occupation	Place of abode	Cher.	Har.	Cater	Hill.
			Astwick				
John	Cockaine	Esq.	Hinksworth CAM	1	1		
John	Squire		Hitchin			1	1
			Barford Magna				
Thomas	Ventrinan			1	1		
John	Whisson		Moredon	1	1		
John	Pickin			1	1		
Thomas	Roberts			1	1		
John	Boston			1	1		
Sandra	Forster	Gent.		1	1		
John	Hart			1	1		
William	Lewis			1	1		
Abraham	Smith			1	1		
John	Williamson			1	1		
John	Willis			1	1		
Richard	Willis			1	1		
John	Pulford			1	1		
James	Gilbert		Abbotsley HUN	1	1		
John	Freshwater			1	1		
Thomas	Wye			1			1
John	Sunbury		Renhold			1	1
William	Brace					1	1
John	Poole		Renhold			1	1
John	Farey		Aynsbury HUN			1	1
Walter	Hancock		Willington			1	1
John	Harwood					1	1
			Blunham				
William	Harding				1		1
Robert	Thomas			1	1		
Joseph	Ravens					1	1
John	Allen					1	1
John	Sellis		Cardington			1	1
Thomas	Bromsall	Esq. High Sheriff				1	1
			Barford parva				
John	Adams					1	1
Serjeant	Battisson					1	1
Thomas	Tingey					1	1
Edward	King					1	1

Christian name	Surname	Occupation	Place of abode	Candidates voted for Cher.	Har.	Cater	Hill.
Robert	Bamford	Clerk				1	1
			Barton				
Edward	Willson			1	1		
Richard	Crouch			1	1		
William	Pryor			1	1		
Robert	Wellborne		St Margarets Westminster	1	1		
Edward	Woodward			1	1		
William	Hopkins		Hertford	1	1		
Arthur	Humphries	Clerk		1	1		
John	Hale				1	1	
Thomas	Feild		Offley			1	1
Matthew	Woodward		Flitton			1	1
Matthew	Stevens					1	1
James	Loe					1	1
Richard	Saxton				1	1	
			Bedford				
Thomas	Lane			1	1		
John	Skelton			1	1		
William	Kitchnall		Shefford	1	1		
John	Bowstred			1	1		
Nicholas	Aspinall	Clerk		1	1		
William	Patenham		Sundrich near Ware	1	1		
Henry	Newman		Sundrich near Ware	1	1		
John	Geary		Artleborow NTH	1	1		
George	Maddy			1	1		
John	Hornbuckle			1	1		
John	Ellson			1	1		
Francis	Walker			1	1		
Thomas	Battisson	Jun.		1	1		
James	Bray			1	1		
Anthony	Cook			1	1		
William	Weale	Gent.		1	1		
John	Wiggins			1	1		
Richard	Divitt			1	1		
John	Towersey	Clerk		1	1		
William	Marthar			1	1		
Richard	Willis	Gent.		1	1		
George	Lockwood		Ampthill	1	1		
Thomas	Carter		Bigleswade	1	1		

Christian name	Surname	Occupation	Place of abode	Candidates voted for			
				Cher.	Har.	Cater	Hill.
Joseph	Willis			1	1		
Alexander	Leith	Clerk		1	1		
John	Goods			1	1		
Thomas	Hawes	Gent.		1	1		
Thomas	Battisson	Sen.		1	1		
John	Robins		Hitchin	1	1		
John	Street		Kempston Hardwick	1	1		
Edward	Veale			1	1		
Samuel	Upton		Millbrook	1	1		
William	Tausley			1	1		
Richard	Prop			1	1		
Thomas	Robinson			1	1		
Thomas	Faldee	Gent.		1	1		
John	Richardson			1	1		
Benjamin	Falkner		London	1	1		
Edward	Markes			1	1		
John	Richardson	Jun.		1	1		
Thomas	Smith			1	1		
John	Crawley			1			
James	Allen			1			
Josiah	Pridmore					1	1
Thomas	Cooper					1	1
Joseph	Smith alias Lyon					1	1
Robert	Bamford					1	1
Robert	Martin					1	1
Thomas	Margetts	Gent.				1	1
Richard	Boston					1	1
John	Daniel					1	1
Stephen	White					1	1
John	Weaver					1	1
Robert	Wood					1	1
Henry	Lowen					1	1
Nathaniel	Bardolph					1	1
John	Plummer					1	1
Thomas	Banes					1	1
William	Dove					1	1
Benjamin	Coleson					1	1
William	Reynolds					1	1
Richard	Wallford		Ailsbury BKM			1	1

Christian name	Surname	Occupation	Place of abode	Cher.	Har.	Cater	Hill.
Lewis	Norman		Keysoe	1	1		
Robert	Grey			1	1		
William	Staines			1	1		
John	Bunyan			1	1		
Daniel	Rich			1	1		
William	Yarnton			1	1		
Thomas	Richards			1	1		
John	Austin			1	1		
Thomas	Peirce			1	1		
William	Thompson			1	1		
Samuel	Massey			1	1		
James	Matthews			1	1		
Henry	Savidge			1	1		
Joseph	Howard			1	1		
Hatton	Eston			1	1		
William	Upton			1	1		
Thomas	Simpson			1	1		
Matthew	Jones			1	1		
Nihholas	Styles			1	1		
Ralph	Smith	Gent.	St Michaels Cornhill	1	1		
Samuel	Tayler			1	1		
William	Matthews			1	1		
John	Cooch			1	1		
Benjamin	Arthur			1	1		
Simon	Tayler			1	1		
Shadrach	Johnson			1	1		
Robert	Clare			1	1		
John	Wadmouth			1	1		
John	Oakley			1	1		
Thomas	Wallsome			1	1		
Isaac	Emery			1	1		
Thomas	Hornbuckle			1	1		
Francis	Brace	Attorney		1	1		
Francis	Brace		Lincolns Inn	1	1		
John	Peppiatt	Gent.		1	1		
Gilbert	Tawill			1	1		
George	Maynard			1	1		
William	Maynard			1	1		
Randall	Tayler			1	1		
Samuel	Spencer			1	1		

Christian name	Surname	Occupation	Place of abode	Cher.	Har.	Cater	Hill.
Thomas	Hammond		St Giles LND			1	1
John	Phillips					1	1
John	Hale					1	1
William	Browne					1	1
John	Franklyn	Sen.				1	1
George	Peirson					1	1
John	Faldoe					1	1
Robert	Negus					1	1
Thomas	Ward					1	1
Thomas	Dew					1	1
Evans	Quick					1	1
John	Berry					1	1
Edward	Wales					1	1
George	Darling		Westham ESS			1	1
Francis	Oakley					1	1
John	Truelove					1	1
Robert	Arthur					1	1
John	Day					1	1
William	Combs					1	1
William	Gascoigne					1	1
William	Risely					1	1
William	Jones	Sen.				1	1
Thomas	Wilks					1	1
William	Reynolds					1	1
Thomas	Ryder		Newport			1	1
William	Dodgson					1	1
Robert	Bell	Esq.				1	1

Beeston

Thomas	Longland				1		
Edward	Walker					1	1
William	Clarke		Bigleswade			1	1
John	Harbutt	Clerk	Westminster	1	1		

Biddenham

Thomas	Faldoe	Clerk		1	1		
Thomas	Faldoe		Shefford	1	1		
William	Harris			1	1		
Richard	Farey			1			1
John	Dawson					1	1
Thomas	Browne		Brumham			1	1
Thomas	Atkins						1

Christian name	Surname	Occupation	Place of abode	Cher.	Har.	Cater	Hill.
Samuel	Fenn					1	1
			Bigleswade				
Robert	Moulton			1	1		
William	Eaton			1	1		
Anthony	Reynolds			1	1		
John	Wright	Esq.		1	1		
Thomas	Caldecott		Longstow CAM	1	1		
Edward	Sparrowhawk		Baldock	1	1		
John	Miles					1	
William	Beaumont		Warden			1	1
Thomas	Magoone					1	
			Billington				
Thomas	Cook					1	1
George	Huxley	Esq.	Red Lyon Street LND			1	1
Henry	Kidgell		Bradnum	1	1		
Robert	Atterbury			1	1		
			Bletsoe				
John	Flint		Bedford			1	1
Luke	Addington			1	1		
Thomas	Battisson		Milton Ernys	1	1		
John	Musgrave			1	1		
Robert	Musgrave			1	1		
John	Lucas			1	1		
Nicholas	Calton			1	1		
Nicholas	Cawthorne		London	1	1		
Thomas	Clark		Stachden	1	1		
Robert	Musgrave		Felmersham			1	1
Thomas	Marling		Keysoe			1	1
Robert	Ashburne					1	1
John	Maxey		Bolnhurt			1	1
Philip	Negus			1	1		
Valentine	Colton	Clerk		1	1		
			Bolnhurst				
Samuel	Gurry					1	1
Smith	Fleetwood		Northampton			1	1
John	Peck					1	1
James	Robinson		Keysoe			1	1
Daniel	Acock					1	1

Christian name	Surname	Occupation	Place of abode	Cher.	Har.	Cater	Hill.
			Brumham				
Thomas	Skevington		Stachden	1	1		
Robert	Richards	Clerk	Oakley	1	1		
			Caddington				
Edward	Bunyan			1	1		
Thomas	Langford		St Stevens HRT	1	1		
Thomas	Taylor		Langley HRT	1	1		
William	Newman			1	1		
Joshua	Hodgkins	Clerk	Kingsley BKM	1	1		
William	Seare			1	1		
John	Byby	Clerk		1	1		
John	Coppin	Esq.		1	1		
William	Bonlstrode			1	1		
William	Noddings			1		1	
Richard	Bannister					1	1
Zachariah	Neale					1	1
			Campton				
John	Goodcheap			1	1		
Joseph	Franklyn		Chicksand	1	1		
William	Rutton	L.D	York Buildings MDX	1	1		
Charles	Ventris	Esq.		1	1		
George	Wilsheire		Stolfold	1	1		
George	Lincolne			1	1		
William	Noddins			1			1
			Cardington				
Joseph	Smith			1	1		
John	Beech			1	1		
William	Chalton		Shefford	1	1		
Robert	Hutson		Bronghton HUN	1	1		
Francis	Meares			1	1		
Barwell	Collins	Clerk	Great Barford	1	1		
John	Willson		Stachden	1	1		
Thomas	Lockington		Christ Church LND	1	1		
Lewis	Atterbury	Clerk	Highgate MDX	1	1		
Thomas	Bygrave			1	1		
William	Spencer			1	1		
Matthew	Cotton					1	1
William	Bull					1	1

Christian name	Surname	Occupation	Place of abode	Cher.	Har.	Cater	Hill.
Thomas	Peck		Bedford	1			1
Samuel	Larkins		Wootton	1	1		
Joseph	Lake		Great Barford			1	1
William	Careless					1	1
William	King		Caxton CAM			1	1
Edward	Cowley		Elstow			1	1
Richard	Houseman		Spittlefields LND			1	1
John	Austin					1	1
Leonard	Willimot					1	1
Samuel	Larkin					1	1
John	Thody					1	1
John	Howard		St Sepulchres LND			1	1
John	Sharrow					1	1
William	Cockaine					1	1
Henry	Whitebread					1	1
Henry	Greene					1	1
Thomas	Redman					1	1
George	Huckle					1	1
John	Hockley		Elstow			1	1
William	Cass					1	1
			Carlton				
Joseph	Chadderton	Clerk		1	1		
William	Knight			1	1		
William	Massome			1	1		
John	Darling		Chellington	1	1		
William	Knight		Pavenham	1	1		
William	Davison		Turvey	1	1		
William	Wootton				1		1
John	Marshall					1	1
William	Frankyln					1	1
Miles	Basterfeild		Bedford			1	1
John	Steff	Jun.				1	1
Roger	Nicholls					1	1
Thomas	Bithery					1	1
John	Honnor					1	1
Thomas	Ashton		Turvey			1	1
Thomas	Whish					1	1
Gideon	Rudd					1	1
Stephen	Hind					1	1
Uriah	Bithray					1	1

Christian name	Surname	Occupation	Place of abode	Candidates voted for			
				Cher.	Har.	Cater	Hill.
William	Steff		Stachden			1	1
			Chalgrave				
Withers	Cheyne			1	1		
John	Odell		Harlington	1	1		
Walter	Foott		Tuddington	1	1		
John	Willisson		Herne	1	1		
William	Shallworth		Winfeild	1	1		
John	Olney			1	1		
Robert	Hawkins					1	1
John	Mawkin					1	1
John	Groome					1	1
Thomas	Olney					1	1
John	Purreott			1	1		
Christopher	Perry		Hockcliffe	1	1		
Edward	Poulton		Hockcliffe	1	1		
William	London			1	1		
Thomas	Keeble		Hockcliffe	1	1		
Thomas	Willis			1	1		
Michael	Olney			1	1		
William	Read			1	1		
Benjamin	Cross			1	1		
Thomas	Buckmaster			1	1		
William	Page			1	1		
John	Osborne			1	1		
John	Olney		Egginton	1	1		
John	Baldry		Houghton Regis			1	1
John	Willcox					1	1
Thomas	Bunker					1	1
John	Edwards					1	1
Daniel	Groome		Tuddington			1	1
			Chellington				
Richard	Wood					1	1
Thomas	Brittanie					1	
Thomas	Ongan		Finchly MDX	1	1		
Thomas	Darling		Chichly BKM	1	1		
			Chaulton				
William	Frankyln			1	1		
Thomas	Mayes		Sundon	1	1		
John	Cutler		Southgate MDX			1	1

Christian name	Surname	Occupation	Place of abode	Cher.	Har.	Cater	Hill.
John	Davis		Sundon			1	1
William	Mayles					1	1
Daniel	Bayly		Aldermanbury LND			1	1
			Clapam				
Alexander	Perring			1	1		
John	Tape	Clerk	Stachden	1	1		
Richard	Colly		Ridgmont	1	1		
William	Negus		Bedford			1	1
John	Negus		Thurleigh			1	1
			Clifton				
Edward	Hill			1	1		
William	Fowler		Southill	1	1		
John	Matthew			1	1		
John	Pedley			1	1		
Thomas	Dilley			1	1		
Matthew	Rogers			1	1		
James	Tayler		Eynesbury	1	1		
Richard	Edwards		Henlow	1	1		
Phillip	Addy	Clerk			1		
Richard	Endersbury					1	1
Edward	Waller		Wallington HRT			1	1
Thomas	Winch					1	1
John	Tingey					1	1
Edward	Ford					1	1
John	Samm		Hitchin			1	1
William	Baker					1	1
John	Fitton					1	1
Samuel	Morris		St Creed Church LND			1	1
			Clophill				
Joseph	Samm			1	1		
William	Linford			1	1		
Laurence	Richardson			1	1		
William	Young		Laighton	1	1		
Sir Pynsent	Chernock	Bart.	Hullcott	1	1		
John	Carter		Hawnes	1	1		
William	Birding					1	1
Henry	Gascoigne					1	1
William	Park					1	1

Christian name	Surname	Occupation	Place of abode	Cher.	Har.	Cater	Hill.
Edward	Park					1	1
John	Carter					1	1
Samuel	Carter					1	1
William	Chapman		Steppingley			1	1
Richard	Waters					1	1
Thomas	Goodwyn					1	1
Nehemiah	Sratton					1	1
Thomas	Waters					1	1
			Cockaine Hatley				
Peter	Clark	Clerk		1	1		
Richard	Cockaine	Esq.		1	1		
Edward	Squire			1	1		
			Colmworth				
Robert	Eastwell		Bedford	1	1		
William	Willis		Wilden	1	1		
James	Morrisson		Baldock HRT	1	1		
Thomas	Clark			1			1
Henry	Underwood		Highfeild HUN	1			
John	Tayler		Bedford			1	1
John	Hillersdon	Esq.				1	1
Francis	Beckett					1	1
Robert	Newman					1	1
Richard	Stringer					1	1
William	Underwood		Highfeilds HUN			1	1
Thomas	Clarke					1	1
Thomas	Bertley		Aynesbury HUN			1	1
Thomas	Cooper					1	1
John	Phillips		Wimple			1	1
Richard	Fisher					1	1
Thomas	Fisher					1	1
Robert	Ives					1	1
Joseph	Hobbs	Clerk				1	1
John	Mason		Bedford			1	1
Thomas	Collins		St Ives			1	1
			Cople				
John	Purser					1	1
Thomas	Collins		St. Ives HUN			1	1
Joseph	Cotton		Chicksand			1	1
David	Jones		Bedford			1	1

Christian name	Surname	Occupation	Place of abode	Cher.	Har.	Cater	Hill.
Matthew	Watts		Duke Street LND			1	1
Thomas	Leonard					1	1
Edward	Marsh					1	1
Edward	Richards					1	1
Robert	Joy			1			1
Thomas	Copperwheat				1		
Stephen	Harding			1	1		
Richard	Brasier	Sen.		1	1		
William	Griggs			1	1		
Oliver	Purser			1	1		
George	Carter			1	1		
Thomas	Atwell		Moulsoe	1	1		
Nicolas	Luke	Esq.		1	1		
			Cranfeild				
William	Olney			1	1		
Abraham	Partridge			1	1		
Timothy	Feild			1	1		
George	Ellis		Hanslop BKM	1	1		
Thomas	Barrot			1	1		
Laurence	Sparkes			1	1		
John	Seamer			1	1		
George	Collins			1	1		
Thomas	Barwick			1	1		
John	Whitlock			1	1		
Francis	Tayler			1	1		
John	Osborne		St James Clerkenwell	1	1		
William	Nash			1	1		
Thomas	Dymoke	Gent.	Newport	1	1		
Michael	Dymoke	Gent.	Bedford	1	1		
Charles	Dymoke	Gent.		1	1		
Jonathan	Lebatt			1	1		
Francis	Duncomb	Esq.	Braughton BKM	1	1		
Ralph	Pools		Marston	1	1		
William	Panirass		Milton BKM	1		1	
John	Field			1		1	
Richard	Partridge			1		1	
Thomas	Burgess		Aspley	1			1
Joseph	Field			1		1	
John	Salmon			1			
Isaac	Dix			1		1	

Christian name	Surname	Occupation	Place of abode	Cher.	Har.	Cater	Hill.
John	Scoff			1	1		
Thomas	Partridge			1	1		
Jacob	Odell					1	1
John	Smithill		North Crawley			1	1
John	Seabrook		Litlington			1	1
John	Higgins		North Crawley			1	1
Thomas	Odell					1	1
Thomas	Baker					1	1
Henry	Wheeler					1	1
Peter	Edwards					1	1
John	Mason		Spalwick HUN			1	1
John	Mead		Stewkley BKM			1	1
Thomas	Franks	Clerk				1	1
John	Fosket		Wishamstead			1	1
Richard	Hartwell					1	1
Michael	Woodward		Marston	1	1		

Crawley

Christian name	Surname	Occupation	Place of abode	Cher.	Har.	Cater	Hill.
Anthony	Rutley			1	1		
William	Gresham			1	1		
Richard	Fowkes		Bletchly BKM	1	1		
William	Gresham			1	1		
Thomas	Sadler			1	1		
John	Caddey		Woodstreet LND	1	1		
John	Brotherton			1	1		
William	Norcliffe	Esq.	Aspley	1	1		
George	Gresham			1	1		
Randolph	Tayler		Ampthill	1	1		
Stephen	Emerton			1		1	
Valentine	Clarke			1		1	
Thomas	Sadler			1		1	
Thomas	Brotherton			1			
Samuel	Palmer			1			1
John	Abraham		Moulsoe BKM			1	1
Francis	Greene		East Claydon BKM			1	1
Robert	Smith		Woolburne			1	1
Henry	Sinfield					1	1
John	Berry					1	1
John	Barnwell					1	1
William	Rolfe					1	1
William	Payne					1	1

Christian name	Surname	Occupation	Place of abode	Candidates voted for			
				Cher.	Har.	Cater	Hill.
John	Sutton					1	1
William	Cooch					1	1
George	Turney					1	1
John	Lavendor					1	1
James	Harding		Southwark			1	1
Thomas	Ingles		St Martins MDX			1	1
Nathaniel	Allbright		Wooburne			1	1
Richard	Coales		Bow Brickhill			1	1
Joseph	Harris		Wooburne			1	1
Robert	Costin		Wooburne			1	1
John	Wellis		Wooburne			1	1
Francis	Huckle		Wooburne			1	1
Richard	Meagre		Great Brickhill	1			
			Deane				
Edward	Martin			1	1		
Thomas	Barry		Shelton	1	1		
Robert	Lamb	Gent.	Great Addington NTH	1	1		
John	Mason		Yelling HUN			1	1
John	York					1	1
Thomas	Fox					1	1
Thomas	Eaton					1	1
John	Marriott					1	1
Austin	Chester					1	1
John	Savage					1	1
Thomas	Mayes					1	1
Jacob	Meele					1	1
Richard	Maston					1	1
Robert	Fox					1	1
Peter	Boundy	Clerk				1	1
Thomas	Boswell					1	1
John	Askew					1	1
Philip	Seyx					1	1
Samuel	Farey					1	1
Theophilus	Leach					1	1
Peter	Farey					1	1
Alexander	Skinner					1	1
Maurice	Cherrey					1	1
Noah	Neale	Esq.	Standford NTH			1	1

Christian name	Surname	Occupation	Place of abode	Candidates voted for			
				Cher.	Har.	Cater	Hill.
			Dunstable				
John	Foxon			1	1		
Richard	Mare			1	1		
Joseph	Rashfield			1	1		
Henry	Ewer			1	1		
Thomas	Billingham			1	1		
Thomas	Vaux	Esq.	Whipsnade	1	1		
Thomas	Crouch			1	1		
William	Webster			1	1		
William	Crossfeild		London	1	1		
Edward	Rolt			1	1		
Marke	Price		Watford	1	1		
Thomas	Groome			1	1		
Henry	Bennell			1	1		
John	Crawley	Gent.		1	1		
John	Wright			1	1		
Richard	London		Hockliffe	1	1		
Richard	Rogers			1	1		
Richard	Groome			1	1		
Jacob	Pueton			1	1		
Henry	Chamberline			1	1		
William	Whittey		Caddington	1	1		
John	Gale			1	1		
George	Gale		Smithfeilds Barrs	1	1		
John	Rennell		St Buttolphs Aldersgate	1	1		
Jonathan	Crouch			1	1		
Charles	Wimpey			1	1		
John	Adams			1	1		
Samuel	Bradwin			1	1		
Thomas	Moreton			1	1		
Joseph	Hartley					1	1
John	Lord	Clerk		1	1		
John	Bass			1	1		
Nathaniel	Groome			1	1		
John	Child		St Fosters LND	1	1		
William	Reynolds					1	1
Richard	Stringer					1	1
John	Haley		Chelsea			1	1
John	Grover		Luton			1	1
Robert	Rose		Bedford			1	1

Christian name	Surname	Occupation	Place of abode	Candidates voted for			
				Cher.	Har.	Cater	Hill.
William	Ellement		Chesham BKM			1	1
John	Cooke					1	1
Robert	Chapman					1	1
John	Purton					1	1
Joseph	Williamson		St Albans			1	1
Richard	Moreton					1	1
George	Knowles					1	1
Henry	Howard		St Alphage LND			1	1
John	Prentice		Aldergate Street			1	1
William	Wilson		St Albans	1	1		
John	Dewberry		Hitchin	1	1		
			Dunton				
John	Fleming			1	1		
Peter	Carvel			1	1		
Robert	Pheasant			1	1		
Edmund	Rudd			1	1		
William	Phillips			1	1		
Michael	Phillips			1	1		
Zachariah	Clare			1	1		
Thomas	Parrott		Hartford HUN	1	1		
Robert	Cock			1			1
John	Keeling			1	1		
John	Ward					1	1
Thomas	Oliffe	Clerk				1	1
			Eaton Bray				
John	Cook			1	1		
Edmund	Stubbs	Clerk	New Market	1	1		
John	Hillyard			1	1		
William	Messider			1	1		
Thomas	Worrall			1	1		
John	Cleasy			1	1		
William	Cook			1	1		
William	Cobb			1	1		
George	Browne			1	1		
Thomas	Prentice			1	1		
William	Wells			1	1		
John	Dymoke			1	1		
Michael	Messider		Luton	1	1		
Thomas	Evans			1	1		
William	Golding			1	1		

Christian name	Surname	Occupation	Place of abode	Cher.	Har.	Cater	Hill.
Thomas	George			1	1		
John	Puttyfoote			1	1		
James	Ashwell			1			1
Richard	Roberts			1			1
Simon	Wood			1			1
Roger	Pursell			1			1
Joseph	Cooper			1			1
Henry	Rogers					1	1
Joseph	Whynott					1	1
John	Sibley		Houghton Regis			1	1
Robert	Cook		Dunstable			1	1
Richard	Ashwell					1	1
William	Hewett					1	1
Richard	Wood					1	1
Joseph	Cook					1	1
Thomas	Fosket					1	1
Thomas	Bruges					1	1
John	Burr					1	1
Richard	Burr					1	1
John	Sandon					1	1
Joseph	Jeffs					1	1
John	Carter	Sen.				1	1
Richard	Adkins					1	1
William	Ashwell					1	1

Eaton Socon

Christian name	Surname	Occupation	Place of abode	Cher.	Har.	Cater	Hill.
John	Moakes			1	1		
Samuel	Luff		Hiddington HUN	1	1		
Leonard	Wright			1	1		
William	Mead		Gamlingay	1	1		
Henry	Boston		Little Gransden	1	1		
John	Peet		Sratton	1	1		
Robert	Lee			1	1		
John	King		Bedford	1	1		
Thomas	Bayster		Alconbury HUN	1	1		
William	Henson		Little Paxston	1	1		
Francis	Attwood			1	1		
Thomas	Savage		Wimbleton SRY	1	1		
Isaac	Emery			1	1		
Weyman	Lee	Esq.	London	1	1		
Richard	Worland		Hinksworth	1	1		

Christian name	Surname	Occupation	Place of abode	Cher.	Har.	Cater	Hill.
Thomas	Atkinson		Gamlingay	1	1		
William	Hatley		St Ives	1	1		
John	Ashcroft	Gent.	Bedford	1	1		
Joseph	Basset	Clerk		1	1		
Robert	Sibley			1	1		
Jonathan	Bell			1	1		
Edward	Flowers			1	1		
Richard	Emery			1	1		
Thomas	Topham			1	1		
James	Topham			1	1		
Samuel	Boston			1	1		
John	Staughton			1	1		
John	Willisson			1	1		
William	Wright			1	1		
Gilbert	Linsey		St Neots	1	1		
John	Topham			1	1		
Thomas	Foster		Bigleswade	1	1		
John	Trott			1	1		
John	Barnes		Eynesbury	1	1		
John	Pratt		Eynesbury	1	1		
James	Lisle		Hitchin	1	1		
Robert	Gray			1	1		
James	Hewett		Everton	1	1		
Richard	Wiles		St Clement Danes	1	1		
John	Hardrett		Highgate	1	1		
Carolinus	Smith		Huntingdon		1		1
Edward	Emery				1		1
John	Gery				1		
Thomas	Linsey		Wyboston		1		
Thomas	Watts					1	1
Samuel	Eden		Tillbroke			1	1
Richard	Smith		Great Staughton HUN			1	1
Henry	Tingey		Little Barford			1	1
John	Quinton		Wellingborow			1	1
Gilbert	Libley					1	1
John	Goodwin					1	1
James	Sparrow					1	1
Thomas	Stocker		Wyboston				1
Edward	Emery					1	1
Henry	Negus		Kimbolton			1	1

Christian name	Surname	Occupation	Place of abode	Cher.	Har.	Cater	Hill.
Abraham	Tayler					1	1
Thomas	Frank					1	1
Thomas	Devereux					1	1
George	King					1	1
John	Wright		Wyboston			1	1
John	Allison					1	1
Jasper	Wagstaffe					1	1
George	Boston					1	1
Thomas	Squire					1	1
John	Edmunds					1	1
John	Mehew					1	1
Simon	Safford					1	1
William	Browne					1	1
Richard	Emery					1	1
John	Flawne					1	1
Joseph	Bell					1	1
William	Frank					1	1
Thomas	Wiles					1	1
George	Wright					1	1
Robert	Wright					1	1
John	Emery		Roxston			1	1
John	Emery		Little Barford			1	1
Joseph	Greene					1	1
William	Baldock					1	1
James	Tayler					1	1
Owen	Dixey		Papworth CAM			1	1
Robert	Lovell		Roxton			1	1
John	Day		Roxton			1	1
William	Wise					1	1
Pallady	Woodward		Goldington			1	1
George	Williams		St Neots			1	1
Henry	Ashley	Esq.				1	1
James	Banks					1	1
Jonathan	Stockeridge					1	1
John	Wright					1	1
John	Stocker					1	1
John	Hoot					1	1
James	Coot					1	1
William	Walgate		Buckden			1	1
John	Moone		St Neots			1	1
William	Rowley					1	1

Christian name	Surname	Occupation	Place of abode	Candidates voted for			
				Cher.	Har.	Cater	Hill.
John	Negus		St Neots			1	1
Thomas	Chesham					1	1
James	Cosens					1	1
Thomas	Bayly					1	1
William	Cooper					1	1
Thomas	Smith					1	1
Samuel	Emery		Great Paxton			1	1
William	Crow					1	1
Philip	Chapman		St Neots			1	1
Thomas	Tingey		Northampton			1	1
Henry	Lowen					1	1
John	Frank					1	1
Edward	Mason		Stanford NTH			1	1
John	Bigg	Esq.	Graffham HUN			1	1
			Eggington				
John	Andrews			1	1		
John	Man		Ivingoe BKM	1	1		
Edward	Gurney		Laighton	1	1		
William	Steevens			1	1		
Thomas	Skittlethorpe			1	1		
Thomas	Stoakes		Woodford ESS	1	1		
Edward	Roberts			1			1
			Elstow				
Thomas	Lucas		St Neots	1	1		
John	Crocker		Bedford			1	1
Robert	Wilsheire					1	1
Thomas	Stoakes		Bedford			1	1
John	Osborne					1	1
John	Newell					1	1
John	Fox					1	1
John	Amcoe					1	1
Mathew	Dymoke					1	1
Ralph	Warren					1	1
Jahn	Savill					1	1
Richard	Andrews					1	1
Samuel	Ballard		St Margarets Westminster			1	1
William	Hillersdon	Esq.				1	1

Christian name	Surname	Occupation	Place of abode	Cher.	Har.	Cater	Hill.
			Evershalt				
Richard	Gregory			1	1		
John	Morrison		Rigmont	1	1		
William	Hide	Clerk		1	1		
William	Houghton			1	1		
William	Houghton			1		1	
William	Parker	Gent.		1			1
William	Deaton			1			1
John	Deaton			1			1
Ambrose	Reddall	Sen.				1	1
James	Franklyn					1	1
John	Cotching					1	1
Henry	Wells					1	1
Henry	Ford					1	1
John	Gregory					1	1
Benjamin	Whitebread					1	1
James	Yarrow					1	1
Robert	Tillcock					1	1
John	Houghton		Brayfield Green NTH			1	1
Samuel	Boteler		Ridgmont			1	1
William	Whitebread					1	1
Humphrey	Tomlinson					1	1
Stephen	Whitebread					1	1
Dixey	Gregory					1	1
Robert	Smith					1	1
Henry	Goldsmith					1	1
John	Reddal					1	1
Richard	Newman					1	1
Thomas	Theed		Wendover BKM			1	1
William	Houghton		Ridgmont			1	1
James	Gregory					1	1
Ambrose	Reddall					1	1
James	Gregory		Bendish HRT			1	1
John	Riston					1	1
John	Reddall					1	1
James	White					1	1
Thomas	Smith					1	1
William	Hopcraft					1	1
John	Symons		St Brides LND			1	1
James	Turney		Wing BKM			1	1

Christian name	Surname	Occupation	Place of abode	Cher.	Har.	Cater	Hill.
Thomas	Buckingham		St Pulchres LND			1	1
William	Plummer		Ratcliffe MDX			1	1
John	Barton					1	1
Robert	Fuller					1	1
William	Gregory		Brayfeild Green NTH			1	1
			Everton				
Philip	Lewis			1	1		
George	Cawcott		Stow CAM	1	1		
Francis	Merriweather	Sen.		1	1		
William	Green		Henlow		1		1
William	Axtel	Esq.	St Peters Poor LND	1			1
Thomas	Dillingham					1	1
			Eyworth				
John	Swaine			1	1		
			Farndish				
Thomas	Islip			1	1		
John	Islip		Addington NTH	1	1		
Thomas	Alderman		Hocott NTH	1	1		
William	Barber	Clerk	Chichly BKM	1	1		
Thomas	Meadwell	Esq.	Geddington NTH			1	1
William	Lamb					1	1
			Felmersham				
George	Alderman			1	1		
Henry	Ventris		St Michael Woodstreet	1	1		
Thomas	Richards		Brunham	1	1		
Thomas	Bodington		London	1	1		
John	Beane		Thurleigh			1	1
Richard	Paine		Milton Ernys			1	1
Robert	Warner		Bedford			1	1
Henry	Amps					1	1
William	Warner					1	1
Matthew	Essex					1	1
William	Ashburne		Pavenham			1	1
William	Aspin	Esq.				1	1
William	Leach	Gent.				1	1
Thomas	Bober	Clerk				1	1
William	Warner					1	1
Thomas	Berry		Little Moor Fields			1	1

Christian name	Surname	Occupation	Place of abode	Cher.	Har.	Cater	Hill.
Stephen	Wood					1	1
Thomas	Allen					1	1
George	Farey		Bedford			1	1
William	Marriott					1	1
			Fenlake				
John	Bundy				1		
John	Peck				1		1
			Flitton				
Henry	Beaumont			1	1		
Thomas	Burrows		Maulden	1	1		
Thomas	Freeman		Leegrave	1	1		
Laurence	Smith		Braughton BKM	1	1		
William	Adams		Greenfield	1			1
John	Crouch					1	1
John	Morrisson					1	1
John	Pennifether					1	1
John	Vincent		St Bultolphs Aldgate			1	1
Edward	Laurence					1	1
Thomas	Laurence					1	1
John	Bonham					1	1
Joseph	Piggott					1	1
Richard	Smith					1	1
Henry	Beaumont					1	1
John	Manfield					1	1
Samuel	Farnell		Silsoe			1	1
John	Allen	Sen.	Silsoe			1	1
Nicholas	Wheel					1	1
John	Wheeler					1	1
			Flitwicke				
Henry	Webb			1	1		
John	Mattham			1	1		
Foster	Green	Jun.		1	1		
John	Underwood			1	1		
Matthew	Freelove			1	1		
Thomas	Howson			1	1		
John	Vaux			1	1		
Matthew	Brazier			1	1		
John	Betts	Jun.	Maulden	1	1		

Christian name	Surname	Occupation	Place of abode	Cher.	Har.	Cater	Hill.
Randal	Mein		Polton	1	1		
John	Collop			1	1		
George	Sole			1	1		
Thomas	Howson			1	1		
John	Franklyn		Ampthill	1	1		
Matthew	Allen			1	1		
Benjamin	Rhodes	Gent.	Silsoe	1	1		
Thomas	Birt					1	1
Thomas	Freelove					1	1
Edmund	Farey					1	1
Thomas	Smith		Evershalt			1	1
George	Swaine					1	1
Gustavus	Sheldon					1	1
Martin	Bullock		Higham Gobion			1	1
John	Hobbs		Bedford			1	1
Foster	Green	Sen.				1	1
Joseph	Tillcock					1	1
William	Pilcarne	Clerk				1	1
William	Chapman		Flitton			1	1
Christopher	Low		Cheapside LND			1	1

Girtford

Christian name	Surname	Occupation	Place of abode	Cher.	Har.	Cater	Hill.
John	Smith			1	1		
Thomas	Adkins			1	1		
Richard	Thurrowgood		Paxston HUN			1	1

Goldington

Christian name	Surname	Occupation	Place of abode	Cher.	Har.	Cater	Hill.
William	Falde	Gent.	Bedford	1	1		
Richard	Walford					1	1
Thomas	Wiffin		Bedford			1	1
James	Wiffin					1	1
John	Wiffin					1	1
Thomas	Goodwin					1	1
William	Wiffin		Bedford			1	1
Thomas	Walford					1	1
Nicholas	Thompson					1	1
Henry	Watson					1	1
John	Whitebread					1	1
John	Sheppard		Kempston			1	1
Thomas	Cleaton		Bocken ESS			1	1
Robert	Cleaton					1	1

Christian name	Surname	Occupation	Place of abode	Cher.	Har.	Cater	Hill.
			Gravenhurst				
Thomas	Goodall			1	1		
John	Smith		North Mimms	1	1		
Robert	Hanscomb	Jun.	Hitchin	1	1		
William	Hanscomb		Clifton	1	1		
Thomas	Burrows		Clophill			1	1
Thomas	Barwick					1	1
John	Dennis					1	1
Peter	De Aranda	Clerk				1	1
			Harlington				
William	Laurence			1	1		
William	Martin			1	1		
William	Morris			1	1		
John	Burr			1	1		
Robert	Morris			1	1		
Arthur	Wingate	Esq.	Bedford	1	1		
William	Woodward			1	1		
James	Farmer			1			1
William	Carter		Pulloxhill			1	1
Daniel	Punter		St Gyles Crippelgate			1	1
John	Dewberry		St Albans			1	1
Richard	Pedder					1	1
			Harrold				
John	Ablestone					1	1
Oliver	Fary					1	1
Edward	Gray					1	1
John	Pratt					1	1
Richard	Gray					1	1
Thomas	Norman					1	1
Thomas	Hartwell					1	1
Edward	Quince					1	1
John	Woolstone					1	1
Alexander	Dawson					1	1
Anthony	Clarke					1	1
Robert	Abraham					1	1
Thomas	Knight					1	1
Thomas	Franklin					1	1
William	Farrer	Esq.	St Andrews Holborn			1	1

Christian name	Surname	Occupation	Place of abode	Cher.	Har.	Cater	Hill.
Edward	Knight		Carlton	1	1		
Robert	Bletsoe			1	1		
John	Bletsoe			1	1		
Thomas	Bletsoe		Boreat	1	1		
Sir Nicholas	Carew		Beddington			1	1
Richard	Wootton			1	1		
William	Somes					1	1
John	Fary					1	1
John	Matthews	Sen.	Newport Pagnell			1	1
Thomas	Knight		Stagsden			1	1
John	Watford		Steventon and Pavenham			1	1

Harroden

Christian name	Surname	Occupation	Place of abode	Cher.	Har.	Cater	Hill.
John	Crofts		Cardington			1	1

Hawnes

Christian name	Surname	Occupation	Place of abode	Cher.	Har.	Cater	Hill.
John	Ivory		Bedford	1	1		
John	Warner			1	1		
Thomas	West			1	1		
William	Woodcraft			1	1		
Edward	Gibson	Clerk		1	1		
Robert	Hills		Potton	1	1		
William	Costin				1		1
Thomas	Berry		Wotton			1	1
Samuel	Maxey					1	1
Richard	Whitridge		Southill			1	1
William	King	Sen.	Caxton CAM			1	1
Richard	Wheeter	Sen.				1	1
Richard	Wheeter	Jun.				1	1
John	Whitridge					1	1
William	Baker					1	1
Francis	Ball					1	1
Thomas	Wheeler		Clophill			1	1
John	Esborne					1	1

Heath and Reach

Christian name	Surname	Occupation	Place of abode	Cher.	Har.	Cater	Hill.
Thomas	Hanwell					1	1
Joseph	Monke		Aspley	1	1		
John	Felts			1	1		

Henlow

Christian name	Surname	Occupation	Place of abode	Cher.	Har.	Cater	Hill.
John	Cooper		Petton		1	1	

Christian name	Surname	Occupation	Place of abode	Candidates voted for			
				Cher.	Har.	Cater	Hill.
John	Samms			1	1		
Pemberton	Bedford	Clerk		1	1		
Robert	Hanscombe			1	1		
Thomas	Trustram		Northamton	1	1		
Humphrey	Standon			1	1		
Thomas	Underwood			1	1		
William	Averne			1	1		
John	Hurst					1	1
George	Edwards	Esq.		1	1		
John	Wright					1	1
			Higham Gobion				
Matthias	Neale		Barton	1	1		
John	Feild		Hitchin	1	1		
John	Cross		New Inn MDX	1	1		
John	Busher		Southwarke			1	1
			Himwicke				
Thomas	Bayes		Stagsden		1		1
James	Turland					1	1
John	Livesay	Esq.				1	1
Francis	Freeman		Archester NTH				
			Hockliffe				
John	Morgan			1	1		
Thomas	Huckins			1	1		
Robert	Gilpin		Chalgrave	1	1		
Benedict	Cole		Layton	1	1		
John	Smith			1	1		
Edward	Hill		London	1	1		
Richard	Cox			1	1		
Edward	Hall			1	1		
John	Hobbs			1	1		
John	Fowler		Ivengoe	1	1		
James	Read		Battlesden	1	1		
Francis	West		Cheapside LND	1	1		
William	Fisher			1	1		
Nathaniel	Poulton			1	1		
Michael	Burton		Battlesden	1	1		
Daniel	Parratt			1	1		
William	Allen		St Margarets Westminster	1	1		

Christian name	Surname	Occupation	Place of abode	Cher.	Har.	Cater	Hill.
Arthur	Debny		Clarkenwell MDX			1	1
Nicholas	Morgan		Hornsey MDX	1	1		
Thomas	Dawbone		Mulsee BKM	1	1		
Edmond	Mann		Great Brickhill	1	1		
Thomas	Gladman		Studham	1	1		
John	Hillersdon		Stokehaman BKM			1	1
Hugh	Dawbone					1	1
			Holliwell				
William	Kingsley	Esq.	Hitchin	1	1		
Francis	Ansell		Higham Parke NTH	1	1		
John	Turner			1	1		
Daniel	Knott			1	1		
William	Alsop		Ickleford HRT	1	1		
Abraham	Watson			1	1		
Thomas	Ansell		Hugington BKM	1	1		
John	Turner		Hitchin			1	1
George	Draper		Hitchin			1	1
			Houghton Conquest				
William	Arnold		Kingstreete LND		1	1	
George	Bird		Southill	1	1		
Edward	Fossy		Maulden	1	1		
John	Langley			1	1		
Henry	Southouse	Esq.	London	1	1		
Stephen	Farrar			1	1		
William	Merrice		Ampthill			1	1
Ralph	Tompkins					1	1
Thomas	Armstrong					1	1
William	Bonner					1	1
Thomas	Smart					1	1
Robert	Clarke			1	1		
John	Riseley					1	1
James	Redman					1	1
Thomas	Hamerston			1	1		
Joseph	Barker	Jun.	Ampthill			1	1
Charles	Copperwheat					1	1
			Houghton Regis				
Thomas	Hawkins					1	1
John	Wallis					1	1

Christian name	Surname	Occupation	Place of abode	Cher.	Har.	Cater	Hill.
John	How					1	1
William	Brittaine					1	1
John	Buckingham					1	1
William	Swaine					1	1
Joseph	Brittaine					1	1
Abraham	Dine		Chalgrave			1	1
Samuel	Hawkins		Hemsleade			1	1
Henry	Willson		Dunstable			1	1
Henry	Parratt		Eversholt			1	1
John	Groome					1	1
John	Norman					1	1
Michael	Messinder					1	1
William	Norman					1	1
Thomas	Palmer					1	1
William	Elmer					1	1
Thomas	Hawkins					1	1
Richard	Pointon		Clophill	1	1		
Richard	Parratt		London	1	1		
Nehemiah	Brandrith	Esq.				1	1
Henry	Brandrith	Gent.				1	1
Matthew	Wingrave					1	1
John	Butterfield					1	1
William	Bourne					1	1
Joseph	Hudnall					1	1
William	Hickstone					1	1
Henry	Tompkins			1	1		
John	Carpenter			1	1		
John	Batchelour		Ridgmont	1			1
James	Large					1	1
Michael	Cooke		Southill			1	1
Francis	Paddan			1	1		
Valentine	Cressey	Clerk				1	1
William	Corbett		Highgate	1	1		
John	Patridge		Egginton	1	1		
Bernard	Turney		Cublington	1	1		
William	Gilmore		Southill	1	1		
William	Newman					1	1
John	Hawkins					1	1
Richard	Gospill					1	1
Simon	Merry					1	1
William	Dine					1	1

Christian name	Surname	Occupation	Place of abode	Cher.	Har.	Cater	Hill.
Thomas	Herbert					1	1
Edward	How					1	1
John	Pipkin		Tuddington	1	1		
John	Prior		Barton			1	1
William	Francis					1	1
William	Valentine					1	1
William	Groome					1	1
Edward	House					1	1
Thomas	Fox					1	1
George	Goring					1	1
William	How					1	1
John	Cooper		Sharpenhoe			1	1
William	Trapp		Minories LND			1	1
Thomas	Buckingham		Ridy HRT			1	1
Thomas	Hawkins		Redbourn HRT			1	1
Thomas	Timberlake					1	1

Hullcutt

Christian name	Surname	Occupation	Place of abode	Cher.	Har.	Cater	Hill.
John	Littlejohn	Clerk		1	1		

Ickwell

Christian name	Surname	Occupation	Place of abode	Cher.	Har.	Cater	Hill.
Humphery	Fish	Sen. Esq.		1	1		
Isaac	Carter			1			
Thomas	Tompion		London			1	1
John	Harvey	Esq.		1	1		

Kempson

Christian name	Surname	Occupation	Place of abode	Cher.	Har.	Cater	Hill.
John	Mann		Wootton			1	1
Matthew	Cary					1	1
George	Wheeler					1	1
William	Sheppard					1	1
John	Leader					1	1
John	Purton					1	1
Joseph	Barker					1	1
Thomas	Barringer					1	1
John	Sheppard		Covington HUN			1	1
Thomas	Bolton		St Albans			1	1
John	Pearce					1	1
Thomas	Cooper					1	1
John	Barker					1	1
Thomas	Remmatt					1	1
Joseph	Barker					1	1

Christian name	Surname	Occupation	Place of abode	Candidates voted for			
				Cher.	Har.	Cater	Hill.
Thomas	Gilpin					1	1
James	Marriott					1	1
Richard	Horton					1	1
Robert	Roback					1	1
James	Gibson					1	1
John	Greene					1	1
John	Eames					1	1
Samuel	Bowers		Bromham			1	1
William	Britaine					1	1
John	White					1	1
Edward	Marshall		Stagsden		1	1	
John	Cater	Esq.				1	1
William	Sanderson					1	1
John	Pearce		Maulden	1	1		
Richard	Blunt					1	1
Robert	Bennet					1	1
John	Reynolds					1	1
Henry	Woodward					1	1
Thomas	David		Bedford			1	1
Zachariah	Mann					1	1
William	Carter	Gent.	Turvey	1	1		
Guy	Hillersdon	Clerk	Castleashby	1	1		
Samuel	Sharpe		Bletsoe			1	1
John	Haynes					1	1
Thomas	Money					1	1
Thomas	Peirson					1	1
William	Boswell					1	1
William	Allen					1	1
Lewis	Haynes					1	1
Joseph	Margets	Clerk				1	1
Samuel	Jackson		Southoe HUN			1	1
John	Bulmore					1	1
John	Pitkin					1	1
Stephen	Jarvice					1	1
John	Peirson					1	1
John	Greene	Sen.	St Sepulchres LND			1	1
John	Green	Jun.	St Sepulchres LND			1	1
John	Radley					1	1
William	Carter		Islington MDX			1	1
Robert	Butcher					1	1
Thomas	Sanders					1	1

Christian name	Surname	Occupation	Place of abode	Candidates voted for			
				Cher.	Har.	Cater	Hill.
Matthew	Dennis	Esq.				1	1
John	Wats					1	1
			Keysoe				
Thomas	Hall		Perleithall	1	1		
George	Tooley	Clerk		1	1		
Thomas	Fullbig		Dunton			1	1
John	Parnell		Croxton	1	1		
Robert	Wotton					1	1
Gilbert	Jackson		Gordington			1	1
Benjamin	Hensman		Steventon			1	1
Richard	Stapleton					1	1
John	Money					1	1
John	Lettice	Clerk	Rushden	1	1		
Eustace	Petty		Bolnhurst	1	1		
Henry	Richards					1	1
Henry	Cole		Little Chelsea MDX			1	1
Richard	Levitt		Kimbolton			1	1
William	Sutton		Straughton Parva			1	1
William	Hills		St Martins in the Fields			1	1
Thomas	Norfield					1	1
Joseph	Henson		Swinshead			1	1
John	Cunnington		Ravensden			1	1
James	Gray		Okenbury HUN			1	1
John	Carter		Olney			1	1
John	Manning					1	1
Thomas	Mayes					1	1
John	Share					1	1
Henry	Haynes					1	1
John	Fulbeck					1	1
Thomas	Shaler		Bow Lane LND			1	1
Robert	Morris					1	1
Hugh	Northfield					1	1
Samuel	Richards					1	1
James	Watford					1	1
John	Nutter		St. Neots			1	1
Bartholomew	Mew		Bedford			1	1
			Knotting				
William	Rider	Esq.		1	1		
John	Sharp	Clerk		1	1		

Christian name	Surname	Occupation	Place of abode	Candidates voted for			
				Cher.	Har.	Cater	Hill.
			Laighton Bendizart				
Richard	Leach			1	1		
John	Procter			1	1		
John	Deane			1	1		
Gabriel	Norcourt			1			1
John	Lake					1	1
Thomas	Carter		Wilshamstead		1		1
Matthew	Harding					1	1
William	Pearson			1	1		
Michael	Higby			1	1		
Hezekiah	Walker		London	1	1		
John	Bonnick			1	1		
Henry	Smith			1	1		
Richard	Scrivener			1	1		
William	Whitamore			1	1		
John	Gregory			1	1		
Thomas	Procter			1	1		
John	Poole		London	1	1		
Joseph	Cooper		Chalgrave	1	1		
Thomas	Procter			1	1		
Thomas	Gurney		Linslet BKM	1	1		
Benedict	Warrall			1	1		
Edward	Ashwell			1	1		
William	Whipping	Jun.		1	1		
Henry	Gregory			1	1		
John	Johnson			1	1		
Arthur	Tarsey			1	1		
George	Whitmore			1	1		
John	Deane			1	1		
William	Whip	Clerk		1	1		
Ralph	Jeffs			1	1		
William	Chaddock			1	1		
Robert	Parratt			1	1		
Robert	Jackson		Stanbridge	1	1		
Thomas	Stonyford		Wooborn			1	1
William	Jeffe					1	1
Matthew	Disney	Clerk		1	1		
Edward	Hannell					1	1
Richard	Ashivell		Oakley	1	1		
Phillip	Layman		London	1	1		

Christian name	Surname	Occupation	Place of abode	Cher.	Har.	Cater	Hill.
John	Mann			1	1		
Thomas	Price					1	1
John	Hollingworth			1			1
William	Staire	Jun.				1	1
Edward	Keeth		Burton Overy LEI			1	1
John	Ashwell			1	1		
Thomas	Lawley			1	1		
Thomas	Walker			1	1		
William	Pratt		South Mims	1	1		
John	West			1	1		
John	Leech		Tuttle Street Westminst	1	1		
Daniel	Leech		St Martins LND	1	1		
William	Theed		Leabourn BKM	1	1		
Joseph	Gurney		Linslead BKM	1	1		
			Layton				
John	Langlord			1	1		
David	Freeman			1	1		
William	Spencer		Batlesden	1	1		
Francis	Dell			1	1		
Richard	Poynton			1	1		
John	Vaux			1	1		
Percivall	Chandler		Solebury BKM	1			1
Leonard	Robinson			1	1		
George	Pratt			1	1		
John	Edge					1	1
William	Fenner					1	1
Michael	Millard		Steeple Clayton BKM			1	1
Thomas	Valentine			1	1		
John	Dishford		Staubridge	1	1		
John	Deane		St Buttolphs Aldersgate	1	1		
Hon Charles	Leigh	Esq.		1	1		
Thomas	Theed	Esq.	Linslade BKM	1	1		
Henry	Clifton		Layton			1	1
Robert	Meads	Gent.	Ailesbury			1	1
John	Cheshire		St Martins MDX			1	1
James	King					1	1
James	Foster		Tring BKM	1	1		
John	Bray		Crawley	1	1		

Christian name	Surname	Occupation	Place of abode	Cher.	Har.	Cater	Hill.
			Langford				
Edward	Griffin					1	1
Samuel	Matthew		Clifton	1	1		
Thomas	Limbury			1	1		
Robert	Skegg			1	1		
John	Hill					1	1
Richard	Ravens					1	1
Edward	Cranfeild		Cardington	1	1		
Edward	Bentley		Astwick	1	1		
John	Wright			1	1		
William	Cooper		Hobne			1	1
John	Hemmin		Stratton			1	1
John	Draper			1	1		
George	Deare		Pollitts HRT			1	1
Thomas	Chambers					1	1
William	Moreton		Biggleswade			1	1
			Ligrave				
William	Prudden			1	1		
Thomas	Prudden			1	1		
Thomas	Swaine			1	1		
			Litlington				
Robert	Feild				1		
John	Bushbye					1	1
Thomas	Staubridge		Elstow			1	1
John	Birt		London			1	1
Humphrey	Hickman			1	1		
Thomas	Clarke					1	1
Richard	Fareman		Tuddington	1	1		
Thomas	Cartwright		Buckden	1	1		
John	Crouch			1	1		
John	Lane		Fletsley	1	1		
William	Feild			1	1		
John	Butler				1		1
Robert	Peake					1	1
John	Dawbone		Mareton	1	1		
John	Wright		Brickhill BKM	1	1		
John	Bedcott		Layton	1	1		
Francis	Bedcott		Layton	1	1		
Charles	Jones	Gent.	London			1	1
Henry	Franklin		Marston	1	1		

Christian name	Surname	Occupation	Place of abode	Cher.	Har.	Cater	Hill.
Hugh	Birt			1			1
John	Bandy			1	1		
William	Cartwright			1	1		
Thomas	Dickins			1	1		
William	Samuel			1		1	
John	Bayes					1	1
Henry	Sibthorpe					1	1
William	Angier					1	1
William	Rawbow					1	1
Abraham	Bigg					1	1
Thomas	Bigg					1	1
John	Plumer					1	1
Thomas	Prior					1	1
Richard	Cleyton					1	1
Thomas	Bonner			1	1		
Sir John	Chester	Bart	Chicheley BKM	1	1		
Joseph	Wagstaff					1	1
			Luton				
Robert	Creed	Clerk	Lathbury BKM	1	1		
George	Caterall			1	1		
Edward	Broading					1	1
Michael	Headon					1	1
John	Gillam					1	1
Edward	Skittlethorp		Dunstable	1	1		
Francis	How					1	1
John	Kilby					1	1
Henry	Harris	Sen.				1	1
Henry	Harris	Jun.				1	1
John	Punter					1	1
John	Fisher					1	1
Joseph	Jaques					1	1
Thomas	Wingrave					1	1
Thomas	Newsam					1	1
John	Ward			1	1		
Thomas	Day			1	1		
Nathan	Skettlethorp			1	1		
Matthew	Gutteridge					1	1
Joseph	Sheppard					1	1
William	Lawford					1	1
Thomas	Morris			1	1		

Christian name	Surname	Occupation	Place of abode	Candidates voted for			
				Cher.	Har.	Cater	Hill.
Thomas	Sibley			1	1		
John	Newman		St James's Square Westminster			1	1
Henry	Cane			1	1		
John	Silbey			1	1		
Clement	Sheppard			1	1		
Benjamin	Munsey					1	1
Daniel	Brown					1	1
Thomas	Smith		Flamstead HRT			1	1
Francis	Wingate Gent.		Harlington	1	1		
John	Tristram			1		1	
Thomas	Davie					1	1
Edward	Ewer			1	1		
John	Roberds		North Mims	1	1		
Thomas	Ekins		Twyfeild NTH	1	1		
Edward	Collins			1	1		
Thomas	Bigg			1	1		
William	Adkinson		Islington	1	1		
Joseph	Gregory		Poleswalden			1	1
John	Punton					1	1
William	Oakley					1	1
Robert	Chankly					1	
Henry	Roberts			1			
William	Blott			1			
Edward	Snokshill			1	1		
Thomas	Sorrey			1	1		
Thomas	Swaine			1	1		
William	Roffe			1	1		
Edward	Place		London	1	1		
Dennis	Brown			1	1		
Samuel	Symons			1	1		
George	Hawkins					1	1
Thomas	Butterfield			1	1		
Abraham	Neale			1	1		
Thomas	Neale		Cadington	1	1		
John	Custerton			1	1		
Ignoll	Howard		St Albans	1	1		
Thomas	Chapman			1	1		
Jeremiah	Barker			1	1		
William	How			1	1		
Thomas	Breanes			1	1		

Christian name	Surname	Occupation	Place of abode	Cher.	Har.	Cater	Hill.
Richard	Meuse			1	1		
Richard	Harlow			1	1		
Samuel	Chace					1	1
Thomas	Albright			1	1		
Charles	Wright		South Mims	1	1		
Abraham	Chapman			1	1		
Thomas	Cranfield		Elstoe	1	1		
Samuel	Slow			1	1		
Thomas	Oney			1	1		
Thomas	Knight			1	1		
Richard	Hill			1	1		
Henry	Ambrose			1	1		
John	Richards			1	1		
John	Clarke			1	1		
Thomas	Mersom	Sen.				1	1
Richard	Circuit					1	1
Nathaniel	Mersom					1	1
Joseph	Birt			1	1		
Alexander	Froglins		Wellin HRT	1	1		
Thomas	Ellingham		Stanbridge	1	1		
Francis	Hopkins					1	1
Thomas	Mersom					1	1
Edward	Winch		Silsoe			1	1
Thomas	Cheney			1	1		
Samuel	Marston					1	1
Robert	Oakley			1	1		
William	Chapman			1	1		
Sir Theophilus	Nappier	Bart.		1	1		
Thomas	Seabrooke		Wilston HRT	1	1		
John	Sherlock			1	1		
Thomas	Smith		St Pauls Covent Garden LND			1	1
William	Underwood			1	1		
Thomas	Bigg		Laurence end HRT			1	1
John	Taylor			1	1		
Robert	Keine			1	1		
Christopher	Eaton	Clerk		1	1		
John	Davis					1	1
John	Davis	Sen.		1	1		
William	Cotton		Billington	1	1		
William	Olney					1	1

Christian name	Surname	Occupation	Place of abode	Cher.	Har.	Cater	Hill.
James	Freeman			1	1		
Richard	Thrussell			1	1		
Jeremy	Oakeley					1	1
Joseph	Adams		Lilley			1	1
John	Cross		Hexton HRT	1	1		
William	Hyorn		Wellingborow			1	1
John	Richards			1	1		
Daniel	Goldsmith			1	1		
John	Prudden			1	1		
Jonathan	Cox			1	1		
Samuel	Cox			1	1		
Robert	Bauldrey					1	1
Sir Joseph	Lawrence		Bishopsgate Street LND	1	1		
Edward	Lawrence		Ware	1	1		
Samuel	Chalton		Harrold			1	1
Archibald	Napier					1	1
Isaac	Cranfield					1	1
Henry	Chapman					1	1
John	Hill					1	1
James	Marshall		Harding HRT			1	1
Joshua	Ironmonger		Ratcliffe Cross LND			1	1
Whitby	Isham		Barnet	1	1		
James	Merlin		Hunsdon HRT			1	1
Edward	Greene					1	1
James	Crawley			1	1		
John	Edwards					1	1
Michael	Coleman					1	1
John	Crawley		St Mary Aix LND			1	1
Anthony	Etherick	Esq.	St Margarots Westmister			1	1
Francis	Stone					1	1
George	Topping		Barkhamstead			1	1
Abraham	Life		Cheston HRT			1	1
Henry	Monke		Biggleswade			1	1
William	Olney					1	1
John	Webb					1	1
Richard	Bigg	Gent.	Kings Walden HRT			1	1
			Marketstreet				
Thomas	Hugnal		Water end HRT	1	1		

Christian name	Surname	Occupation	Place of abode	Candidates voted for			
				Cher.	Har.	Cater	Hill.
Charles	Wright		Chellington	1	1		
Edward	Bridon					1	1
William	Mayles			1	1		
Thomas	Seer			1	1		
William	Barr			1	1		
William	Varney			1	1		
Robert	Prior		Nailsworth CAM	1	1		
John	Cock		Chellington	1	1		
John	Alberry		Alberry HRT			1	1
John	Hedges		Tharcutt Hadley		1	1	
			Marston				
John	Richardson		Ampthill CAM [sic]	1	1		
Thomas	Bird	Gent.	Perkenhall	1	1		
John	Denbigh		Ridgmont	1		1	
Edward	Sumerlin		Wootton			1	1
Thomas	Warburton		Harding	1	1		
William	Wheeler					1	1
Thomas	Woodcraft			1	1		
Thomas	Beckerfield		Leighton	1	1		
Stephen	Taylor			1	1		
John	Day			1	1		
John	Betsworth			1		1	
Thomas	Baker			1	1		
Thomas	Lane		Bletley BKM	1	1		
John	Richardson			1	1		
Francis	Buss			1	1		
John	Fowler			1	1		
Samuel	Wheeler			1	1		
William	Crouch			1	1		
John	Hobbs			1	1		
Robert	Roe			1	1		
Edward	Snagg	Esq.	Ampthill	1	1		
William	Pearce			1	1		
Samuel	Hall		Rushden NTH	1	1		
Thomas	Pearce			1		1	
John	Impey		Great St Bartholomews LND	1	1		
Mathew	Snagg		Braughton HRT	1	1		
William	Marston		Hempstead			1	1
George	Baker		Ridgmont	1	1		
Esdras	Marshall		Hitchin	1	1		

Christian name	Surname	Occupation	Place of abode	Cher.	Har.	Cater	Hill.
Jeremy	Bosworth		Ampthill	1	1		
John	Tuffnaile		Elstow			1	1
William	Atwell		Eggington	1			1
John	Wilcocks					1	1
Moses	St. Eloy	Clerk				1	1
William	Smith	Gent.	Astwood			1	1
John	Sugars		Goldington	1			1
Thomas	Ablethite			1	1		
			Maulden				
Henry	Ward					1	1
William	Astrey					1	1
John	Webb					1	1
William	Jennings					1	1
Thomas	Feild					1	1
John	Jennings					1	1
John	Charles					1	1
John	Betts	Sen.		1	1		
Ralph	Kilby			1	1		
John	Rentham			1	1		
William	Betts		Maulden	1	1		
Edward	Randal			1	1		
Matthais	Tompkin			1	1		
Henry	Bennet		Ampthill	1	1		
John	Wardell			1	1		
Thomas	Underwood			1	1		
William	Pedder		Ampthill	1	1		
George	Winwright			1	1		
John	Quait			1	1		
Robert	Read			1	1		
William	Crouch		London	1	1		
Richard	Allen	Clerk		1	1		
William	Bowden		Ampthill	1	1		
Richard	Woodsey			1	1		
Ebenezer	Chandler		Bedford			1	1
Lancelot	Clerk		St Alhallows LND			1	1
George	Bonskill			1	1		
Matthew	Linford			1			1
Francis	Child			1	1		
John	Hill	Sen.		1	1		
John	Hill	Jun.		1	1		

Christian name	Surname	Occupation	Place of abode	Cher.	Har.	Cater	Hill.
Melchburne							
John	Bass			1	1		
Meppershall							
Towers	Ashcroft	Clerk	Bedford	1	1		
William	Blundell			1	1		
Thomas	Wilshier			1	1		
Robert	Goodal		Howell LIN	1	1		
Robert	Chamberlin		Stamford LIN	1	1		
William	Giddins		Shefford			1	1
Milbrooke							
Francis	Circuit			1	1		
Robert	Scarborow			1	1		
Thomas	Huckle					1	1
Henry	Hardacre	Clerk		1	1		
William	Brace			1	1		
John	Huckle			1	1		
William	Fisher					1	1
Charles	Richards		Ampthill	1	1		
Thomas	Hunt		Litlington			1	1
John	Fountaine			1	1		
Richard	Peach			1	1		
John	Liceman		Southwarke			1	1
Milton Byrant							
Joseph	Johnson	Esq.		1	1		
William	Livesay			1	1		
Edward	Gibbs			1			1
Edward	Herbert					1	1
Francis	Smith					1	1
John	Impey		Bulloxhill			1	1
Edward	Higgs			1	1		
William	Staire		Layton	1	1		
John	Waters		Tuddington	1	1		
Joseph	Clements		Layton			1	1
Francis	Wheeler		Batlesden	1			
William	Capell			1			
William	Harris			1			
Henry	Collins		Battlesden	1			
William	Turner		Wooburn	1			1

Christian name	Surname	Occupation	Place of abode	Candidates voted for			
				Cher.	Har.	Cater	Hill.
George	Monke			1			1
William	Fossey		Luton			1	1
John	Harbert		Tuddington			1	1
Francis	Cooke	Sen.				1	1
Francis	Cooke	Jun.				1	1
William	Ashby					1	1
			Milton Ernys				
John	Crutchly		Warden	1	1		
Oliver	Dix			1	1		
John	Parrat				1		
John	Adington			1	1		
John	Lawkins	Clerk		1	1		
John	Morgan			1	1		
William	Benton		Radwell			1	1
William	Gee		Huntingdon			1	1
			Mogerhanger				
Joseph	Adams		Buckbrooke NTH			1	1
Simon	Sperry					1	1
			Northill				
Isaac	Thomas		Tempsford			1	1
John	Carter				1		
George	Mordant			1	1		
Thomas	Walker		Sandy	1	1		
Joseph	Baker		Warden	1	1		
John	Mordant	Sen.	Caldecott	1	1		
Richard	Audley Briton		Sandy	1	1		
Edward	Rose			1	1		
Thomas	Day		Warden	1	1		
Richard	Stacey		Sandy	1	1		
Thomas	Tompion			1	1		
Richard	Barr			1	1		
John	Mordant	Jun.		1	1		
Thomas	Huns			1	1		
John	Atterton			1	1		
Samuel	Bull		Bedford	1	1		
Edward	Woodward		St. Pauls Church Yard	1	1		
John	Mordant			1	1		

Christian name	Surname	Occupation	Place of abode	Cher.	Har.	Cater	Hill.
Thomas	Wells		Tempsford	1	1		
Charles	Amey		Balsam CAM			1	1
Thomas	Croote		Renhold			1	1
Owen Thomas	Bromsall	Esq.				1	1
Humphry	Fish	Esq.				1	1
Capel	Barrow	Clerk		1	1		
Richard	Titford		Willington			1	1
John	Greene					1	1
James	Jennings					1	1
John	Hitchcock					1	1
Simon	Kitman					1	1
James	Day		Warden	1	1		

Oakley

Christian name	Surname	Occupation	Place of abode	Cher.	Har.	Cater	Hill.
Giles	Smith			1	1		
Giles	Smith		Kempston			1	1
John	Stoakes					1	1
Symon	Gale					1	1
Joseph	Phillips		Bromham			1	1
John	Pennington	Gent.	Bedford	1	1		
Robert	Stoakes		Clapham			1	1
William	Paine		Steventon			1	1
Richard	Knight					1	1
John	Cumberland					1	1
Joseph	Cooke		Spaldwick HUN			1	
Richard	Dickson				1		1
John	Harley			1	1		
Thomas	Harvey			1	1		
William	Wood			1	1		
Thomas	Smith					1	1

Odel

Christian name	Surname	Occupation	Place of abode	Cher.	Har.	Cater	Hill.
Thomas	Elmer					1	1
Sir Rowland	Alston	Bart.				1	1
Vere John	Alston	Clerke				1	1
Laurence	Cumberland					1	1
William	Matthews					1	1
Thomas	Halfehead					1	1
Thomas	Matthews					1	1

Pavenham

Christian name	Surname	Occupation	Place of abode	Cher.	Har.	Cater	Hill.
Thomas	Knight			1	1		

Christian name	Surname	Occupation	Place of abode	Cher.	Har.	Cater	Hill.
William	Goodman		Wellingborough	1	1		
Thomas	Crane			1	1		
Henry	Bull		Burton Latimore NTH	1	1		
Robert	Tole			1	1		
William	Rawlins			1	1		
Robert	Clare					1	1
Thomas	Clare					1	1
John	Spencer					1	1
William	Lambert					1	1
Thomas	Hipwell					1	1
Thomas	Cooch		Fensham			1	1
Richard	Lambert					1	1
William	Morris					1	1
			Potsgrave				
John	Peel		Soulbury BKM			1	1
Edward	Botsford					1	1
			Pertenhall				
John	Meanly		Bolnhurst				1
John	King	D.D	Chelsea	1	1		
Robert	Paradine	Clerk		1	1		
Edward	Warner		There and Keyso	1	1		
William	Gilbert		Peterborow	1	1		
Thomas	Arnold		Kimbolton			1	1
Edward	Rolt	Esq.	Sachum HRT	1	1		
John	Ibbott			1	1		
Robert	Wright		Kimbolton			1	1
Thomas	Pentloe		Kimbolton			1	1
William	Watson		Cambridge			1	1
Thomas	Hunt					1	1
Charles	Gisby		Kimbolton			1	1
John	King		Kimbolton			1	1
Samuel	Brown		Woodford NTH	1	1		
Simon	Bass					1	1
			Potton				
John	Langham					1	1
Edward	Rolt					1	1
Richard	Thorne			1	1		
John	Smith			1	1		

Christian name	Surname	Occupation	Place of abode	Cher.	Har.	Cater	Hill.
Thomas	Augier			1	1		
Thomas	Millard			1	1		
Richard	Malden				1		
William	Bushby		London	1	1		
John	Pedley			1	1		
Thomas	Ward			1	1		
George	Ridgley			1	1		
Thomas	Haukin			1	1		
John	Adkins			1	1		
George	Pedley			1	1		
William	Coke			1	1		
Robert	Burges			1	1		
Nathaniel	Philip		Hatfield	1	1		
John	Raymond			1	1		
Robert	Smith		London	1	1		
George	Whiskin			1	1		
James	Smith		London	1	1		
William	Beech					1	1
John	Carrier					1	1
Abraham	Kirby			1	1		
Nicholas	Phipp					1	1
Richard	Austin					1	1
John	Phipp					1	1
John	Bunburry					1	1
			Puddington				
Richard	Marshall		Hinwick			1	1
Adam	Sturges					1	1
William	Bamford	Clerk				1	1
Henry	Wagstaffe		Newport			1	1
Richard	Wagstaffe					1	1
William	Seers					1	1
Richard	Orlebar	Esq.				1	1
			Purton				
William	Hobbs		Stevenly		1	1	
			Pulloxhill				
John	Goldsmith		Thames Street LND			1	1
John James	Le Port	Clerk	Silsoe			1	1
Peter	Burges					1	1
Thomas	Vincent		Bedford			1	1

Christian name	Surname	Occupation	Place of abode	Candidates voted for			
				Cher.	Har.	Cater	Hill.
Henry	Flecken			1	1		
Thomas	Osborne		Offley HRT			1	1
Charles	Nichols	Esq.	Hitchin	1	1		
Edward	Bishop			1	1		
John	Rants		Newport	1	1		
William	Smith					1	1
Thomas	Hollis		Trinty Minoryes			1	1
George	Chalkley		Polewald HRT			1	1
Thomas	Crouch		Clifton			1	1
John	Gamble					1	1
Benjamin	Bishop					1	1
William	Sheppard		Astyberry			1	1
Bernard	Halfepenny	Esq.	Enfield MDX	1	1		
John	Ravensden		Warden		1		1
			Radwell				
Robert	Rogers		Kettering NTH			1	1
Theophilus	Rogers		Northampton			1	1
Oliver	Rands	Gent.				1	1
John	Tapp					1	1
John	Mulsoe					1	1
Robert	Norman					1	1
			Ravensden				
Joseph	Watford					1	1
Joseph	Wagstaffe	Esq.	Sharnbrooke			1	1
Thomas	Watford		Knotting	1	1		
Richard	Seely					1	1
Robert	Podmore		Bishopsgate Street	1	1		
Samuel	Levitt		St Olives Southwarke	1	1		
Thomas	Tulley	Esq.	Westminster			1	1
			Renhold				
Joseph	Hookham			1	1		
William	Beecher	Esq.				1	1
			Ridgmont				
Thomas	Cooke	Sen.				1	1
William	Ellord		Meppershall		1	1	
Richard	Whitebread					1	1
Richard	Cooke				1		
John	Knight				1		1

Christian name	Surname	Occupation	Place of abode	Cher.	Har.	Cater	Hill.
John	Clarke		Hackney			1	1
Richard	Newman			1	1		
Nicholas	Maschall			1	1		
John	Austin					1	1
Thomas	Hollingworth			1	1		
Francis	Low	Esq.	Grays Inne	1	1		
William	Bidsey					1	1
Thomas	Robins					1	1
Thomas	Kent					1	1
John	Mastall			1	1		
Henry	Maulden					1	1
William	Buttler					1	1
Robert	Morrison	Sen.				1	1
Robert	Burnett		Spittlefeild LND			1	1
Thomas	Cooke					1	1
Richard	Colly		Clophill	1	1		
			Risely				
Richard	Sansome		Biggleswade			1	1
John	Benfeild					1	1
William	Camberlaine					1	1
John	Sellby					1	1
John	James					1	1
John	Wildman					1	1
Robert	Crofts		Bedford	1	1		
Joseph	Barringer		Earlsey	1	1		
Robert	Rootham		Great Barford	1	1		
William	Underwood		Wellingbrough	1	1		
Richard	Flint			1	1		
Nathaniel	Rowlett		Kimbolton	1	1		
William	Tisam		London	1	1		
William	Woodham		Arington NTH	1	1		
Francis	Gray			1	1		
John	Risely		Bletsoe	1	1		
Edward	Litchfeild			1	1		
William	Sheppard	Gent.	London	1	1		
William	Feild		Mongrave HRT	1	1		
Thomas	Bletsoe	Esq.	Oxford	1	1		
John	Peacock			1	1		
William	Woodward			1	1		
Thomas	Rootham			1	1		

Christian name	Surname	Occupation	Place of abode	Cher.	Har.	Cater	Hill.
Francis	Lee		Tilbrooke	1	1		
Thomas	Bourn			1	1		
Thomas	Gale			1	1		
John	Woodward			1	1		
Edward	Litchfeild			1	1		
John	Allen			1	1		
George	Snagge		Maulden	1	1		
Thomas	Elliott			1	1		
John	Harding	Clerk		1	1		
John	Love					1	1
Thomas	Dawson					1	1
John	Henson		Swinshead			1	1
Thomas	Searle		Tedworth HUN			1	1
			Roxton				
Isaac	Clark		Colmworth			1	1
William	Aspland					1	1
Richard	Thorowgood		Cople	1	1		
Lancelot	Luke		Blunham	1	1		
Samuel	Luke		Potton	1	1		
John	Carelesse		Gamlingay	1	1		
Robert	Child			1	1		
John	Barnett			1	1		
Richard	Keyford			1	1		
Thomas	Cartwright			1	1		
John	Reuse	Clerk			1		
Thomas	Kippest		Wilden		1		1
Thomas	Child					1	1
Thomas	Robinson					1	1
Thomas	Day					1	1
William	Andrews	Sen.	St Bennets Pauls Wharfe	1	1		
John	Scarborow		Great Straughton			1	1
			Sandy				
John	Richardson					1	1
Robert	Whitefeild			1	1		
Nicolas	Cole		Gamlingay	1	1		
William	Ghitefeild			1			
John	Webb		St Neots	1	1		
James	Deane		Potton	1	1		
George	Cooke		Tempsford	1	1		

Christian name	Surname	Occupation	Place of abode	Cher.	Har.	Cater	Hill.
William	Christmas			1	1		
Baron	Brittaine			1	1		
John	Ayres			1	1		
John	Stevens			1	1		
Richard	Vintner			1	1		
William	Walker			1	1		
John	Rolt		Great Barford	1	1		
Robert	Fennell			1	1		
John	Cupis			1	1		
John	Underwood			1	1		
David	Sutton			1	1		
John	Brittaine			1	1		
John	Tilcock			1	1		
Henry	Atkins				1		
Jonathan	Hooker	Clerk		1	1		
William	Radwell			1	1		
William	Underwood			1	1		
Richard	Richardson	Sen.		1	1		
Richard	Richardson	Jun.		1	1		
William	Tingey				1		
Richard	Carter			1	1		
John	Cage				1		
William	Banes			1	1		
Joseph	Keech			1	1		
William	Halfhide		Northill	1	1		
Thomas	Mayes			1	1		
John	Sutton		Southill	1	1		
John	Skilleter			1	1		
Samuel	Sutton			1	1		
John	Lambys		Narboise, HUN		1		
Lewis	Monox	Esq.				1	1
Richard	Britaine				1	1	
John	Langley					1	1
John	Hurt					1	1
Robert	Garner				1	1	
George	Mayes				1	1	
John	Adkins			1	1		
William	Pipp		Norton HRT	1	1		
John	Austin		Hertford	1	1		
Thomas	Vintner					1	1
John	Richardson			1	1		

Christian name	Surname	Occupation	Place of abode	Candidates voted for			
				Cher.	Har.	Cater	Hill.
Thomas	Glover			1	1		
Edward	Biller		Kimbolton			1	1
Thomas	Richardson			1	1		
John	Asher		Coventry	1	1		
William	Asher		Coventry	1	1		
John	Bishop					1	1
Richard	Bishop				1		
Thomas	Skilleter	Sen.				1	1
Robert	Robinson		Willington			1	1
William	Bromsall		Bedford			1	1
			Salford				
John	Field			1	1		
William	Lovell			1	1		
Ambrose	Reddall			1	1		
William	Phillips			1	1		
			Straton				
Sir John	Cotton	Bart.		1	1		
			Stanbrooke [Sharnbrook]				
John	Ellion					1	1
Joseph	Roberts		Carlton			1	1
William	Wiles					1	1
John	Aspin	Esquire				1	1
Thomas	Erne		Bletsoe	1	1		
Joseph	Godfrey	Gent.		1	1		
Thomas	Sheffeild					1	1
Thomas	Hayes		Radwell			1	1
William	Phillipps			1	1		
William	Campton		Rushden	1	1		
George	Alsopp			1	1		
William	Wadmough		Renhold			1	1
John	Hipwell				1		1
William	Jordan		St Baddlesall Foster Lane			1	1
John	Belton	Clerk				1	1
Richard	Reech					1	1
William	Risely					1	1
Thomas	Browne		Tower-Street LND			1	1
Joshua	Browne					1	1
Aaron	Harper					1	1

Christian name	Surname	Occupation	Place of abode	Cher.	Har.	Cater	Hill.
John	Jaques					1	1
Thomas	Scrivener					1	1
Israel	Willimote					1	1
Philip	Norman					1	1
Thomas	Savage					1	1
William	Bayes					1	1
Robert	Riseley		Bedford			1	1
			Shefford				
Francis	Whitebread			1	1		
Francis	Wells			1	1		
John	Dow			1	1		
John	Willows			1	1		
William	Walsome		Patten	1	1		
William	Pateman			1	1		
Matthew	Greene			1	1		
John	Austin			1	1		
William	Towers		London	1	1		
John	Norris				1		
Thomas	Palmer			1	1		
Samuel	Peinton			1	1		
George	Fennel			1	1		
Henry	Bonner		Wilshamstead	1	1		
Thomas	Seaward		Newport	1	1		
George	Chapman			1	1		
Daniel	Pointon				1		1
Thomas	Samin					1	1
Wendover	Benboe		Tinewich BKM			1	1
			Sharpenhall				
George	Feilder		London	1	1		
Thomas	Corey					1	1
			Shelton				
Nathaniel	Mason		Queenbith LND			1	1
Thomas	Corey					1	1
			Shitlington				
Robert	Prior		Trinity College Cambridge	1	1		
Grey	Longville	Esq.				1	1
John	Elliot		Hexton HRT		1		

Christian name	Surname	Occupation	Place of abode	Cher.	Har.	Cater	Hill.
Henry	Coleman			1	1		
John	Hanscombe		Cambridge			1	
Robert	Pryor		Cambridge	1	1		
Thomas	Adkins			1	1		
John	Trussel			1	1		
William	Griggs		Standon	1	1		
Abraham	Burrows		London	1	1		
Robert	Pryor		Cambridge	1	1		
Thomas	Coleman			1	1		
Samuel	Brawne			1	1		
Thomas	Ashton			1	1		
Mathew	Lacey			1	1		
Daniel	Carter			1	1		
Rodert	Field		Meppershall		1		
Henry	Whitebread			1	1		
Thomas	Costin		Wilshamstead	1	1		
Thomas	Rust			1	1		
John	Ireland		Hitchin			1	1
Robert	Pryor		Cambridge	1	1		
Thomas	Joyce		Hitchin	1	1		
Edward	Jennings		Redbourn HRT	1	1		
James	Crouch			1	1		
John	Burrows			1	1		
George	Fowler					1	1
Thomas	Elmer		Offley		1	1	
Richard	Pearce		Ickleford			1	1
Edward	Tapster		Barton			1	1
Joseph	Honour				1	1	
John	Hanscombe		Purton		1	1	
Richard	Sheppard	Esq.	Hitchin			1	1
Heylock	Kingsley	Esq.	Hitchin	1	1		
John	Hinton					1	1
Edward	Brittaine		Southill			1	1
William	Ceely		Kimpton HRT			1	1
			Silsoe				
Henry	Godfrey					1	1
John	Grubb		Hartingfordbury HRT			1	1
William	Fowler		Meppershall		1	1	
Henry	Gwynn		Biggleswade	1	1		
Thomas	Caton					1	1

Christian name	Surname	Occupation	Place of abode	Cher.	Har.	Cater	Hill.
Thomas	Giddins					1	1
Thomas	Bishop					1	1
William	White					1	1
John	Allen	Jun.				1	1
Thomas	Sanim					1	1
Charles	Millway					1	1
John	Gwynn					1	1
			Souldrop				
John	Hanger			1	1		
John	Richards			1	1		
Joseph	Eden			1	1		
			Southill				
George	Inskipp					1	1
George	Nodes	Gent.		1	1		
Thomas	Hawkins			1	1		
John	Barber			1	1		
Roger	Layton			1	1		
Thomas	Hawkins			1	1		
Thomas	Collop			1	1		
Philip	Randall			1	1		
Thomas	Inskipp		Ramerick HRT	1	1		
Samuel	Parker		London	1	1		
Thomas	Feild		Bedford	1	1		
Thomas	Alborne			1	1		
Edward	Hurst			1	1		
Nathaniel	Tayler			1	1		
James	Wilson			1	1		
John	Sole			1	1		
Thomas	Fage			1	1		
John	Carrington		Broome	1	1		
Nicholas	Osborne			1	1		
William	Randall			1	1		
Edward	Jefferson			1	1		
John	Kilby		Ickleford			1	1
Samuel	Bedford	Clerk			1		1
John	Cole		Shefford	1	1		
Robert	Osborne		Hawnes	1	1		
Thomas	Lenton					1	1
John	Glinster		Risden HRT	1	1		
Thomas	Finch				1		1

Christian name	Surname	Occupation	Place of abode	Candidates voted for			
				Cher.	Har.	Cater	Hill.
Sir George	Bing					1	1
Thomas	Usher			1	1		
Thomas	Hawkins				1		1
John	Abbot			1	1		
George	Inskipp			1	1		
Thomas	Dilly					1	1
John	Harrewden					1	1
			Stachden				
Thomas	Neman					1	1
Samuel	Noble		Olney BKM			1	1
Edward	Adams			1	1		
Benjamin	Rogers	Clerke	Bedford	1	1		
John	Thurlow Brace		Ashtwood			1	1
Francis	Hoyle			1	1		
James	Allen					1	1
			Stanbridge				
John	Emerton			1	1		
John	Andrew		Harpenden HRT	1	1		
Ralph	Baldwin		Ashwell	1	1		
Richard	Whynot			1	1		
Henry	Barnes					1	1
Edward	Cooper			1	1		
Richard	Cooper		Chalton			1	1
Henry	Honour			1	1		
John	Knoxhill					1	1
John	Allen			1	1		
John	Goodspeed			1	1		
Thomas	Stanbridge					1	1
Thomas	Tearle		Hockcliff	1	1		
John	Impey			1	1		
Giles	Gifford					1	1
Richard	Prentice		South Mims			1	1
William	Gold		Hockliffe			1	1
			Stanford				
Thomas	Baldwin		Ashwell	1	1		
Thomas	Usher			1	1		
Joseph	Randal			1	1		
Francis	Hoddel		Calderot	1	1		

Christian name	Surname	Occupation	Place of abode	Cher.	Har.	Cater	Hill.
John	Layton		Hawnes	1	1		
Thomas	Inskipp					1	1
			Steppingley				
John	Farmer			1			1
John	Matthews			1	1		
Matthew	Dutton					1	1
John	Farrow		Flitwick	1	1		
William	Emerton			1			1
Maurice	Abbot	Esq.				1	1
Robert	Jones					1	1
Thomas	Hudson					1	1
Mathew	Dutton		Buckingham			1	1
			Stevington				
Thomas	Cox		Stagsden			1	1
Thomas	Lawrence					1	1
Jonathan	Skevington		Turvey	1	1		
Lewis	Pake		Bromham	1			
George	Fern	Clerke		1	1		
William	Falde	Gent.	Bedford	1	1		
			Stondon				
Joseph	Tompson		Hitchin			1	1
Samuel	Leach	Clerk		1	1		
James	Bazely			1	1		
John	Lilly		Dunstable	1	1		
Matthew	Lawrence		Dunstable	1	1		
John	Meager					1	1
			Stopeley				
John	Piggot		Sundon	1	1		
Francis	Turner		London	1	1		
Francis	Young					1	1
Francis	Piggot			1	1		
John	Stone					1	1
			Stoefold				
Henry	Rumbold					1	1
Edward	Berry			1	1		
Matthew	Bennet					1	1
Joseph	Frost		Kettering	1	1		
Edmond	Crouch			1	1		

Christian name	Surname	Occupation	Place of abode	Candidates voted for			
				Cher.	Har.	Cater	Hill.
John	Plumer		Shittington	1	1		
Nicholas	Reynolds			1	1		
Benjamin	Harris			1	1		
Abraham	Taylor			1	1		
Thomas	Cox			1	1		
John	Wright			1	1		
William	Gore			1	1		
John	Cooper			1	1		
Henry	Squire					1	1
John	Heath		Hitchin			1	1
Miles	Freeman					1	1
John	Ford					1	1
William	Kichener					1	1
John	Bennet					1	1
William	Bennet					1	1
William	Lytton	Esq.	Knebworth HRT	1	1		
John	Bouchier		Enfeild MDX			1	1
Thomas	Taylor					1	1
Charles	Stevens					1	1
Edward	Purton					1	1
			Staughton parva				
Owen	Goodchild			1	1		
William	King		Southoe HUN	1	1		
Henry	Fell			1	1		
Robert	Worrall			1	1		
Thomas	Smith			1	1		
John	Dennis					1	1
John	Barrell		Bushmead			1	1
Thomas	Haynes					1	1
Thomas	Crow					1	1
Thomas	Paine		St Neots			1	1
John	Woodhouse	Esq.	Barkhamstead HRT	1	1		
John	Freeman		Spaldwick HUN			1	1
			Stretley				
Thomas	Spriggins					1	1
William	Bur		Harlington	1	1		
Richard	Langley		Sundon	1	1		
James	Smith			1	1		
Francis	Ausell			1	1		

Christian name	Surname	Occupation	Place of abode	Cher.	Har.	Cater	Hill.
				Candidates voted for			
Thomas	Spriggins			1	1		
Lawrence	Smith			1	1		
John	Biscoe		St Georges Puttolphs Lane	1	1		
Hugh	Smith			1	1		
Walter	Ryon	Esq.	Essex	1	1		
James	Byss		Hartingford Berry	1	1		
Richard	Roe					1	1
Thomas	Evans		Barton			1	1
			Studham				
William	Barnes			1	1		
Edward	Waterton			1	1		
Thomas	Gladman			1	1		
Daniel	Puttenham		Ivinghoe BKM	1	1		
William	Church			1	1		
John	Traverse		Kings Langley	1	1		
Thomas	Trott		Hempstead	1	1		
John	Halsey		Redbourne HRT	1	1		
Edward	Marriot					1	1
Adrian	Martin			1	1		
Richard	Messider			1	1		
Richard	Halsey			1	1		
			Sundon and Sutton				
John	King			1	1		
Abraham	Saunders					1	1
Richard	Carter					1	1
William	Randall					1	1
John	Robinson			1	1		
Matthew	Watts			1	1		
William	Crawley					1	1
John	Ashby			1	1		
Thomas	Gregory			1	1		
James	Smith			1	1		
Roger	Dawson			1	1		
Thomas	Samm			1	1		
Thomas	Cheney	Esq.		1	1		
John	Groome			1	1		
Richard	Halsey			1	1		
Thomas	Tuffin		Wendover BKM			1	1

Christian name	Surname	Occupation	Place of abode	Candidates voted for			
				Cher.	Har.	Cater	Hill.
Lawrence	Leach		St James Westminster	1	1		
John	Tennant			1	1		
John	Wester					1	1
John	Bide	Esq.	Hemstead HRT			1	1
John	Odgar	Gent.	Curricott HRT			1	1
Edward	Buckingham		Ridge HRT			1	1
			Tempsford				
Thomas	Howen		Bedford			1	1
William	Bishop		Blunham, there, and Sandy		1	1	
James	Randall		Tadlow	1	1		
Christopher	Eyre		Ashton HRT	1	1		
Francis	Merriweather		Everton		1		
Robert	Hawkins	Clerk	Goldington	1	1		
William	Day					1	1
Richard	Hatley		London	1	1		
John	Denn				1		1
Henry	Wallis			1	1		
George	May			1	1		
Gerrard	Awdley		Gamlinegay			1	1
John	Wood				1	1	
John	Whiston			1	1		
Richard	Stewart			1	1		
			Tebworth				
John	Olney					1	1
Daniel	Parrat		Layton	1	1		
George	Drinkwater			1			1
Henry	Osborne			1	1		
George	Shaw			1	1		
			Thorncott				
William	Ravens					1	1
			Thurleigh				
Henry	Empson					1	
Samuel	Dudley	Clerk	Bryars Hardwick WAR			1	1
Joseph	Mann		Brumham			1	1
John	Gale		London			1	1
William	Erle		Wilden		1		

Christian name	Surname	Occupation	Place of abode	Cher.	Har.	Cater	Hill.
Charles	Watford				1		1
Christopher	Dixon	D.D	Church-Prampton NTH	1	1		
Thomas	Walker		Ravensden		1		1
James	Erne		Ravensden			1	1
John	Powers	Clerk		1	1		
John	Savage			1	1		
Joseph	Easton			1	1		
Henry	Cooper			1		1	
John	Bodington					1	1
Peter	Gregory					1	1
Daniel	Erne					1	1
John	Watford		Layton Stone HUN			1	1
John	Hervey	Esq.	Bedford			1	1
Richard	Parker					1	1
Robert	Ashurst	Esq.	Distaffe Lane LND			1	1
Ephraim	White		St. Ives			1	1
			Tilbrooke				
John	Putterill					1	1
John	Day					1	1
John	Law					1	1
William	Smith		Cavington HUN and Dean			1	1
William	Foster	Clerk		1	1		
Thomas	Allen		Deane			1	1
Thomas	Sheppard					1	1
Thomas	Sheppard		Kimbolton			1	1
			Tillsworth				
John	Ball			1	1		
John	Prentice			1	1		
Abell	Haddis			1	1		
			Tingey				
Thomas	May					1	1
John	Norman		Ingosfield LIN	1	1		
Richard	Lawson		Steppingly			1	1
			Tottenhoe				
John	Ginger					1	1
Thomas	Diez					1	1
Henry	Herbert		Tillsworth			1	1

Christian name	Surname	Occupation	Place of abode	Candidates voted for			
				Cher.	Har.	Cater	Hill.
Daniel	Groome		Hornsey MDX	1	1		
Robert	Hasle		St Albans			1	1
Thomas	Martin			1			1
Richard	Gadburry		Dunstable			1	1
Michael	Mouse			1	1		
John	Robins					1	1
Thomas	Martin	Jun.				1	1
Thomas	Hensman			1	1		
Henry	Hobbe		Purton			1	1
Thomas	Samus		Watford	1	1		
Joseph	Viez					1	1
Joseph	Mouse					1	1
Gabriel	Knophill			1	1		
William	Sherriffe			1	1		
Robert	Ironmonger			1	1		
Thomas	Scrivener			1	1		
William	Fowler			1	1		
Samuel	Bryerlegg					1	1
John	Dodd					1	1
Thomas	Tompkins					1	1
John	Gladburry		Kibsworth HRT	1	1		
John	Branklin			1	1		
Thomas	Pratt					1	1
John	Underwood					1	1
William	Collins					1	1
John	Festen		Kingsworth HRT	1	1		
Thomas	Berkley					1	1
Thomas	Vize					1	1
Henry	Whitehead					1	1
Robert	Tompkins			1	1		
Grandsund	Smith		Kingsworth HRT	1	1		
Matthew	Mead		St Magnes LND			1	1
John	Myers		Higham Gobion			1	1
			Tuddington				
John	Gurney		Cranfeild	1		1	
Thomas	Burr		Houghton Regis			1	1
Thomas	Goldsmith	Sen.				1	1
Thomas	Goldsmith	Jun.				1	1
William	Stevens			1	1		
John	Lord	Clerk		1	1		

Christian name	Surname	Occupation	Place of abode	Cher.	Har.	Cater	Hill.
Joseph	Potts					1	1
Thomas	Harris					1	1
Edward	Fisher					1	1
George	Catheral		Luton	1		1	
Thomas	Bull					1	1
John	Strange			1		1	
Richard	Souldiar		Hempstead	1	1		
Henry	Bowles		Watford	1	1		
William	Godfrey		Harlington	1	1		
Matthew	Bishop			1	1		
Jonas	Porter			1	1		
George	Winwright			1	1		
Bernhard	Stannyfoot			1	1		
Jonathan	Norris			1	1		
Richard	Pufford			1	1		
Francis	Pufford			1	1		
George	Pufford			1	1		
Hugh	Cook			1	1		
Thomas	Potts			1	1		
James	Stone		Layton	1	1		
George	Shaw			1	1		
Thomas	Roe			1	1		
Andrew	Cross		Clerkenwell	1	1		
George	Sutton			1	1		
Thomas	Odell		Dunstable	1	1		
John	Harris					1	1
Christopher	Bennell					1	1

Turvey

Christian name	Surname	Occupation	Place of abode	Cher.	Har.	Cater	Hill.
John	Skevington			1	1		
Robert	Bodington		Carlton			1	1
William	Friend	Clerk	East Burnham BKM	1	1		
John	Bodington			1	1		
Thomas	Bull			1	1		
Lewis	Tisoe					1	1
John	Skevington		Stagsden	1	1		
William	Skevington					1	1

Warden

Christian name	Surname	Occupation	Place of abode	Cher.	Har.	Cater	Hill.
Sir Samuel	Ongley			1	1		
William	Smith	Esq.				1	1

Christian name	Surname	Occupation	Place of abode	Candidates voted for			
				Cher.	Har.	Cater	Hill.
John	Mackdowell	Esq.		1	1		
William	Palmer	Esq.	Ladbrook WAR	1	1		
			Westoning				
Abraham	Dix			1	1		
Richard	Bosgrave		Holborn	1	1		
George	Barber		Bednal Green MDX	1	1		
Thomas	Cox		Hornsey MDX	1	1		
Edward	Burr			1	1		
Henry	Vaux			1	1		
Daniel	Woodward			1	1		
William	Olney			1	1		
Richard	Mebcroft			1	1		
Nicholas	Martin		Poleswarden HRT			1	1
William	Feild		Ampthill	1	1		
Thomas	Backhurst		Harlington	1			1
Thomas	Sheppard		Brumham			1	1
			Whipsnade				
Ralph	Mason			1	1		
John	Clark	Clerk		1			
William	Jarman	Gent.	Gaddesden HRT	1	1		
John	Vaux	Esq.		1	1		
			Willington				
			Wilden				
John	Conquest		Bolnhurst				1
Thomas	Gilbert		Keysoe	1	1		
William	Farey		Bletsoe			1	1
William	Smith					1	1
Henry	Ekins					1	1
John	Emery		Bolnhurst			1	1
John	Throckmorton		Warrington			1	1
Simon	Davison			1	1		
Thomas	Lake					1	1
Alpheus	Dix					1	1
Thomas	Smith		Renhold			1	1
John	Nodes	Clerk		1			1
John	Church		Staughton Parva			1	1
Robert	Clark		St Andrews Holborne			1	1

Christian name	Surname	Occupation	Place of abode	Cher.	Har.	Cater	Hill.
Libeas	Eastwell					1	1
William	Smith					1	1
Richard	Wagstaff					1	1
John	King					1	1
William	Church		Cardington			1	1
William	Walker		Ravensden		1		1
Thomas	Wagstaff					1	1
Richard	Smith					1	1
			Wilshamstead				
John	Baldwin			1	1		
Thomas	Ashurst		Hawnes	1	1		
William	Cawne	Clerk	Wavendon BKM	1	1		
Richard	Pangborne		Wavendon BKM	1	1		
William	Tompkins	Jun.		1		1	
Easter	Warren		Olney BKM			1	1
Jonathan	Baldwin		Ashwell	1	1		
William	Bedles	Gent.		1	1		
John	Dearmer		Shefford	1	1		
William	Birt		Wotton HRT	1	1		
John	Woodcraft			1	1		
John	Osborne		Ampthill	1	1		
Nathaniel	Pearce				1		1
William	Edwards	Esq.	Bedford	1	1		
John	Abbot		Cardington	1	1		
John	Cooke			1	1		
Martin	Yorke		Tuddington			1	1
William	Thorne			1			1
Samuel	Richardson	Clerk		1	1		
William	Tompkins			1	1		
John	Pennyfather		Clophill			1	1
Sir Thomas	Sanders Seabright	Bart.	Flamstead	1	1		
William	Dearmer				1		1
Sir Ralph	Ratcliffe		Hitchin			1	1
James	Cox					1	1
William	Crane					1	1
			Wimington				
William	Wiles					1	1
Richard	Newcombe	Clerk		1	1		
John	Church			1	1		

Christian name	Surname	Occupation	Place of abode	Candidates voted for			
				Cher.	Har.	Cater	Hill.
Thomas	Scriven	Clerk	Twywell NTH	1	1		
Thomas	Mason					1	1
Thomas	Smith		Rushden NTH			1	1
			Wingfeild				
Thomas	Chaplin		Bedford	1	1		
			Wooburne				
William	Ashby		Wavendon BKM	1	1		
Robert	Sinfeild					1	1
Thomas	Walton			1	1		
Henry	Clarke		Bow Brickhill BKM	1	1		
Thomas	Phipps		Silsoe	1	1		
Nicholas	Sanders					1	1
Thomas	Ireland					1	1
Daniel	Giles		Wichloe BKM			1	1
Richard	Smith			1	1		
Jeremias	Ruberds					1	1
Francis	Turner		Westminster			1	1
Thomas	Croote					1	1
Henry	Woolhead					1	1
Daniel	Newcombe	Clerk				1	1
Symon	Taylor	Jun.				1	1
William	Walbanke					1	1
Simon	Taylor	Sen. Gent.				1	1
Joseph	Newcombe	Clerk				1	1
			Wootton				
Thomas	Russell					1	1
Thomas	Juggins		Newport Pagnell			1	1
John	Green					1	1
John	Hill					1	1
Matthew	Hill					1	1
Thomas	Bird		Cople	1	1		
Thomas	Fensham		Haughton Conquest	1	1		
Robert	Graves	Esq.	Harrode BKM	1	1		
Thomas	Hills			1	1		
Richard	Brockhurst		Turvey		1		
Andrew	Moore	Clerke		1		1	
Edward	Money		Ampthill			1	1

Christian name	Surname	Occupation	Place of abode	Candidates voted for			
				Cher.	Har.	Cater	Hill.
John	Bonner		Houghton Conquest			1	1
John	Clarke		Houghton Conquest			1	1
Robert	Hinde		St Andrews Holborn			1	1
John	Goddard					1	1
William	Wiles					1	1
John	Quarry					1	1
Thomas	Mee					1	1
Humphry	Fensham					1	1
Henry	Hill					1	1
John	Miller		Sherington BKM			1	1
Robert	Pemberton	Gent.	Eynsbury			1	1
John	Read		Stepney MDX			1	1
Edward	Shaw		Cripplegate LND			1	1
William	Read		Spittle Fields LND			1	1
John	Rogers					1	1
John	Hill					1	1
Samuel	Barber					1	1
John	Fowkes					1	1
			Westlingworth				
Roberr	Bristow				1	1	
Nicholas	Rosel			1	1		
John	Pearson		Kempson			1	1
Robert	Weston					1	1
James	Eakins		Bedford	1	1		
Edward	Squire		Hatley	1	1		
John	Burton		Eyworth	1	1		
George	Newell			1	1		
Thomas	Endersby			1	1		
John	Blowes		Eyworth	1	1		
William	Cosby			1	1		
Thomas	Abbis		Eyworth	1	1		
Robert	Handley			1	1		
John	Pitchers			1	1		
James	Blowes			1	1		
John	Berenschall	Clerke			1	1	
William	Edey					1	1
Richard	Millard				1	1	
Daniel	Lewis					1	1

Christian name	Surname	Occupation	Place of abode	Candidates voted for			
				Cher.	Har.	Cater	Hill.
Thomas	Gifford				1	1	
William	Peacock		Huntington			1	1
Vigorous [Vegerous]	Edwards		St Pulchers LND			1	1
Tomas	Squire			1	1		
			Wyboston				
Richard	Frank		Stow CAM			1	1
Levit	Pearson	Clerk	Finelly NTT	1	1		
			Yeilden				
William	Lynne		Stanwick NTH	1	1		
Matthew	Wiles			1	1		
John	Joyce				1		
Henry	Lamb		Newton BKM	1	1		
Pawlet	St. John	Clerk		1	1		

Tables

Table 1. County Election Results by Hundreds, 1685–1715

1685 Election

Name	Chernocke	Boteler	Russell	Monoux
Willey	43	31	73	60
Stodden	32	25	57	50
Barford	72	73	73	57
Manshead	108	113	210	182
Redbornestoke	144	141	119	111
Flitt	95	87	39	31
Biggleswade	149	145	32	29
Clifton	53	54	20	16
Wixamtree	76	79	35	31
Bedford Town	43	54	49	44
Out Voters recorded under parishes				
TOTAL	**841**	**904**	**744**	**634**

1705 Election

Name	Russell	Gostwick	Chernocke	Harvey
Willey	132	149	89	49
Stodden	118	123	63	33
Barford	148	191	70	27
Manshead	288	208	358	115
Redbornestoke	212	185	233	110
Flitt	109	94	161	130
Biggleswade	43	71	119	76
Clifton	52	50	82	70
Wixamtree	67	82	72	64
Bedford Town	59	97	68	25
Out Voters recorded under parishes				
TOTAL	**1408**	**1279**	**1239**	**764**

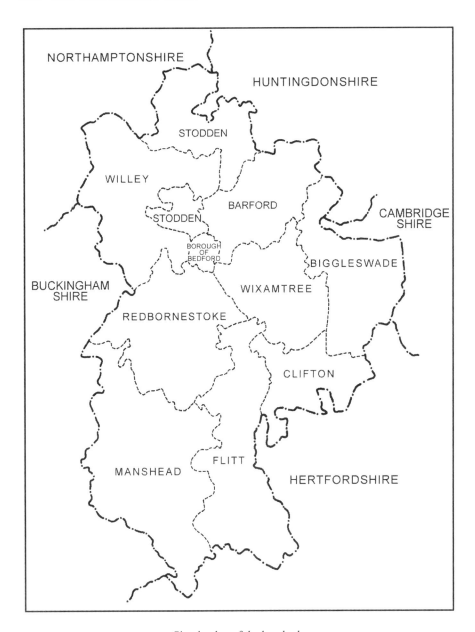

NORTHAMPTONSHIRE

HUNTINGDONSHIRE

STODDEN

WILLEY

BARFORD

STODDEN

CAMBRIDGE
SHIRE

BOROUGH
OF
BEDFORD

BIGGLESWADE

BUCKINGHAM
SHIRE

WIXAMTREE

REDBORNESTOKE

CLIFTON

MANSHEAD

FLITT

HERTFORDSHIRE

Simple plan of the hundreds

1715 Election

Name	Chernocke	Harvey	Cater	Hillersden
Willey	75	80	132	137
Stodden	68	70	101	99
Barford	75	85	127	134
Manshead	341	306	252	269
Redbornestoke	199	185	214	208
Flitt	137	144	131	127
Biggleswade	110	133	62	43
Clifton	94	99	54	52
Wixamtree	74	82	56	63
Bedford Town	44	44	86	86
Out Voters recorded under parishes				
TOTAL	**1241**	**1264**	**1254**	**1233**

Table 2. 1685 County Election: Analysis of Votes by Parish

Place	Boteler	Chernocke	Russell	Monoux
Ampthill	23	17	5	2
Arlesey	2	1	4	3
Astwick	1	1	0	0
Gt Barford	12	8	8	6
Lt Barford	3	3	0	0
Barton	9	9	0	0
Battlesden	1	0	2	1
Bedford	54	43	49	44
Biddenham	3	2	0	0
Biggleswade	12	12	1	1
Billington	1	1	1	1
Bletsoe	2	0	4	5
Blunham	8	8	10	10
Bolnhurst	1	1	5	5
Bromham	4	4	0	0
Campton	4	4	0	0
Cardington	5	7	20	16
Carlton	3	3	6	6
Chalgrave	11	11	1	0
Chellington	2	2	2	0
Clapham	1	1	1	1
Clifton	8	7	4	1
Clophill	9	9	2	2
Cockayne Hatley	3	3	0	0
Colmworth	0	0	11	11
Cople	9	9	2	2
Cranfield	20	21	1	1
Dean	3	2	6	5

Place	Boteler	Chernocke	Russell	Monoux
Dunstable	18	15	13	10
Dunton	0	0	11	11
Eaton Bray*	3	3	9	9
Eaton Socon*	48	48	11	11
Edworth	0	0	1	1
Eggington	0	0	1	1
Elstow	1	0	13	12
Eversholt	1	1	21	19
Everton	7	7	1	1
Eyeworth	3	3	1	1
Farndish	1	1	0	0
Felmersham	4	3	12	11
Flitton	3	3	10	10
Flitwick	10	11	2	2
Goldington	3	3	7	6
Gravenhurst	4	3	2	1
Harlington	5	4	1	1
Harrold	7	4	22	17
Haynes	3	3	3	3
Henlow	10	10	0	0
Higham Gobion	1	1	0	0
Hockliffe	9	1	10	3
Houghton Conquest*	9	9	0	0
Houghton Regis*	2	2	27	26
Hulcote	2	3	0	0
Husborne Crawley	1	1	18	17
Kempston	12	9	22	23
Keysoe	2	0	18	16
Knotting	0	0	2	2
Langford	1	1	6	6
Leighton	27	27	21	19
Lidlington	27	29	7	6
Luton	46	39	14	8
Markyate	2	2	1	1
Marston	3	3	12	12
Maulden	24	24	2	2
Meppershall	4	4	1	1
Milbrook	9	9	1	1
Milton Bryan*	0	6	11	8
Milton Ernest*	1	1	1	1
Northill	18	18	2	2
Oakley	5	4	4	4
Odell	0	0	7	7
Pavenham	2	1	3	3
Pertenhall	2	0	5	3
Potton	28	27	4	3

Place	Boteler	Chernocke	Russell	Monoux
Pulloxhill	4	2	7	7
Ravensden	0	0	5	5
Renhold	0	0	4	4
Ridgmont	5	6	13	9
Riseley	16	15	5	4
Roxton	7	7	9	9
Salford	4	4	0	0
Sandy	56	54	2	1
Sharnbrook	1	0	2	1
Shefford	10	10	7	7
Shillington	20	20	5	5
Southill	27	27	0	0
Stagsden	3	3	0	0
Stanbridge	5	4	8	7
Staughton, Lt	0	0	5	5
Steppingley	2	2	1	1
Stevington	1	1	3	2
Stondon	5	5	1	1
Stotfold	5	5	8	7
Streatley	3	3	0	0
Studham	0	0	2	2
Sundon	15	15	1	1
Sutton	3	3	0	0
Tempsford	8	8	4	4
Thurleigh	4	2	2	2
Tilbrook	0	0	4	4
Tilsworth	5	6	0	0
Tingrith	3	3	0	0
Toddington	5	5	20	16
Totternhoe	3	3	5	5
Turvey	5	4	5	4
Warden	3	3	1	1
Westoning	5	3	6	3
Whipsnade	4	4	0	0
Wilden	6	3	18	15
Willington	6	7	0	0
Wilstead	4	4	19	19
Woburn	0	2	15	12
Wootton	1	1	11	11
Wrestlingworth	24	24	0	0
Yelden	1	1	1	0
Unallocated	14	14	3	0
TOTAL	**841**	**904**	**744**	**634**

(Official total given in the Document)

*   With voters marked as coming from Eaton, Houghton or Milton it is often difficult to know which of the two parishes with those names is being referred to.

Table 3. 1695 Election: Analysis of Votes by Parish

Place	Duncombe	Browne
Ampthill	27	0
Arlesey		
Aspley Guise	10	0
Astwick		
Gt Barford	0	1
Lt Barford		
Barton	2	0
Battlesden	4	0
Bedford	48	7
Biddenham	0	1
Biggleswade		
Billington	7	0
Bletsoe		
Blunham	1	0
Bolnhurst		
Bromham		
Caddington	18	0
Campton		
Cardington	7	1
Carlton		
Chalgrave	25	0
Chellington		
Clapham	2	0
Clifton	0	1
Clophill	7	1
Cockayne Hatley	1	0
Colmworth	4	2
Cople	1	2
Cranfield	31	0
Dean	1	0
Dunstable	45	0
Dunton		
Eaton Bray	13	0
Eaton Socon	0	9
Edworth		
Eggington	7	0
Elstow	2	1
Eversholt	25	0
Everton	1	0
Eyeworth	1	0
Farndish	1	0
Felmersham	0	1
Flitton	12	0
Flitwick	11	0

Place	Duncombe	Browne
Goldington	1	0
Gravenhurst		
Harlington	17	0
Harrold	5	0
Haynes		
Henlow	0	3
Higham Gobion		
Hockliffe	11	0
Houghton Conquest	17	0
Houghton Regis	26	0
Hulcote	3	0
Husborne Crawley	19	0
Kempston	25	2
Kensworth	1?	0
Keysoe	1	0
Knotting	1	0
Langford		
Leighton	45	0
Lidlington	23 +1?	0
Luton	17	10
Markyate		
Marston	29	0
Maulden	9	0
Melchbourne	0	1
Meppershall		
Milbrook	7	0
M. Bryan	17	0
Milton Ernest	2	0
Northill	3	0
Oakley	6	0
Odell		
Pavenham	5	0
Pertenhall		
Potsgrove	1	0
Potton	2 +1?	3
Pulloxhill	10	1
Ravensden	3	0
Renhold	1	0
Ridgmont	20	0
Riseley	0	3
Roxton	1	7
Salford	3	0
Sandy	10	0
Sharnbrook	2	0
Shefford	0	3
Shillington	0	1

Place	Duncombe	Browne
Souldrop	5	0
Southill	0	3
Stagsden	5	0
Stanbridge	15	0
Staughton, Lt	0	2
Steppingley	4	0
Stevington	1	0
Stondon		
Stotfold		
Streatley	2	0
Studham	1	0
Sundon	21	0
Sutton	0	1
Tempsford	1	0
Thurleigh	10	2
Tilbrook		
Tilsworth	6	0
Tingrith	2	0
Toddington/Chalton	37	0
Totternhoe	18	0
Turvey	3	2
Warden		
Westoning	10	0
Whipsnade	2	0
Wilden	9	2
Willington	0	4
Wilstead	12	6
Woburn	17 +1?	0
Wootton	15	0
Wrestlingworth	4	0
Yelden		
TOTAL	**1108**	**906**

(Official total given in Document)

Note: the names of the voters who were likely to have voted for Browne in his own East Bedfordshire area were not recorded. They probably went to a Biggleswade poll.

Table 4. 1705 County Election: Analysis of Votes by Parish

Place	Russell	Gostwick	Chernocke	Harvey	Total voters
Ampthill	5	5	35	26	38
Arlesey	12	12	2	1	14
Aspley Guise	18	8	27	11	35
Astwick	3	3	1	1	4
Gt Barford	16	21	7	6	26
Lt Barford	1	2	3	1	4
Barton	2	1	7	6	8
Battlesden	0	1	1	0	1
Bedford	59	97	68	25	134
Biddenham	2	3	5	3	7
Biggleswade	1	2	7	5	8
Billington	2	1	4	4	6
Bletsoe	3	5	5	1	9
Blunham/Moggerhanger	5	7	7	8	14
Bolnhurst	2	2	2	2	3
Bromham	2	1	0	2	3
Caddington	1	0	7	61	7
Campton	0	0	8	7	8
Cardington	31	37	13	7	46
Carlton	15	15	5	4	20
Chalgrave	7	6	18	5	24
Chellington	3	2	4	2	7
Chicksands	No Return				
Clapham	1	1	1	0	2
Clifton	11	12	6	5	17
Clophill	3	4	19	14	21
Cockayne Hatley	0	1	2	0	2
Colmworth	14	16	4	2	18
Cople	9	14	4	0	14
Cranfield	16	10	33	17	41
Dean	24	24	1	1	25
Dunstable	23	21	43	7	63
Dunton	6	7	11	11	18
Eaton Bray	17	11	24	1	37
Eaton Socon	87	95	29	17	118
Edworth	No Return				
Eggington	0	0	7	5	7
Elstow	13	14	1	0	15
Eversholt	36	27	10	1	40
Everton	1	2	7	5	8
Eyeworth	2	1	1	2	3
Farndish	0	0	4	4	4
Felmersham/Radwell	21	24	8	4	30
Flitton	5	5	19	15	24

Place	Russell	Gostwick	Chernocke	Harvey	Total voters
Flitwick	11	5	21	7	25
Goldington	12	15	2	.1	16
Gravenhurst	1	1	4	4	5
Harlington	8	6	19	7	24
Harrold	16	18	16	13	33
Haynes	11	11	6	5	17
Heath & Reach	1	1	0	0	1
Henlow	7	7	6	4	13
Higham Gobion	2	3	3	2	5
Hockliffe	3	3	16	3	19
Holwell	2	2	2	2	4
Houghton Conquest	9	7	8	6	15
Houghton Regis	38	36	13	6	49
Hulcote	0	1	1	1	2
Husborne Crawley	28	18	17	5	37
Kempston	52	54	11	2	63
Keysoe	23	24	4	3	28
Knotting	0	0	1	1	1
Langford	10	10	6	6	16
Leighton	20	13	62	21	75
Lidlington	22	15	25	9	40
Luton/Leagrave	56	47	79	58	127
Market Street	1	1	0	0	1
Marston	8	10	32	21	40
Maulden	6	6	22	18	28
Melchbourne	2	2	0	0	2
Meppershall	1	1	8	5	8
Milbrook	4	2	9	7	12
Milton Bryan	18	6	1	2	26
Milton Ernest	2	2	6	4	8
Northill	4	11	26	27	36
Oakley	10	10	10	2	20
Odell	3	4	5	1	7
Pavenham	7	13	7	0	15
Pertenhall	12	12	2	2	14
Podington	2	2	12	10	14
Potton	3	4	20	17	23
Potsgrove	No return				
Pulloxhill	11	9	9	5	18
Ravensden	5	6	4	2	9
Renhold	5	6	4	2	9
Ridgmont	17	16	4	0	21
Riseley	19	18	24	15	41
Roxton	1	17	16	0	17
Salford	0	0	6	5	6
Sandy/Beeston	10	26	40	33	56

Place	Russell	Gostwick	Chernocke	Harvey	Total voters
Sharnbrook	10	11	5	1	16
Shefford	6	6	18	15	25
(Shefford?) Hardwick	0	0	1	1	1
Shelton	6	6	0	0	6
Shillington	10	9	37	34	46
Souldrop	1	1	3	1	4
Southill	14	17	16	17	32
Stagsden	2	2	2	0	4
Stanbridge	2	2	17	10	19
Staughton, Lt	7	13	9	1	16
Steppingley	9	3	6	0	9
Stevington	6	6	0	0	6
Stondon	0	0	2	2	2
Stotfold	20	21	9	8	29
Streatley	1	2	6	4	7
Studham	6	5	7	5	12
Sundon	17	12	19	4	29
Sutton	No Return				
Tempsford	3	9	7	3	12
Thurleigh	24	25	4	3	28
Tilbrook	6	6	2	1	8
Tilsworth	0	0	2	1	2
Tingrith	3	2	2	1	4
Toddington/Chalton	21	16	41	3	58
Totternhoe	15	14	22	6	36
Turvey	6	5	2	1	7
Warden	2	1	5	4	6
Westoning	8	8	2	2	10
Whipsnade	0	0	4	3	4
Wilden	10	14	13	1	18
Willington	23	31	1	1	4
Wilstead	19	13	19	5	32
Woburn	16	14	3	1	19
Wootton	21	21	8	2	27
Wrestlingworth	2	3	14	10	17
Wymington	2	3	10	9	13
Yelden	3	3	1	1	4
Official total given in Document					
	1239	**1276**	**1408**	**764**	**2563**

Table 5. 1715 County Election: Analysis of Votes by Parish

Place	Chernocke	Harvey	Cater	Hillersden	Totals of votes
Ampthill	34	32	10	10	86
Arlesey	4	4	8	8	24
Aspley Guise	24	19	11	13	53
Astwick	1	1	1	1	4
Gt Barford	15	16	6	7	44
Lt Barford	0	0	5	5	10
Barton	7	9	6	4	26
Battlesden	0	0	0	0	0
Bedford	44	44	86	86	260
Biddenham	4	3	3	5	15
Biggleswade/ Holme	7	9	1	1	18
Billington	2	2	2	2	8
Bletsoe	10	11	4	5	30
Blunham/ Moggerhanger	0	2	9	9	20
Bolnhurst	0	0	5	5	10
Bromham	2	2	0	0	2
Caddington	10	9	3	2	24
Campton/ Shefford	7	6	0	1	14
Cardington	13	17	20	22	72
Carlton	6	7	18	20	51
Chalgrave	28	26	11	13	78
Chellington	2	2	2	1	7
Chicksands	0	0	0	0	0
Clapham	3	3	2	1	9
Clifton	8	9	9	9	35
Clophill	6	6	9	9	24
Cockayne Hatley	3	3	0	0	6
Colmworth	4	4	16	17	41
Cople	8	8	8	9	35
Cranfield	28	19	20	14	82
Dean	3	3	21	21	48
Dunstable	34	34	15	14	97
Dunton	8	10	3	3	24
Eaton Bray	22	18	17	22	79
Eaton Socon	41	46	66	69	222
Edworth	0	0	0	0	0
Eggington	7	6	0	1	14

Place	Chernocke	Harvey	Cater	Hillersden	Totals of votes
Elstow	1	1	13	13	28
Eversholt	8	4	37	39	88
Everton	3	0	1	3	12
Eyeworth	1	1	0	0	2
Farndish	4	4	2	2	12
Felmersham	4	4	21	21	50
Flitton/Silsoe	5	7	26	26	64
Flitwick	16	16	13	13	58
Goldington	1	1	13	13	28
Gravenhurst	4	4	4	4	12
Harlington	8	7	3	4	22
Harrold	5	5	21	21	52
Haynes	6	8	10	12	36
Heath & Reach	2	2	1	1	6
Henlow	8	9	3	2	22
Higham Gobion	3	3	1	1	8
Hockliffe	20	20	3	3	46
Holwell	7	7	2	2	18
Houghton Conquest	7	8	10	9	34
Houghton Regis	12	11	47	48	118
Hulcote	1	1	0	0	2
Husborne Crawley	16	10	23	21	70
Kempston	3	4	53	53	113
Keysoe	5	5	28	28	66
Knotting	1	1	0	0	2
Langford	7	7	8	8	30
Leighton	66	59	16	19	160
Lidlington	18	18	17	18	71
Luton/Leagrave	66	66	37	34	203
Market Street	0	0	0	0	0
Marston	28	26	11	9	74
Maulden	22	21	11	12	66
Melchbourne	1	1	0	0	2
Meppershall	5	5	1	1	12
Milbrook	8	8	4	4	24
Milton Bryan	12	4	9	12	37
Milton Ernest	5	5	2	2	14
Northill	18	20	11	12	61
Oakley	5	6	10	10	31
Odell	7	7	0	0	14

Place	Chernocke	Harvey	Cater	Hillersden	Totals of votes
Pavenham	6	6	9	9	30
Pertenhall	7	7	9	9	32
Podington	0	1	10	11	22
Potton	19	24	8	3	54
Potsgrove	0	0	2	2	5
Pulloxhill	5	6	12	13	36
Ravensden	3	3	4	4	14
Renhold	1	1	1	1	4
Ridgmont	8	7	14	13	41
Riseley	26	26	9	9	70
Roxton	7	11	8	7	33
Salford	4	4	0	0	8
Sandy/Beeston	40	55	18	10	123
Sharnbrook	5	6	21	21	53
Shefford	15	16	2	3	36
Shelton	0	0	2	2	4
Shillington	24	27	14	11	76
Silsoe	1	2	11	10	24
Souldrop	3	3	0	0	6
Southill	32	34	7	10	83
Stagsden	3	3	4	4	14
Stanbridge	10	10	7	7	34
Staughton, Lt	16	6	6	6	24
Steppingley	4	2	5	7	18
Stevington	4	3	2	2	11
Stondon	4	4	2	2	12
Stotfold	12	12	13	13	50
Streatley	10	10	3	3	26
Studham	11	11	1	1	24
Sundon/Sutton	14	14	9	9	46
Tempsford	8	12	5	4	29
Thurleigh	5	7	14	14	40
Tilbrook	1	1	7	7	16
Tilsworth	3	3	0	0	6
Tingrith	1	1	2	2	6
Toddington/ Chalton	26	23	16	13	78
Totternhoe	15	14	21	21	71
Turvey	5	5	3	3	16
Warden	3	3	1	1	8
Westoning	11	10	2	3	26
Whipsnade	4	3	0	0	7

Place	Chernocke	Harvey	Cater	Hillersden	Totals of votes
Wilden	3	3	13	14	33
Willington	0	0	0	0	0
Wilstead	18	18	7	9	52
Woburn	5	5	13	13	36
Wootton	5	5	25	24	59
Wrestlingworth	13	10	7	6	36
Wymington	3	3	3	3	12
Yelden	4	5	0	0	9
	1241	**1231**	**1221**	**1228**	**4893**

Out County voters

Ampthill	2	2	2	2	8
Arlesey	3	3	1	1	8
Aspley Guise	8	8	1	1	18
Astwick	1	1	1	1	4
Barford, Great	2	2	1	1	6
Barton	2	2	1	1	6
Bedford	5	5	6	6	22
Biggleswade	2	2	0	0	4
Billington	0	0	1	1	2
Bletsoe	1	1	0	0	2
Bolnhurst	0	0	1	1	2
Caddington	3	3	0	0	6
Campton	1	1	0	0	2
Cardington	3	3	3	3	12
Chellington	2	2	0	0	4
Clifton	1	1	3	3	8
Colmworth	1	1	5	4	11
Cople	1	1	2	2	6
Cranfield	6	5	4	3	18
Dean	1	1	2	2	6
Dunstable	6	6	5	5	22
Dunton	1	1	0	0	2
Eaton Bray	1	1	0	0	2
Eaton Socon	18	19	18	19	74
Eggington	1	1	0	0	2
Elstow	1	1	1	1	4
Eversholt	0	0	8	8	16
Everton	1	2	0	1	4
Felmersham	2	2	3	3	10
Flitton	1	1	1	1	4
Gravenhurst	2	2	0	0	4
Harlington	0	0	3	3	6
Harrold	1	1	3	3	8

Henlow	1	1	1	1	4
Higham Gobion	2	2	1	1	6
Hockliffe	7	7	2	2	18
Holwell	4	4	2	2	12
Houghton Conquest	1	2	1	0	4
Houghton Regis	3	3	4	4	14
Husborne Crawley	3	2	5	5	15
Kempston	1	1	6	6	14
Keysoe	2	2	7	7	18
Langford	0	0	1	1	2
Leighton Buzzard	14	13	3	4	38
Lidlington	4	4	2	2	12
Luton	13	13	15	15	56
Markyate	2	3	2	1	8
Marston Moretaine	5	6	2	1	14
Maulden	1	1	1	1	4
Meppershall	2	2	0	0	4
Milbrook	0	0	1	1	2
Milton Ernest	0	0	1	1	2
Northill	1	1	2	2	6
Oakley	0	0	1	0	1
Pavenham	2	2	0	0	4
Pertenhall	4	4	6	6	20
Potsgrove	0	0	1	1	2
Potton	4	4	0	0	8
Podington	0	0	2	2	4
Pulloxhill	3	3	4	4	14
Ravensden	1	1	2	2	6
Ridgmont	1	1	2	2	6
Riseley	7	7	1	1	16
Roxton	2	2	1	1	6
Sandy	7	8	1	1	17
Sharnbrook	1	1	2	2	6
Shefford	2	2	1	1	6
Shelton	0	0	1	1	2
Shillington	7	9	8	7	31
Southill	4	4	1	1	8
Stagsden	1	1	1	1	4
Stanbridge	2	2	1	1	6
Steppingley	0	0	1	1	2
Stondon	0	0	1	1	2
Stopsley	1	1	0	0	2
Stotfold	2	2	2	2	8
Staughton , Little	2	2	2	2	8
Streatley	4	4	0	0	8
Studham	4	4	0	0	8
Sundon/Sutton	1	1	4	4	10

Tempsford	3	3	1	1	8
Thorncote/Thurleigh	1	1	5	5	12
Tilbrook	0	0	2	2	4
Tingrith	1	1	0	0	2
Totternhoe	5	5	3	3	16
Toddington	3	3	2	2	10
Turvey	1	1	0	0	2
Warden	1	1	0	0	2
Westoning	3	3	1	1	8
Whipsnade	1	1	0	0	2
Wilden	0	0	3	3	6
Wilstead	5	5	2	2	14
Woburn	2	2	2	2	8
Wootton	0	0	5	5	10
Wrestlingworth	0	0	2	2	4
Wymington	1	1	1	1	4
Yielden	2	2	0	0	4

Bibliography

Manuscript Sources

Bedfordshire and Luton Archives and Records Services
Archdeaconry of Bedford Court Case Papers (ref. ABCP)
Assize Records (ref. HSA)
Bedford Borough Archives (ref. BOR B)
Chester Archive (ref. CH)
Harvey Archive (ref. HY)
Lists of Bedfordshire Clergy (ref. Fasti)
Miscellaneous collections (ref. Z)
Orlebar Archive (ref. OR)
Registration Various (ref. RV)
Russell Archive: Bedford Settled Estate (ref. R)
Russell Archive: Holland (ref. RH)
Russell Archive: Ossory (ref. RO)
Trevor Wingfield Archive (ref. TW)
Wade Gery Archive (ref. GY)
Wade Gery and Brackenbury Archive (ref. WG)

Lincolnshire Archives
Massingberd Archive (ref. M. (G).)

Printed Sources

Beckett, J.V., *The Aristocracy in England 1660–1914* (Oxford, 1986)
Bell, Patricia, ed., *Episcopal Visitations in Bedfordshire 1706–1720*, BHRS, vol. 81 (Woodbridge, 2002)
Blakiston, G., *Woburn and the Russells* (London, 1980)
Brown, J., *John Bunyan (1622–1688): his Life, Times and Work*, tercentenary edn, rev. F.M. Harrison (London, 1928)
Cardigan, Earl of, *The Life and Loyalties of Thomas Bruce: a biography of Thomas, Earl of Ailesbury and Elgin, gentleman of the bedchamber to King Charles II and to King James II 1656–1741* (London, 1951)
Chambers, C. Gore, 'Political history', *The Victoria History of the County of Bedford* (London, 1908), vol. 2, pp. 17–72
Collett-White, James F.J., *Inventories of Bedfordshire Country Houses 1714–1830*, BHRS, vol. 74 (Bedford, 1995)
Colley, L., *In Defiance of Oligarchy: the Tory Party 1714–60* (Cambridge, 1982)
De Beer, E.S. ed., *The Diary of John Evelyn* (London, 1955)
English Historical Documents 1660–1714, ed. Andrew Browning. English Historical Documents, vol. 8. (London, 1953)
Fea, A., *The Loyal Wentworths* (London, 1928)

Finberg, H.P.R., 'The Gostwicks of Willington', *The Gostwicks of Willington and other studies*, BHRS, vol. 36 (Streatley, 1956), pp. 46–146

GEC, *Complete Baronetage* (Exeter, 1900–9), 6 vols

GEC, *The Complete Peerage of England Scotland Ireland Great Britain and the United Kingdom extant extinct or dormant*, new edn rev. and enlarged by the Hon. Vicary Gibbs (London, 1912), 14 vols

Godber, J., *History of Bedfordshire 1066–1888* (Bedford, 1969)

Godber, J., *The Story of Bedford* (Luton, 1978)

Godber, J., *Wrest Park and the Duke of Kent (Henry Grey 1671–1740)*, Elstow Moot Hall leaflet No. 7 (Bedfordshire County Council, 1977)

Hatton, R., *George I*, new edn (New Haven and London, 2001)

Henning, B.D., *The House of Commons, 1660–1690*, The History of Parliament (London, 1983), 3 vols

Holmes, G., *British Politics in the Age of Anne*, rev. edn (London, 1987)

Holmes, Geoffrey and W.A. Speck, *The Divided Society: Party Conflict in England 1694–1716*, Documents of Modern History (London, 1976)

O'Byrne, R.H., *The representative history of Great Britain and Ireland, comprising biographical and genealogical notices of the members of parliament from 1 Edward VI, 1547 to 10 Victoria, 1847* (London, 1848), Part 1: Bedfordshire

Orlebar, F. St J., *The Orlebar Chronicles in Bedfordshire and Northamptonshire, 1553–1733 or The Children of the Manorhouse and their posterity* (London, 1930)

Oxford Dictionary of National Biography, ed. H.C.G. Matthew and Brian Harrison. (Oxford, 2004), 67 vols

Speck, W.A., *Reluctant Revolutionaries: Englishmen and the Revolution of 1688* (Oxford, 1988)

Thomson, Gladys Scott, ed., *Letters of a Grandmother, 1732–1735, being the Correspondence of Sarah, Duchess of Marlborough, with her granddaughter, Diana, Duchess of Bedford* (London, 1944)

Thomson, Gladys Scott, *Life in a Noble Household 1641–1700* (London, 1937)

Thomson, Gladys Scott, *The Russells in Bloomsbury 1669–1771* (London, 1940)

Wigfield, W.M., ed., 'Recusancy and Nonconformity in Bedfordshire, illustrated by select documents, 1622–1842', BHRS, vol. 20 (Aspley Guise, 1938), pp. 145–229, 243–9

Index of Personal Names

Surnames are grouped according to similar spelling, sound or proved variants, based on the *Index of Bedfordshire Probate Records 1484–1558*, compiled by Alan F Cirket. London, British Record Society, 1994, 2 volumes.

Pages references may contain more than one occurrence of the indexed name.

Bayley, Bayly, Daniel 172; Francis 24; John 14, 26, 54; Thomas 57, 182; William 26
Bayster, Thomas 179
Bazely, James 218
Beachamp, Beachampt, Beachmpt, James 70; Nicholas 70; Thomas 70
Beadle, Beadles, Mr 156, 157; Mrs 157; William 49; see also Bedells
Beale, John 15, 93, 109; Samuel 15; Thomas 123
Beane, John 184; Thomas 15; William 147
Beard, John 56
Beaufort, Duchess of 42
Beaumont, Henry 26, 53, 185; Thomas 26, 109, 138; William 14, 92, 110, 168
Becher, William 70, 133
Beckerfield, Thomas 202
Becket, Beckett, Edward 26; Francis 14, 56, 70, 173; Robert 70; Simon 51, 70; Thomas 15, 70; William 23, 32, 70, 90
Bedcott, Francis 122, 197; John 15, 53, 54, 122, 126, 197; Thomas 54, 85,160; William 161
Bedells, Bedles, Biddell, Thomas 70, 88; William 14, 148, 226; see also Beadle
Bedey, David 139
Bedford, Dukes of, see Russell; Mr 157; Pemberton 15, 59, 113, 189; Samuel 9, 14, 59, 216; William 15, 58
Bedles see Bedells
Beech, John 57, 114, 169; William 26, 208
Beecher, Sir William xxv, 3; William 209
Bell, Edward 22, 32; John 95; Jonathan 180; Joseph 106, 181; Lewis 23; Richard 22, 32; Robert 70, 91, 167
Belton, John 213
Bembow, Benboe, Wendover 137, 214
Benfeild, John 15, 210
Bennell, Bennill, Christopher 147, 224; Henry 177
Bennet, Bennett, Henry 32, 127, 203; John 32, 139, 141, 219; Matthew 141, 218; Robert 193; Thomas 54, 125; William 141 219
Bennill see Bennell
Bentinck, Hans Willem, 1st Earl of Portland 67
Bentley, Edward 119, 197; Thomas 141; William 70
Benton, William 128, 205
Berenschall, John 228
Berkeley, Berkley, Bertley, Thomas 173, 223; William 9, 41; see also Betley
Berridge, Edward 26
Berry, Edward 218; George 15; John 15, 26, 50, 70, 89, 101, 107, 109, 167, 175; Richard 26, 100; Robert 26, 70; Samuel 88; Thomas 15, 104, 113, 184, 188; William 70, 88, 100
Bertley see Berkeley
Berwick, Thomas 111
Best, Bartholomew 132; John 85, 161; Thomas 142
Bethray see Bitherey
Betly, Richard 24; see also Berkeley
Betsworth, John 202
Bett, Betts, John 15, 54, 126, 185, 203; Lewis 32; William 15, 127, 203

Bicher, W. 9
Biddell see Beddells
Bide, John 221
Bidsey, William 210
Bigg, Abraham 26, 57, 122, 198; John 124, 182; Richard 124, 201; Thomas 14, 198, 199, 200
Bigrave, Thomas 95
Biller, Edward 213
Billingham, Samuel 49; Thomas 177; William 26
Bing see Byng
Bings, Daniel 70
Birchmore, Brichmore, Perchmore, John 49; Richard 15, 20; William 15
Bird, George 15, 115, 190; John 150; Richard 103; Thomas 126, 202, 227; William 148; see also Burt
Birden, Birding, William 15, 172
Birdsey, John 26; Thomas 26, 53, 133; William 26
Birkhead, Joseph 15
Birt see Burt
Biscoe, John 142, 220
Bishop, Bisshop, Bishopp, Benjamin 209; Edward 24, 132, 209; Francis 15, 135, 136; John 15, 135, 213; Matthew 224; Richard 213; Thomas 216; William 221
Bitherey, Bitheray, Bethray, Bithery, Bithray, Bithwray, John 96; Thomas 23, 32, 95, 170; Uriah 170
Blackhurst, Thomas 128; see also Backhurst
Bland, Robert 14, 48; William 15, 55
Blanes, William 70
Blatt, William 51
Bletsoe, Francis 113; John 26, 112, 188; Joseph 26, 57, 109; Richard 70; Robert 112, 188; Thomas 112, 133, 188, 210
Blew, Blow, Blowes, James 15, 151, 228; John 15, 151, 228
Blewitt, John,70
Blith, Robert 15
Blood, John 150
Blott, John 139; William 22, 32, 56, 199
Blow, Blowes see Blew
Blundell, Blundall, G. 9; Sir George 14; William 127, 204
Blunt, Richard 59, 193; William 124
Bober, Thomas 184
Boddington, Bodington, John 147, 222, 224; Robert 224; Thomas 109, 130, 184; William 14
Boffe, Daniel 26
Bolesby, John 70
Bolton, John xxii, 14, 70, 109; Thomas 117, 192; William 85, 128
Bonet, F 64
Bonfield, John 113; Michael 149; Robert 70; William 70, 89
Bonham, John 185
Bonlstrode see Boulstred
Bonner, Edward 94; Henry 110, 214; John 26, 109, 228; Thomas 15, 52, 122, 198; William 15, 115, 190
Bonnick, Jeremiah 51; John 195

Bruges, Thomas 179

Bryerlegg, Samuel 223

Buckingham, Abraham 54; Edmond 143; Edward 221; Gabriell 15; Henry 24, 49; John 15, 26, 191; Richard 116; Samuel 58, 116; Thomas 26, 116, 184, 192

Buckingham, Duke of, *see* Villiers

Buckland, Simon 101

Buckmaster, Edward 15; Edwin 103; Joseph 15; Thomas 56, 95, 171

Bull, Henry 130, 207; John 55, 130; Samuel 123, 205; Thomas 147, 224; William 95, 169

Bullhead, Henry 150

Bullmer, Bulmore, John 117, 193

Bullock, Martin 186

Bumstead, Bumsted, Richard 51, 87

Bunburry, John 208

Bundy, James 15; John 185; Nathaniell 26; Robert 24

Bunion *see* **Bunyan**

Bunker, Roger 50; Thomas 26, 96, 171; Timothy 156, 157

Bunn, John 52

Bunyan, Bunyon, Bunion, Bunnyon, Edward 58, 169; John xvi (illus), xix, 1, 8, 10, 38, 71, 91, 166; Samuel 140; William 26

Bur, Burr, Edward 24, 49, 147, 225; Hesekiah 147; John 15, 22, 32, 52, 56, 111, 179, 187; Richard 179; Thomas 223; William 14, 22, 56, 142, 219

Buraet, John 128

Burges, Burgess, Burgis, Henry 108; Peter 26, 208; Robert 131, 208; Thomas 174

Burgoyne, Sir Roger xxiv

Burnet, Burnett, Gilbert, Bishop of Salisbury 45, 46; Robert 210

Burrows, Burrow, Burrowes, Burrough, Burroughes, Abraham 215; John 15, 138, 215; Richard 93; Robert 87, 162; Samuel 117; Thomas 15, 26, 71, 185, 187; William 26

Burry, Thomas 15

Burt, Birt, Hugh 198; John 15, 50, 57, 197; Joseph 123, 200; Thomas 186; William 226

Burton, Edward 141, 151; John 228; Michael 189; Richard 50

Bush, Francis 55, 126; Luke 146; William 135

Bushby, Bushbey, Bushbye, Francis 122; John 50, 122, 197; Matthew 15; Thomas 26, 53; William 15, 122, 208

Busher, John 189

Buss, Francis 202

Butcher, Henry 53; Robert 116, 193

Butfield *see* **Butterfield**

Butler, Buttler, James 14; John 53, 197; Samuel 107; William 210

Butterfield, Butfield, John 191; Thomas 119, 199

Button, Richard 26; Thomas 71

Byby, John 169

Bygrave, Thomas 169

Byng, Bing, family xxv; George, 1st Viscount Torrington xxi; Pattee xxi, xxiv, xxv; Sir George 217; *see also* **Bings**

Byss, James 220

Byworth, Robert 54, 86, 162

Caddey, John 175

Cadwell, John 96

Cage, John 212

Calamy, James 15, 129

Caldecott, Thomas 168

Calton, Caulton, Colton, Nicholas 168; Valentine 71, 92, 168

Campion, Thomas 26

Campton, William 213

Cane, Henry 199; John 123; Thomas 86; *see also* **Cawne**

Canfield, Isaac 123; William 55

Canterbury, Archbishop of, *see* Sancroft

Capell, William 204

Capon, John 51, 121, 138; Thomas,139

Carden, Ralph 146; *see also* **Garden**

Cardigan, Earl of (author) 38

Careless, Carelesse, John 211; William 94, 170

Carew, Matthew 117; Sir Nicholas 188

Carey, Maurice 101; Walter 108

Carpenter, John 57, 116, 191

Carr, Anthony 15; Thomas 51; William 16, 52

Carrier, John 208

Carrington, John 15, 139, 216

Carter, Alderman 155; Daniel 138, 215; Edward 16, 57; George 174; Isaac 192; John 16, 26, 32, 51, 57, 104, 119, 129, 172, 173, 179, 194, 205; Joseph 125; Matthew 23, 32; Richard 111, 143, 212, 220; Robert 27; Samuel 173; Thomas 15, 16, 26, 49, 57, 71, 129, 140, 164, 195; Willam 55, 58, 98, 109, 117, 187, 193

Carteret, Henry Edward xiii, 66; John, 2nd Baron Carteret, xxiv

Cartwright, Cartright, Catwright, John 26, 56; Thomas 121, 197, 211; William 122, 198

Carvel, Carvell, Carvill, Carville, Edward 146; John 51, 147; Peter 101, 178

Carver, Samuel 119

Cary, Matthew 192; Walter 15

Cass, William 170

Castle, Richard 148

Castleton, John 26

Cater, John xiii, xiv, xxii, xxiv, xxvi, 118, 153, 154, 158, 159, 160, 193, 233, 242, 243, 244, 245; Squire 63

Caterall, Catterall, Catheral, Catherall, Cautherell, George 56, 123, 147, 198, 224; John 16

Catlin, Samuel 125

Caton, Robert 114; Thomas 215

Catwright *see* **Cartwright**

Caudwell, Cawdwell, John 32, 50

Caulton *see* **Calton**

Cautherell *see* **Caterall**

Cawcock, George 16

Cawcott, George 184

Cawne, William 48, 55, 148, 226; *see also* **Cane**

Cawthorne, Nicholas 168

Cayson, John 71

Guest, John 57
Gurney, Gurny, Edward 54, 146, 182; George 48, 147; John 223; Joseph 196; Leonard 74;, Simon 133; Thomas 28, 51, 74, 88, 100, 117, 120, 195
Gurry, Samuel 28, 93, 168
Gutteridge, Daniel 59; Matthew 125, 198; Richard 110; William 56
Gwyn, Gwynn, Henry 139, 215; John 138, 216; Thomas 28
Gyles see Giles

Haddis, Abell 222
Haddock, Walter 28
Haggis, 155; William 74; see also Hoggis
Hailey, George 162
Hains see Haynes
Haithwaite, Edward 74
Hale, John 88, 164, 167; Oliver 18; Robert 121; William 108
Hales, Thomas 18
Haley, John 177
Halfepenny, Bernard 132, 209; Thomas 18
Halfehead, Halfhead, Edmund 17; John 18; Thomas 17, 206; William 111
Halfhide, William 212
Hall, Edward 9, 24, 32, 49, 86, 189; John 18; Richard 28; Samuel 202; Thomas 28, 118, 194; William 28, 94
Hallton, Edward 101
Halseby, Thomas 118
Halsey, John 142, 220; Richard 220; Thomas 96
Hamerston, Thomas 53, 115, 190
Hammond, Hamond, Richard 23, 28, 33; Thomas 167
Hams, Thomas 129
Hancock, John 18, 74; Thomas 74; Walter 59, 88, 163
Handley, Hanley, Hanly, Robert 18, 151, 228
Handscomb see Hanscombe
Hanger, John 54, 216; Robert 51
Hanley see Handley
Hannell, Hanwell, Edward 28, 56, 113, 195; S 9; Shem 18; Thomas 188; William 122
Hanover, Electors of 65
Hanscomb, Hanscombe, Handscomb, Edward 112; James 138; Jeremy 18; John 18, 215; Robert 52, 113, 187, 189; William 17, 28, 138, 141, 187
Hanwell see Hannell
Harbert see Herbert
Harborough, John 28
Harbutt, John 167; see also Herbert
Hardacre, Henry 127, 204
Harden, Thomas 51; William 57
Harding, James 100, 176; John 88, 134, 211; Matthew 93, 195; Richard 126; Stephen 98, 174; Thomas 18; William 163
Hardrett, John 180
Hare, Charles 94
Harley, John 206; Robert, 1st Earl of Oxford and Mortimer, 64, 153

Harlow, Richard 18, 122, 200
Harman, Thomas 162
Harper, Aaron 213; Oliver 18; Richard 105; Thomas 95; William 18
Harrewden see Harrowden
Harriott, Richard 28
Harris, Abell 51, 144; Benjamin 219; George 18; Henry 18, 124, 124, 198; John 58, 146, 224; Joseph 176; Robert 28, 128; Thomas 99, 224; William 28, 167, 204
Harrison, Harrisson, John 28; Edward 74; Thomas 132, 146; William 74
Harrowden, Harrowdine, Harrewden, John 18, 28, 217; Thomas 18; William 93
Hart, John 88, 163
Hartley, Joseph 177
Hartwell, John 28, 51; Joshua 18; Richard 175; Thomas 112, 187
Harvey, Hervey, family 63; John xiv, xx, xxii, xxiv, xxv, xxvii, 11, 17, 59, 67, 68, 85, 116, 144, 153–60, 192, 222, 231, 233, 239–245; Richard 85; Thomas 18, 55, 58, 85, 206; William 130
Harway, Thomas 56
Harwood, John 88, 163
Haseldine, Aslendine, John 24, 111
Hasle, Robert 223
Hatley, Richard 221; William 180
Haughton, Adam 55
Haukin, Thomas 208
Hauley, Thomas 136
Hawes, Haws, John 18, 52; Thomas, 75, 85, 91, 160, 165
Hawkins, Edward 28; George 199; Jeffrey 104; Jeptha 28, 50; John 28, 48, 116, 128, 191; Nicholas 75; Robert 18, 28, 96, 116, 143, 171, 221; Samuel 191; Thomas 18, 28, 54, 56, 59, 97, 116, 119, 131, 139, 190, 191, 192, 216, 216, 217; William 103, 108
Hawks, Paul 28
Haws see Hawes
Hawthorne, Thomas 28, 108
Haxby, Thomas 18
Hayes, Hays, Thomas, 75, 90, 136, 213; see also Hey
Haynes, Haines, Hains, Heyns, Heynes, Ambrose 86; Edward 28; Henry 18, 92, 118, 194; John 117, 193; Lewis 18, 118, 193; Thomas 18, 142, 219; William 57
Headon , Michael 198
Hearn, John 141
Heath, Gregory 125; John 219
Heatson, Thomas 115
Hebbs, Henry 28, 55; John 28, 48, 114
Hedding, Joseph 28
Hedges, John 202
Heed, William 92
Helder, Richard 10, 28, 59, 93, 132; Thomas 57
Hemmin, John 197
Henceman see Henseman
Henderson, David 74; John 74
Hensman, Henseman, Henceman, Benjamin

194; John 74, 91; Thomas 109, 145, 223;
William 118
Henson, John 134, 211; Joseph 194; William 179
Herbert, Harbert, Edward 128, 204; Henry 222;
John 49, 128, 146, 205; Ralph 54; Thomas 54,
146, 192; William 128; *see also* **Harbutt**
Herman, Thomas 87; William 147
Herne, Stephen 74
Herring, Thomas 28
Hervey *see* **Harvey**
Hewes, Thomas 162
Hewett, Hewitt, James 104, 107, 180; John 28;
Robert 106; Thomas 18, 104; William 106,
179
Hewlatt, Thomas 28
Hey, William 18; *see also* **Hayes**
Heynes, Heyns *see* **Haynes**
Heyward, Henry 102; William 18
Hickman, Henry 18; Humphrey 122, 197;
Thomas 18; William 18
Hickson, Andrew 161; William 122
Hickstone, William 191
Hide, George 10, 17; William 183
Higby, Michael 195
Higgins, Edward 149; Henry 117; John 50, 56, 98,
117, 175
Higgs, Edward 28, 50, 127, 204; John 28, 59,
74–5, 91; Thomas 51, 130, 149
Higham, Richard 18
Hildersdon *see* **Hillersden**
Hill, Edward 18, 172, 189; Henry 51, 52, 150,
228; John 18, 49, 50, 56, 119, 123, 127, 150,
197, 201, 203, 227, 228; Matthew 150, 227;
Richard 123, 200; Robert 28; Samuel 18;
Thomas 18, 52, 150; *see also* **Hills**
Hillersden, Hillersdon, Hildersdon, Elizabeth
(née Farrer) xxi; Guy 118, 193; John 28, 51,
75, 114, 173, 190; T 9; Thomas xiii, 12, 23,
32, 40, 41, 45, 46, 59, 63, 242–5; William xiii,
xiv, xxi, xxii, xxiv, 75, 107, 153, 154, 158, 159,
160, 182, 233
Hillow, Edward 102
Hills, James 105; Michael 75; Ralph 18, 144;
Robert 188; Roger 75; Thomas 227; William
28, 75, 118, 194; *see also* **Hill**
Hillyar, Hillyard, John 104, 178; Lewis 75
Hinckley, Christopher 126
Hind, Hinde, John 54; Morgan 111; Robert 117,
228; Sebastian 75; Stephen 170; Thomas 75
Hinkly, Christopher 54
Hinton, Henry 28, 86; John 215
Hipwell, John 51, 136, 213; Thomas 130, 207
Hitchcock, John 28, 129, 206
Hive, John 97
Hobbs, Hobb, Hobbe, Daniel 143; Henry 223;
John 57, 113, 114, 125, 186, 189, 202; Joseph
144, 173; Matthew 32; Thomas 56; William
145, 208
Hobson, John 133
Hockley, John, 170
Hoddel, Francis 217
Hodden, John 18

Hodgis, Henry 143
Hodgkins, Hodgskins, Joseph 94; Joshua 169
Hoggis, John, 18; *see also* **Haggis**
Hoight, Francis, 57
Holcott, John 125
Holden, Thomas 148
Holdstock, Joseph 75; Robert 28
Holliman, Stephen 28
Hollingsworth, Hollingworth, Hollinworth, John
18, 54, 120, 196; Matthew 28; Thomas 86,
133, 160, 210
Hollis, Thomas 132, 209
Holloway, John 75, 149; Samuel 18, 98
Hollowley, Christopher 18
Holmes, Holms, Geoffrey (author) 42; Thomas
124; William 28, 117
Holt, Barnard 54; Baron 18; Edward 49
Hone, Bernard 145
Honeyford, Bernard 146
Honnor, Honer, Honner, Honour, Henry 18, 50,
120, 217; John 170; Joseph 28, 137, 138, 215;
Richard 18; Thomas 28
Honyborn, Edward 94
Honylove, Thomas 75, 89
Hood, Richard 96
Hooden, Michael 124
Hooker, Jonathan 18, 212
Hookham, Hookam, John 55; Joseph 209
Hoot, John 181
Hooton, Hootton, John 58, 144; Michael 118; *see
also* **Houghton**
Hopcraft, William 183
Hopkins, Francis 124, 200; John 50, 99; Nicholas
28, 55, 147; Samuel 88; William 18, 164
Hornbuckle, Hornebuckle, John 75, 164;
Thomas 166; William 55, 75, 89
Horseford, William 151
Houghton, Horton, Adam 18, 114; John 183;
Richard 193; Thomas 57; William 108, 183;
see also **Hooton**
House, Edward 192
Houseman, Richard 94, 170
Howard, Henry 178; Ignoll 199; John, xix, 75, 94,
125, 170; Joseph 75, 166; Simon 75; Thomas
94; William 75
Howe, How, Edward 116, 192; Francis 125, 198;
Henry 116; John 191; Thomas 18, 87, 162;
William 50, 115, 123, 192, 199
Howen, Thomas 221; *see also* **Ouen**
Howes, Hows, Francis 52; Henry 56; Timothy 28
Howland, Elizabeth, wife of 2nd Duke of Bedford
44
Howsen, Howson, John 110; Thomas 110, 185,
186
Hoyl, Hoyle, Francis 156, 217
Hubbins, Benjamin 18; Thomas 23, 28, 33, 49, 117
Huckins *see* **Huggins**,
Huckle, Francis 176; George 28, 94, 170; John
204; Joseph 88; Thomas 54, 94, 127, 204
Hudnall, Hugnal, Joseph 191; Thomas 201
Hudson, Hutson, Robert 169; Thomas 52, 110,
140, 218

Index of Places

Places are indexed under county, then generally by parish. Hamlets and houses are indexed under their parish. A section at the end of the index lists places where the county has not been identified. Spelling variations are noted in round brackets where they are significant or might cause confusion with similarly named places, especially in counties other than Bedfordshire.

Subject Index